TONY MACAULAY grew up in the 1970s  Road – an experience that has s writing. Following successful spell he has gone on to spend more thar and reconciliation both in Northe

also a writer and broadcaster, and has contributed regularly to Radio Ulster for more than ten years. His first two books, *Paperboy* and *Breadboy*, were critically acclaimed bestsellers. The sequel to these, *All Growed Up*, was released in 2014.

BREAD BOY

TEENAGE KICKS AND TATEY BREAD: WHAT PAPERBOY DID NEXT

TONY MACAULAY

BLACKSTAFF PRESS

First published in 2013 by
Blackstaff Press
4D Weavers Court, Linfield Road
Belfast, BT12 5GH
With the assistance of
The Arts Council of Northern Ireland

Reprinted 2014, 2016

Typeset by CJWT Solutions, St Helens, England

Printed and bound by CPI Group UK (Ltd), Croydon CR0 4YY

A CIP catalogue for this book is available from the British Library

ISBN 978 0 85640 910 3

www.blackstaffpress.com

Follow Tony on Twitter @tonymacaulay

For Wesley – the best of the
Belfast breadmen

CONTENTS

INTRODUCTION

I was a breadboy. This never made it on to my CV. So, just for the record, the dates of employment were 1977–79. The place was Belfast.

Early every Saturday morning, I delivered freshly baked bread to the consumers of the Upper Shankill. On a good day Belfast was as familiar and comforting as a warm buttered soda farl. But on a bad day, Belfast was hard and sour, like a dry stale wheaten bannock.

I was a breadboy. Aged fourteen. Just starting out, like a fresh plain loaf newly dispatched from the ovens of the Ormo bakery. Full of hope and innocent optimism. A tiny crumb on the streets of a city still feeding off ancient rivalries, that were well past their sell-by date. Yearning for peace, but living through troubles.

And yet, as you will learn from the slices of life on these pages, I was happy with my calling. I was a good breadboy. I delivered.

ALL GROWN UP

I was all grown up now, so I was. Fourteen years old and nearly shaving. My career had just taken off as impressively as *Thunderbird 3* blasting off from Tracy Island. In spite of the fact that jobs were a rarity in Belfast, I had just secured my second major contract of employment. For a few short years I had been a mere paperboy, but paper rounds were just for wee kids. Now I was a man, I had left such childish things behind. I had hung up my dirty canvas paper bag for good because it was time for me to move on to bigger and better things.

While most boys of my age were still struggling to get a job stacking shelves in the Co-op, I had been headhunted to work as executive assistant to Leslie McGregor, the head breadman in the last Ormo Mini Shop in Belfast. My career trajectory was on a steeper incline than a petrol bomb hurtling over the peace wall. I had been appointed to the highly responsible position of breadboy to the Upper Shankill. I had made it.

My predecessor in the position had been sixteen years old and had resigned to do A levels so he could get a good job in the bank and move to Bangor. From the vast pool of potential breadboys in the whole of the Upper Shankill, Leslie had chosen me. He had spotted my retail abilities as if he was a talent scout searching for the latest brilliant football player for Linfield. The only two essential criteria in the job specification for a breadboy were no thieving and no giving cheek to the pensioners. Leslie had either heard it through the grapevine or directly from Rev. Lowe, the minister of Ballygomartin Presbyterian Church, that I met both of the essential criteria. I was a wee good livin' fella who went to grammar school and everyone knew I had been an exemplary paperboy. My excellent customer service reputation had gone before me, up and down the streets of the Upper Shankill like a flute band in July. Leslie must have learned of my reputation as the only pacifist paperboy in West Belfast. I was only ever an observer of riots and never a participant. No petrol bomb had ever crossed my palms. While other boys may have wanted to wear dark glasses like the brigadier in the UDA, I longed to wear a leather jacket like the Fonz in *Happy Days*, except my mammy wouldn't let me. And so I had been handpicked from a throng of young hopefuls, the same way the casting director had chosen the new blonde Charlie's Angel, after Farah Fawcett-Majors left to become a big film star. Leslie hadn't asked for a written reference from my previous employer, Oul' Mac, the newsagent, which was lucky because it might have presented a difficulty. Writing had never been Oul' Mac's preferred method of communication. But I understood from Titch McCracken – one of my former paperboy colleagues who overheard the conversation while shoplifting brandy balls at the newsagents – that I had received an excellent verbal recommendation from my previous employer.

'Aye, that wee lad's a quare lot better than all them other cheeky wee thievin' shites!' Oul' Mac had said without hesitating, even for a drag of his cigarette. I understood that Leslie accepted this as a most satisfactory reference from a previous employer.

I realised that this glowing commendation from Oul' Mac would be hard to live up to but I was very ambitious and determined to continue my climb up the employment ladder. I knew Leslie was a master breadman who took no nonsense, so I committed myself wholeheartedly to learning my new trade and continuing my professional development. I was well aware that I was in an extremely privileged position. Leslie's van was not just any old bread van. It was the very last Ormo Mini Shop in Belfast. Of course, there had been other Ormo Mini Shops in the recent past, but most had been burnt either to block a road to free Ireland or to create a barricade to save Ulster. Leslie's Ormo Mini Shop was the last one of its kind in the whole of Northern Ireland and so the only one left on the planet. This reminded me of the dodo in my biology book at Belfast Royal Academy. Ormo Mini Shops were almost extinct. Can you imagine the responsibility of becoming the only breadboy in the whole wide world still serving customers from such an endangered vehicle? My job was completely unique. I was the only one. It was just like being the Secretary of State for Northern Ireland, except nobody hated you.

Everybody wanted bread and so everyone needed me. I would be delivering one of the essential services. Only water and electricity and Harp lager were more important. No one in Belfast could survive without the sustenance of a sliced white pan loaf and a ready supply of potato bread. Our city was more divided than ever and yet we were completely united in our love for the humble soda farl. It didn't seem to matter what foot you kicked with when you were toasting Veda bread. We all adored it! I wondered if our shared love of bread provided a common bond, which held out some hope for peace in the future. Who would care about a United Ireland or a United Kingdom, as long as we had a fresh malt loaf on the table? I was a dreamer, so I was.

The last Ormo Mini Shop in Northern Ireland was a wonder to behold. Motorbikes being crashed by Evil Knievel enthralled my wee brother, and my big brother was most impressed with Ford Capris in car chases in *The Sweeney*, but I alone was in awe of the Ormo Mini Shop. As the name suggests, it was, in fact, a miniature mobile shop. A marvel of engineering, it had great bulk and reasonable speed. On a busy day, or if there was a suspected hijacker on the street, it could reach speeds of up to 25 mph. This wondrous vehicle was grander than my father's Ford Escort respray and more welcome than a Shankill black taxi when the buses were off. It was a completely square, giant tin-box of tasty goodies on wheels. It was the most mouthwatering moving object to arrive in our street since the poke van. The Mini Shop was longer than a milk van and a rag-and-bone cart joined together and almost the height of a double-decker bus before burning. The diesel engine made a clattery purr as loud as any bin lorry and certainly noisier than the lemonade van. You knew when the Ormo Mini Shop was approaching your street because it growled up the road, leaving all the pathetic, traditional little bread vans from the other bakeries cowering at the red, white and blue kerbstones in submission to its greatness. The breadmen in those other old-fashioned bread vans had to dismount and walk around to the rear of their vans to access the loaves using a long wooden pole to withdraw drawers full of bread onto the street. They used the same poles to protect their produce from marauding gangs of children. Leslie did not have such problems. He simply had to step out of his spacious driver's cab and into the shop, surrounded by shelves heaving with freshly baked bread. And all of this under cover and protected from the ever-present Belfast rain and the odd stone or brick outside. If a gang of wee hoods approached, Leslie could simply close the door and drive off to safety. This was twentieth-century bread service, on the move, in your own street and with a roof. Of course, you didn't need to rely on the roar of the engine to let you know the Ormo Mini Shop was coming. It played a little tune just like the poke man's van, but slightly less melodious. When you pressed the red button in the driver's cab a cheery tune crackled out from a speaker at the back.

'Diddledee ding, diddledee ding, diddledee ding.'

At first I enjoyed the power and novelty of being able to send out diddledee dings to the people of the Upper Shankill at five-minute intervals every Saturday morning. But after a very short time the repetition of the tune began to irritate me as much as Boney M singing 'Ma Baker' every half hour on Radio Luxembourg. I soon noticed that the diddledee dings seemed to annoy the more hung-over customers on the Saturday mornings after the Friday nights before. So we didn't play it so much around the Twelfth of July because there were usually a lot of hangovers about then and the tune sounded nothing like 'The Sash' anyway. I noticed that Leslie used his diddledee dings sparingly and only outside the homes of customers who still hadn't paid for last week's bread.

The only other vehicle to drive up our street with an inside of a capacity similar to the Mini Shop was a British Army Saracen. In Belfast, guns and bombs were as common as a loaf of bread. The Ormo Mini Shop was a tank of sorts, except our war was with Mother's Pride, the rival bakery whose muffins were a major threat. While the tanks had soldiers with guns inside we had apple turnovers with cream. The Mini Shop seemed to be bigger on the inside than the outside – just like the TARDIS, the favoured mode of transport of my hero Doctor Who, with the curly hair and the big long scarf. I sometimes imagined our Mini Shop was actually a time machine that could take me back in time to see dinosaurs roaming the Black Mountain when it was a big volcano. Or forward in time to the year 2000 to see Belfast with no paramilitaries roaming the streets.

The Ormo Mini Shop was so spacious that four or five people could walk around inside at the same time, as long as they hadn't eaten too many of our gravy rings and Florence cakes. The Mini Shop had shelves of bread and pastries and soft drinks and crisps and sweets on all four walls. There were mouthwatering delights from floor to ceiling, apart from at the entrance to the driver's cab and a small window at the back. New customers would always marvel at the fact that this amazing vehicle even had 'a wee windie at the back'. This window was important, not just for providing natural light to the shop, but also for looking back to check if any customers were running after you because you gave them the wrong change or sold them a blue, mouldy barmbrack. It was also useful when I had to play look-out for hijackers hiding up the entries. The fizzy drinks could occasionally be problematic because they often exploded on opening due to all the movement going over potholes where buses had burnt, but most of the other merchandise was warm, fresh, inviting and relatively inert.

Apart from its other many attractions, the most tantalising and memorable feature of the Ormo Mini Shop was the smell. Unlike me, after my only bottle of Brut aftershave had run out, it never smelt bad on a Saturday morning. You see, bath day wasn't until Sundays. The interior of the Mini Shop was filled with the mouthwatering aroma of freshly baked bread. I loved this smell. It was addictive. Every time I entered the van at six thirty each Saturday morning the seductive scent wafting from still warm loaves, fresh from the oven, made me long for noon when my labours would be finished for another week. Then I could hurry home with free fresh soda and potato bread that my father would add to a magnificent Ulster fry, which he cooked while listening to Big T playing Billie Joe Spears on Downtown Radio.

Leslie liked me, so he did. He said I was a good, honest boy because I went to church after getting saved at the Good News Club on my holidays at the caravan in Millisle. This was of vital importance to Leslie. It meant you wouldn't steal money from the till or nick a Wagon Wheel from the confectionery shelf even though you really wanted to. Anyway, the big bread bosses at Ormo HQ on the Ormeau Road checked Leslie's takings and stock every week so it was very important that every penny and every single crumb was accounted for.

Leslie was universally regarded as the most trustworthy and honest person in the whole of the Upper Shankill. He took a Sunday School class, taught the Bible to the Boys' Brigade on a Sunday morning (even when some of the boys were still hungover from a bottle of Mundies up an entry the night before) and he looked after all the money in the church. He was like Mother Theresa, only bigger and much, much more Protestant. Leslie was a big good livin' man, which meant that he didn't drink or smoke or say 'fuck' a lot like most men. I never saw him drink so much as a shandy and I never once heard him call Mr Black from No. 13, the rudest of all customers, 'a curnaptious oul' bastard' even though this was clearly the most apt description. Leslie was very holy but I realised that he must have had sex a few times because he had young children. I suppose he had to do something to pass the time when he wasn't serving bread or at church or at meetings in the Orange hall.

Leslie must have been thirty or something but he looked like he was much older. He always wore old-fashioned slacks with braces and a shirt and tie under his white coat, just like my chemistry teacher, except Leslie's white coat was bakery regulation rather than scientific attire. Leslie was tall but he was quite overweight from snacking on the pastry temptations that were always surrounding him. He had thin brown hair combed to the side with Brylcreem and very clear white skin and rosy cheeks like a Free Presbyterian. Leslie was a Grand Worshipful Something or Other in the Orange Order but he was more of an old school, Bible-and-bowler-hat Orangeman than the new, petrol-bomb-and-paramilitary kind.

'Yer man's an awful good big crater,' explained my mother, 'Sure he's in the Black as well as the Orange.'

I wasn't quite sure what this meant because I was unschooled in the details of the Loyal Orders, but my mother was clearly very impressed.

Leslie wanted more wee good livin' boys in the Orange Order instead of under-age drinkers and so he regularly encouraged me to join the Junior Orange Lodge. In spite of his power as my employer and his persuasiveness, I declined these entreaties because I liked the few Catholics I knew and anyway my atheist father had pronounced, 'No son of mine is joinin' no Orange Order!' My father had decided when the Troubles started that the sash his father wore should remain as a relic in the roof-space.

In cleanliness and purity Leslie was the complete opposite of my first employer, but he shared Oul' Mac's difficulties in the dental department. He had very few teeth for a man of his age and most of those that remained seemed to be at risk. Even though he didn't smoke, his vulnerable incisors were stained a malt-loaf colour. It must have been all the wee cups of tea and sugary traybakes pressed upon him by the ladies at church meetings. While it was true that Leslie could not be tempted with strong liquor, he was a sucker for a caramel square. On Saturday mornings I feared that several strong bites into a stale fruit scone would precede the demise of his last few teeth, but they seemed to soldier on undaunted, just like Leslie's views on matters of politics and religion. My bread mentor utilised his limited tooth supply very well, though, giving a pleasant smile to most of the customers.

Although Leslie was almost completely without sin, he did

have one serious weakness – he loved a good gossip almost as much as Big Aggie in our street. Unfortunately I suffered greatly as a result of this weakness. A bread run that should have taken three hours sometimes took six because Leslie spent far too long with every customer talking about what was happening on the Road, who was bad with their nerves, who had taken a stroke, who had run off with her fancy man and why we were being sold down the Dublin Road, again and again. He spread the latest news throughout the Upper Shankill faster than David Dunseith on *UTV Reports*. He started every outpouring of gossip with the same words: 'C'mere til a tell ye!'

Some customers, who were nosey or lonely or both, enjoyed every story and would hang on Leslie's every word while clutching their pastries. I noticed others would wince at the sound of 'C'mere til a tell ye!' As an unwelcome story unfolded in the claustrophobic confines of the Mini Shop the bored customer would slowly edge backwards down the steps with their loaves in their arms, attempting to escape a ten-minute monologue about a certain customer who 'thinks she is something but never pays her bread bills'. Sometimes I was fascinated by the insights Leslie had into what was going on in the Troubles. He was something of an authority on the security policies of the RUC and the British Army and he gave the impression that he played an important advisory role for MI5. But on other occasions I was bored rigid when he repeated for the millionth time the same story about Mrs Piper's affair with a man from a gospel hall up the Newtownards Road 'and her that good livin' and all'. I wanted to be finished my labours not gossiping about the neighbours. My mind often wandered towards more exciting preoccupations like music and movies and outer space and Judy Carlton. Judy Carlton was in my chemistry class. She was lovely, so she was. She had gorgeous blue eyes like Lynda Carter and I wanted her to be my very own personal Wonder Woman. I wanted to finish work and get home to practise my cracked Spanish guitar so that I could play like yer man in Queen with the curly hair. I wanted to listen to ABBA's *Arrival* album on the stereogram in the sitting room and stare at Agnetha in a white jumpsuit beside a helicopter on the cover.

Following my appointment to the post of breadboy the first major challenge was to waken up in time to do the job. When Leslie informed me that he would pick me up at our house at 6.30 a.m. on my first Saturday, I nodded knowingly, but inside I was thinking, 'How am I going to get up at six o'clock every Saturday morning?' This was extremely early for any morning of the week never mind a Saturday when everyone else was having a good lie-in. At least my paperboy shifts had been during waking hours, even if I had often delivered my forty-eight *Belfast Telegraphs* in the early evening darkness. I wondered if I would ever get a job you did in the light.

Fortunately there had been enormous strides forward in the technology of the humble alarm clock. I was able to buy a new-fangled digital radio alarm clock from the *Great Universal Club Book* for just twenty weeks at 79p. 'Digital' meant it wasn't old-fashioned and round with hands. It was made of impressive white plastic and you couldn't get anything more modern than plastic. My granny complained that nearly everything was plastic now, even Union Jacks on the Twelfth. My plastic timepiece had four digital numbers that clicked down to tell the time in 24-hour-style. It made the time look all space-age like in *Space 1999*. The digital clock radio hummed quite loudly when you plugged it in and this kept me awake at night, but it was very good at waking me up at six o'clock on a Saturday morning. The radio alarm clicked on just in time for the news on Downtown Radio to tell me who had been shot last night. This was followed by *Eamonn Mallie's Farming Round-up*, which inexplicably gave the price of cows in Ballymena. Inevitably I sometimes pressed the wrong button or the provos pressed a very different button to blow up the electricity sub-station and the radio alarm didn't go off at all. On these mornings I would be wakened by the sound of a distant and dreamy diddledee ding, diddledee ding, diddledee ding. I then woke up with a start and realised I had missed the news and the price of pigs in Portadown and Leslie was outside our front door impatiently pressing his button and waking up the whole street. This did not go down well with the rest of my family. My father would be furious at being wakened so early on his day off after a long week at the foundry and would bang the wall between our bedrooms shouting unsympathetically, 'Will ye get up, ya lazy wee glipe!'

Even my ever-patient mother was tested. I could hear her mutter to my father from beneath the bedclothes, 'Oh my God, Eric, I don't know what we're gonna do with that wee lad. He lives on cloud cuckoo land, so he does!'

Mammy usually went to bed very late because she was always sewing a dress for a swanky lady up the Malone Road to wear to a dinner dance for the lifeboats. My big brother would be similarly upset because he needed every last minute of sleep before getting up to play rugby for the Glorious First XV rugby team at Belfast Royal Academy's playing fields in Mallusk, over the mountain. He would save his anger for later in the day in the middle of the most exciting part of *Doctor Who*: 'Are you so busy havin' dirty dreams about Judy Carlton that ya can't even wake up for your wee job as Leslie's skivvy, ya big fruit?'

Fortunately for him I was a blessed peacemaker and more concerned about how the Doctor was going to escape from certain death by the Daleks, so I responded with a silent sneer.

The only member of my family who was not upset at being wakened early on a Saturday morning was my wee brother. He had worked out that he could still go back to sleep for another few hours, but he was happy that it was Saturday morning and very soon it would be time to get up to try to swap his Lego for Kerplunk on *Noel Edmonds Multi-Coloured Swap Shop*.

In spite of my occasional lapses in professional punctuality, these were happy and exciting days. After all, this was the era of *Saturday Night Fever* and *Star Wars*. Most of the old cinemas in Belfast had been burnt down but we all queued up outside the few remaining ones in the city centre to see these most amazing movies of all time. I couldn't decide whether I wanted to be Luke Skywalker or John Travolta. All the wee girls in our street fancied John Travolta because he was good at disco dancing in a white suit but Luke Skywalker saved the universe from the terrifying Darth Vader with a lightsaber. Of course, we all knew that Darth was really just the Green Cross Code Man dressed up in a black suit, but Luke was still a hero anyway because he piloted the first spaceships without visible strings.

Breadmen aside, it was the era of exceptionally nice teeth. The Bee Gees smiled with big white gnashers because they were number one every week on *Top of the Pops* and Jimmy Carter smiled all the time because he was number one in the White House in America. I smiled a lot too but not one of my molars was as white as a Bee Gee's.

In between sewing buttons, my mother laughed at Benny Hill chasing girls in their bras and fancied Des O'Connor. My father laughed when Morecambe and Wise made fun of Des and said he couldn't really sing at all. It was a time when my family was safe and happy and everyone was still alive, apart from my other granda, but we were getting closer to the years of Carlsberg Special and the tears.

Denim ruled the fashion world. Everyone had denim jeans with decent flares and most boys up our way had denim jackets. I wanted one too but Mammy still wouldn't let me because she said Wrangler jackets were just for wee hard men who were nothing but 'gatherups and scruffs from down the Road' and 'none of them nice wee fellas at BRA wear them oul' jackets'. Even the most popular aftershave was called Denim. I still hadn't started shaving, but I longed for my first bottle the same way my big brother had longed for his first bottle of Harp. Denim was a more subtle fragrance than my first aftershave Brut, and mercifully it included no misleading instruction to 'splash it all over'. The advertisements on TV showed a lovely woman's hand popping the buttons of a denim shirt on a man with a hairy chest. This commercial presented me with everything I wanted most in the world in just thirty seconds – a cool denim shirt, a hairy chest, a bottle of Denim and a lovely woman's hand. The bottle of Denim seemed the most immediately achievable so I saved up my breadboy pay to buy my first bottle from Boots beside the City Hall, where Ian Paisley shouted and you got the bus.

There were other distractions from my work like the Troubles and Blondie and Space Invaders and small pets from Gresham Street. I was learning to become a great actor – like Roger Moore – in school plays and I was beginning to travel the world with other wee deprived kids from West Belfast. I was acquiring new skills all the time, such as how to be a missionary for Jesus and how to snog properly at the Westy Disco. I had my share of worries too, like rugger boy bullies and exams at school and gunmen in the streets and bombs at the shops.

Yet in spite of these distractions I stuck purposefully to my new career path, as stubbornly as a jam sponge falling face down on the floor of the Mini Shop. I soon learned the vital difference between a pan loaf and a plain loaf and within a few weeks I was as much a fixture in the Ormo Mini Shop as the van was a presence in the puddled streets of the Upper Shankill.

However my first day as a breadboy was to be a memorable day for all the wrong reasons. This was because in the very same week that my new career was born, The King died, so he did.

2

THE KING IS DEAD

The life of Elvis, The King, ended on Tuesday and the career of Tony, the breadboy, began on Saturday. I awoke with a start to the six o'clock news. In my dreams I had slept in at least a dozen times. I had spent the night intermittently waking up in a panic before realising it was just another dream. In one of these nightmares, Leslie had sacked me before I even got the chance to deliver a single bap. He had kicked me down the steps of the Ormo Mini Shop in front of the whole street. Angry neighbours threw potato farls at me as I stood in the middle of the road in my pyjamas. In another dream my punishment for being late was to be beamed up to the planet Skaro to be exterminated by a thousand Daleks and the Doctor didn't arrive at the last minute to save me with his sonic screwdriver. As I surfaced enthusiastically from beneath the sheets I briefly recalled another dream involving Olivia Newton-John, but this had had a much more pleasant outcome.

I always had a feeling of dread when the news came on because I was afraid someone I knew had been shot or blown up. But this morning the main news was that Elvis was still dead. A medley of the Elvis rock and roll years ensued and this ensured I got up immediately. This was not the best time to admit it publicly but I never liked Elvis. At my guitar lessons on Friday nights with Mr Rowing, I had been forced to play 'Love Me Tender' and 'Cheating Heart'. All I really wanted to learn was the latest number one hit like 'Knowing Me, Knowing You' by ABBA or 'Don't Give Up On us Baby' by Hutch (without Starsky), which was written by a man with exactly the same name as me! All that 'Blue Suede Shoes' lip-curling from the young thin Elvis seemed so old-fashioned to me, especially compared to the very latest progressive rock of Smokie. I was bored by the incessant repeats on television of all those old films of Elvis with a flowery garland round his neck on a beach in Hawaii singing songs to nice ladies in coconut bras and grass skirts. And the more up-to-date, fat Elvis was even worse, crooning ballads in Las Vegas in a white sequinned catsuit which showed considerable strain in the belly region. Of course my mother and my granny loved Elvis. Granny loved him more than Valium. She cried during 'Are You Lonesome Tonight?' and said 'he's still a lovely wee fella, so he is' when it was obvious that he was far from wee, so he was. Meanwhile my mother's adoration of The King was not without a certain dietary critique. Mammy regularly referred to the expanding Presley waistline as a cautionary lesson when she caught me eating peanut butter on a spoon straight from the jar: 'You don't wanna end up lookin' like Elvis, love, nigh, do ye?'

For some unknown reason all the Protestant paramilitaries adored Elvis, even though he sang a song about crying in the chapel which sounded very Catholic to me. I doubted if Elvis had ever held the string on the banner in the parade on the Twelfth when he was a wee boy. In fact, I was pretty sure there was no Twelfth of July in America because they had the Fourth of July instead. I had never seen an Orange parade on *The Waltons* but having said that I was convinced that John Boy and his family were Protestants because they looked very like people from Ballymena and Grandma Walton looked like the sort of woman who would make a delicious apple tart for the Field.

Anyway, in spite of any clear evidence of loyalist leanings, Elvis was still the mascot of the UDA and he was always 'pick of the pops' at the UVF drinking club down the Road. Every paramilitary had Elvis sideburns, which must have itched something desperate underneath their balaclavas.

On this monumental morning of my bread delivery debut I knew everyone in the whole world, apart from me, was grieving for The King. But I soon realised that this could provide me with an unexpected opportunity to shine on the first day of my new job. Unlike everyone else, I was not distracted by grief and so I could focus entirely on my induction. I knew I could dazzle Leslie with the excellent customer delivery skills I had acquired during my former career as a paperboy. Furthermore, I knew from experience that the people of the Upper Shankill still wanted fed no matter how bad things were on the streets or in the wider world. People still needed bread to live, with or without Elvis, and so I pressed manfully onward with my new career.

I tiptoed down the thinning shag-pile on the stairs and gently opened the front door, trying hard not to waken anyone in the family. As I stepped out into the bright August morning I could smell Dad's best red rose bush beside the front door and I could hear wee birds chirping in the hawthorn bushes up the fields at the end of our street. Our houses were the last ones before the fields began a steep climb up the Black Mountain. It was all grass and nettles and cows' clap at the end of our street. A few doors away, Mr Oliver had clipped his hedge into the shape of a big rooster, and a little robin redbreast was sitting on top of it. I almost expected the hedge to do a 'cock-a-doodle-do'.

I gently closed the front door and strode purposefully down our thoroughly bleached front step towards the rest of my career. Leslie was waiting for me at the top of the steep steps into the Mini Shop, smiling with every tooth he could muster.

'Well, young fella, are you all set?' he asked encouragingly.

'Aye!' I replied, monosyllabically.

Before we drove off, Leslie sat me down in the driver's cab and acquainted me with the ropes. He started off with the basics. The most fundamental information was the difference between a plain loaf and a pan loaf. Until this day I had been unaware of the distinction between the two types of loaf. A pan loaf was longer and smoother and whiter and a plain loaf was shorter and fatter and rougher. It was a little confusing for me to begin with because in some ways a pan loaf was plainer, and certainly blander than a plain loaf. A pan loaf had a soft crust and was good for making sandwiches for the Sunday School excursion while a plain loaf had a dark crispy crust that was great for dunking in a can of tomato soup. It occurred to me that pan loaves and plain loaves were a bit like Protestants and Catholics in Northern Ireland, basically the same but with a slightly different consistency underneath their crusts.

To my great disappointment, Leslie advised me that the two responsibilities I longed for the most would initially be denied me. The first task from which I was forbidden was putting money in the till. I wasn't sure whether this restriction meant that Leslie thought I couldn't count or that I might thieve, but either way I was slightly affronted. Did he think I was a wee hood who would steal the money? Did he not know I was a wee good livin' fella that had never shoplifted a single sweetie mouse in Oul' Mac's newsagents? Or did he think I couldn't do the sums even though I had come top of the class in a maths exam at BRA and only smart people went there? I had collected paper money for years. I had never thieved and always counted correctly even when under attack from wee hoods and robbers. I had been top of the class in maths for years, until Timothy Longsley started revising and beat me in every exam.

The second forbidden task was an even bigger disappointment. I was not allowed to push the big red diddledee ding button. I could understand not being allowed to handle the money because most wee lads thieved, but there was no good reason why I should not be allowed to press the button. This was outrageous! Did he think I was going to break it? I knew how to press a button. I did it every day on my cassette recorder. I was fourteen years old after all. I was not a kid like my wee brother who broke his *Star Wars* R2-D2 robot by pressing the 'speak' button too hard. I suspected that Leslie was just keeping all the best jobs for himself. I knew he would regret this. What would have happened if Bjorn and Benny had kept all the lead vocals for themselves instead of giving them to Agnetha and Frida? Patrick Walsh, who played violin better than me at the School of Music, said Protestants kept all the best jobs for themselves. I thought this couldn't be true because my father got sent a bullet to his locker at the foundry for giving a Catholic a job, but here was evidence that Patrick might have a point after all.

As we proceeded on my virgin bread run, Leslie continued with the induction process. He advised me of a whole range of policies and procedures. I could barely take it all in. Leslie explained in very serious tones that Procea loaves were medicine bread for people who were allergic or something. This made him look and sound like a bread doctor in his white coat, apart from the big Ormo butterfly on the pocket.

As we crisscrossed the estates of the Upper Shankill on that first Saturday morning, the master breadman explained a whole set of dos and don'ts. I was to keep an eye on wee hoods who came into the shop. Leslie explained that these characters did not normally get up early on Saturday morning – a relief after my experiences as a paperboy – so if they ever came into the van, I was to consider them shoplifters. I also gleaned that I should never permit customers to open a fizzy drinks can within the confines of the Mini Shop: 'Them wee minerals explode because of us goin' over all them oul' security ramps.' To my delight I was then informed that damaged goods should never be sold, but always kept aside for our mid-morning break, to wash down with a can of Lilt. Even on that very first morning I was tempted to deliberately drop and damage a delicious-looking Victoria sponge.

Once Leslie had exhausted all of the official requirements of the job he suggested that a good breadboy would also make a good junior Orangeman and member of the Boys' Brigade. I declined invitations to join both institutions by explaining that I was already a scout and my atheist da did not allow me to join the Orange.

'That father of yours has some quare funny ideas,' commented Leslie.

This was not the first time I had heard such a remark. Daddy preferred to disagree than to agree with everybody else.

I soon discovered that only listening to Leslie would never fully equip me for my newfound profession. I had to learn from experience and the only way to develop skills in customer relations was to deal with an assortment of customers. I knew I was going to have to be sensitive to the grief attending almost every customer because of the recent demise of The King. It was a particularly dark morning in the Upper Shankill. It was like Ian Paisley himself had died.

We started the bread round in my own street. Mrs Piper was the first to enter the Mini Shop that morning, clutching her large black leather handbag and repeatedly pulling her unbuttoned cardigan across her expansive bosom. Mrs Piper's breasts always confused me. The older I got the more difficult I was finding it not to look at breasts. It was strange, as if breasts had special magnets inside them, drawing my eyes in their direction. If a woman had big breasts like Raquel Welch then she was usually dead sexy and your eyes just kept on looking at them even when you tried to stop. But when it came to Mrs Piper's ample bosom I had to try not to look in the first place. There was nothing sexy about Mrs Piper and yet the magnets in her breasts seemed to work just like Raquel Welch's. It was difficult because her bosom was very large by any standard and also because she never smiled and always stared at you like you had been up to something sinful. As a result of this stern countenance I tried not to look at her face either. This left very few remaining parts of Mrs Piper that I could comfortably look at. However, today I did look at her face because she entered the van crying. Mrs Piper was in mourning over the death of The King.

'Och God love him. He's in a better place nigh,' she wept. 'He was a lovely wee good livin' fella and he sang all them lovely gospel songs, so he did.'

I was surprised at Mrs Piper's distress over the dead Elvis because I knew for a fact that she strongly disapproved of sinful rock music. Mrs Piper was very saved indeed. She had once complained to the Rev. Lowe that my da was a devil in sheep's clothing because he was the DJ, playing Showaddywaddy to 'them poor innocent wee children', at the Westy Disco in the church hall. She had clearly never been inside the Westy Disco to meet the innocents.

Mrs Piper was convinced that Elvis was saved because he sang 'How Great Thou Art' with such feeling. She seemed to be much more forgiving of Elvis's sins than anybody else's. She bought a small white plain and a packet of German biscuits. I couldn't understand why these biscuits were called German because I never saw any German soldiers eating them in all those black and white war movies. As Leslie revved the engine and pressed the diddledee ding button to head towards the next stop, I wondered if Kimberley Mikados and Coconut Creams were called Irish biscuits in Germany.

After several more grief-stricken Elvis fans arrived seeking bread and crumbs of comfort, we crawled up the street to Mrs Grant's house. Leslie explained that she rarely entered the van itself, God love her, because her Richard was always bad with his pains, so I had to bring her bread order to the front door.

'Och look at you, ya wee crater!' she exclaimed as she answered the doorbell. 'You're all grown up nigh and doin' the bread for Leslie McGregor!'

Mrs Grant had a way of stating the obvious but I liked her because she had tipped me well as a paperboy. The poor woman had an awful lot to contend with because of her Richard and her only son, who was a genius at a university in England and never came home to see her.

'Thanks, love,' she said, as I conscientiously closed her front gate behind me. Up until this point it had been the first Elvis-free conversation of the morning. Everyone was saying how terrible it all was and it reminded them of when some brilliant president in America was shot dead and they all remembered what they were doing that day too. But Mrs Grant belatedly joined in the wake with the comment, 'There will only ever be one Elvis Presley!'

I nodded sensitively, like one of the undertakers from Wilton's on the Crumlin Road. I hoped that Mrs Grant was right, but within a year there were at least a dozen Elvises in Belfast alone.

As we turned the corner into the next street, on our way towards the main Ballygomartin Road, Leslie gave me the bad news that I had to deliver two plain and a wheaten bannock to Mr Black in No. 13. Mr Black had a grumpy oul' bake and two greyhounds that barked and snapped at your ankles. With his limited social skills it was unsurprising that he never joined us inside the Mini Shop. Instead, I had to leave his bread beside his back door, on the kitchen windowsill, which was always sticky with white gloss paint. I was hoping that this would require no interpersonal interaction with Mr Black, but on that very first morning his barking greyhounds attempting to chew on my Dr Martens must have wakened him. Just as I was escaping he opened the back door in his dressing gown, which made him look like George out of *George and Mildred* on UTV.

'Yer late!' he accused.

'Sorry, Mr Black, it's my first week and Elvis is dead.'

'And leave them dogs alone, ya wee hallion!' he added, ignoring my explanation.

Mr Black retrieved his bread from the windowsill and slammed the door without so much as a thank you for my services or a word of commiseration on the passing of The King. As I climbed back into the van with an obvious scowl on my face, Leslie said, 'C'mere til a tell ye, son! Never mind that oul' fella. See him. He's hateful til everyone except them there dogs of his.'

I appreciated this support from my line manager. Leslie was being protective. He had clearly realised already that I was going to be good, and in turn I understood that employee satisfaction was high on his agenda.

The Saturday morning bread round involved circling the whole of the Upper Shankill. We started out in my street of neat semis and then went down the Road to all the old red-brick terraced houses. Next, we skirted the enemy territory of Ardoyne, where the IRA lived, to serve the pensioners who lived in small houses with metal grilles on their windows on the peace line. Then we turned back up the hill to serve the big estate where they had a green for the Eleventh boney and a community centre for the paramilitaries. Next, we drove along another high peace wall that protected us from the other side. And finally, tired from all our labours, we crossed the main road dividing the Council estate from our posh three-bedroom semis and we slowly retraced our tracks back to my house again.

I already knew most of the customers in my street. In fact I even had a previous customer service relationship with most of them from being a paperboy and doing wee jobs for ten pence a go as a Scout during Bob-a-Job week. However once we headed down the Road and around the big estate I met all sorts of new customers.

Miss Adams lived in one of the very neat old terraced houses with a tiny front garden on the main road. I was fairly certain Miss Adams wasn't related to Gerry. She was in her seventies and had never married. She was what my mother called 'a spinster and a real lady', like my Great Aunt Maud who wore pearls and spoke proper and lived in a nursing home. I sometimes noticed Miss Adams at church in a fur coat on Remembrance Sunday. Her father had been a soldier in the Great War but he had been dead now much longer than Elvis. Miss Adams was so thin and fragile I feared she would snap in two if she slipped on the steep steps up into the van, but thankfully on my first morning on duty she avoided any such trauma.

'Good morning Miss Adams,' said Leslie politely.

'Good morning Mr McGregor,' she replied.

'Lovely day!' commented Leslie.

'Gives rain,' replied Miss Adams.

'What can I do for you this morning, Miss Adams?' asked Leslie.

'Just a small pan and a chocolate Swiss roll, please, if you don't mind, Mr McGregor,' Miss Adams responded pleasantly.

It sounded more like *Are You Being Served?* on BBC1 than the Ormo Mini Shop up the Shankill.

'Dreadful business about that young singer,' said Miss Adams. 'He was such a nice young man.'

Then she looked at me and added, as if in some way connecting me with the late Elvis Presley, 'Only always do your very best, young man, as your very best is only always what you can do.'

As we departed, this riddle rang in my ears. I couldn't quite work it out but I assumed Miss Adams meant that I should try to do a good job delivering the bread.

I feared that the next section of the bread round would be a more dangerous part of the job, serving pensioners on the peace line beside Ardoyne. However it turned out to be very peaceful on the peace line so early on Saturday morning. Petrol bombers mustn't have used amazing white plastic digital alarm clocks at the weekend. The only hazards were the remains of riots from the night before. Leslie had to swerve round broken bottles and smashed red bricks on scorched tarmac. All the little houses were very similar along this road and all the old ladies wore the same housecoats and had the same hairstyle of slightly pink hair in curlers. It was like serving bread to a street full of Hilda Ogdens from *Coronation Street*. Almost everyone got one pan and one plain with two soda farls and two potato farls. This was their bread for the week. Everyone paid out of the same red leather purses and said 'Thanks very much nigh, love.'

One of our customers on the peace line was Mrs McAllister. She lived in a house with metal grids across all the windows, to stop stones and petrol bombs getting in, with her only daughter who was in a wheelchair. Their house looked like a big hamster cage but if you looked through the metal grids you could see beautiful Delft horses on the inside windowsills looking out at you.

'Here, take in a Coke for the wee girl in the wheelchair, son. She's not right, you know, but she loves a wee mineral,' said Leslie.

I did as I was bid and Mrs McAllister's daughter shrieked with delight at the sight of the can of cola. She had one of the happiest faces I had ever seen, even though she lived in a wheelchair in a house with caged windows on the peace line. Maybe there were advantages to being 'not right'. I was very pleased to meet her. She pointed to a picture of Elvis on the wall and chuckled. Mrs McAllister had torn The King out of the *Sun* and stuck him up on the wall of her working kitchen beside the Queen. I pointed and chuckled too and felt quite evil for doing so.

Once we left the peace line behind we relaxed on our way back up the main road, past Oul' Mac's newsagent shop and towards the big estate. This was the longest uninterrupted drive of the day and it provided a brief repose from bread, before the busiest part of the morning in the council estate where people queued up to get into the Mini Shop. Leslie whistled a hymn as we travelled onward. I think it was 'Bread of Heaven'.

The first customers to arrive in the van when we stopped in the estate were Mr and Mrs Rosbottom. The Rosbottoms weren't just fat, they were what my biology teacher called obese, and I soon learned why.

'Six pan, four plain, four boxes of gravy rings, eight soda, eight tatie farls, two boxes of Tunnock's teacakes, four Cokes, a packet of coconut slices and three of them there packets of chocolate digestive biscuits, love,' said Mrs Rosbottom. This was too much bread and confectionery for a new breadboy to remember in one go, so I had to ask her to repeat the order several times. Mrs Rosbottom was smaller than her husband and this made her appear exceptionally round. She reminded me of one of my wee brother's favourite toys – a Weeble which wobbled but never fell down, no matter how many times you pushed it over. I had an urge to knock over Mrs Rosbottom just to see if she would bounce up again. Mr Rosbottom was bigger than his wife both vertically and horizontally and he was a man of very few words. I gradually learned that his main function on a Saturday morning was to transport most of their huge stock of goods into the house. However, he did make one remark that first morning, given the exceptional circumstances. 'He's not dead, ye know. He's still alive,' he whispered in Leslie's ear, as he burdened the steps beneath him.

'That's it, brother. Praise the Lord!' agreed Leslie, clearly mistaking the remark as devotion to Jesus rather than Elvis.

'That'll keep youse goin' over the weekend,' said Leslie as the couple headed towards the steps with several kilograms of bread loaded in their chubby arms.

'Themuns must have a powerful lot of children to feed,' I said to Leslie as we drove off in the considerably lightened van.

'No, son, them two live on their own.'

For some strange reason my first encounter with the Rosbottoms made me feel hungry.

Billy Cooper's wee granny with the curlers was next to enter the van. She was not a woman for small talk and simply presented her weekly request.

'A pan, a plain, two soda and two pataita,' she said.

The next customer on the estate was a Very Important Man. In fact he was THE most important man in the whole neighbourhood. Big Duff was a paramilitary with tattoos and big gold rings and an Ulster Flag hanging from his bedroom window all year round. Everyone in the estate was dead scared of him because if you didn't give him money for the loyalist prisoners or if you mixed with Catholics, apart from to hurt them, then he could get you put out of the estate. He never carried out the intimidation personally because he was too busy running the bar in the community centre. Instead he got wee hard lads – the ones at my primary school who couldn't read – to put on balaclavas to do his dirty work for him. Leslie tiptoed around Big Duff and was very careful about what he said to him, as if he was someone really important like the prime minister or Gloria Hunniford. I liked Big Duff even less than I liked Elvis. The King was hard to listen to but at least he never got anyone kneecapped for robbing the post office. I was afraid that if Big Duff found out I was a teenage pacifist who tried not to hate Catholics too much, I would be banished from ever delivering another soda farl on his estate.

But in spite of my fear and resentment of Big Duff, I understood that this week must have been a difficult time for him because of Elvis and all. So I attempted to make a customer–provider connection.

'I'm sure you're ... er ... ragin' about Elvis, Big Duff,' I faltered, as I handed the paramilitary a pan loaf.

I was making small talk with a real live paramilitary. I hoped Jesus wouldn't mind. I genuinely couldn't think of any 'thou shalt not talk to paramilitaries' in the Bible, not even in the King James version. I had never encountered such a reputedly dangerous man before, although it was rumoured one year when I was wee boy that the Santa whose knee I sat on in the grotto in town was actually a brigadier in the UDA.

'Listen to me, son,' he replied with a definite air of power. I obeyed and, as my nervous fingers dug into his pan loaf, he continued, 'You see, there's themuns that's born for greatness and there's themuns that's nat! And Elvis Presley was ...' – his voice cracked with emotion – 'The King!'

I was shocked. Big Duff was filling up. This did not correspond with his reputation. He wiped a tear from his eye and rubbed his nose on the Ulster tattoo on the back of his hand. I had not expected these emotions from a loyalist leader. It had never occurred to me that paramilitaries cried, especially not over American rock and roll singers.

Then Big Duff composed himself and announced, 'My community regrets the passing of a great man!'

Although I disagreed with this pronouncement, I realised that when Big Duff said 'my community' you weren't allowed to contradict him or you wouldn't be allowed in 'his community' any more.

I dutifully handed him his pan loaf and he departed the van with a walk of great authority. Leslie sighed and quickly pressed the diddledee ding button and this satisfactorily changed the atmosphere. As we drove off I looked back at Big Duff through the rear window. I could just make out a hole in the side of his pan loaf where my fingers had pierced the packaging during the tense encounter. I prayed that he wouldn't notice or I would be in big trouble. I imagined Big Duff chasing me in his Ford Cortina like in *The Sweeney* and catching up with me in a dead-end entry and forcing me to replace the loaf or else.

Halfway through the estate, we parked beside the bins at the back of the chippy where no customers would disturb us. It was 10 a.m. and time for my first mid-morning break and we tucked into a mortally damaged box of apple turnovers. Just as we were finishing our cans of Lilt, my old mate Philip Ferris arrived at the van to ask for change of a ten-pound note for his mother's coalman. This was typical of Philip Ferris. Not only did he enter the van while the workers were officially off duty, but he also had the cheek to ask for a currency exchange service without so much as an apology for failing even to buy a crumb of bread. But at least Philip provided some relief from the incessant adoration of Elvis, which had dominated my first day as a breadboy. As he climbed down the steps of the van with ten one pound notes stuffed in the breast pocket of his Wrangler jacket I realised we had not yet commiserated.

'Did you hear about Elvis?' I enquired.

'Elvis Presley? So what! He was ballicks!' replied Philip.

Philip was usually very annoying because he was never impressed by anyone, apart from Geordie Best, but on this one instance I had to concur with his assessment. However Philip's use of bad language in Leslie's presence did not go down well at all.

'C'mere til a tell ye, wee lad,' interjected Leslie, 'Any more of that oul' cursin' of yours and I'll tell your da and you'll be off the BB football team next year!'

I could tell by Phillip's face that he took this threat very seriously. However as he walked off sulkily I am sure I heard a further muffled 'ballicks' from under his breath.

When we finally arrived back in my street that first Saturday morning, Leslie pulled up the handbrake with a sigh of satisfaction at a job well done.

'Well done, young lad!' he said. 'You'll do all right, so you will!'

I glowed in the light of this professional praise.

Leslie presented my with my £3.50 wages which I had already spent in my head on a fish supper and a plastic *Millennium Falcon*. As a bonus he presented me with a damaged packet of potato farls and a dented crusty loaf. I thanked my boss politely, jumped down the steps of the van in one leap and ran into the house proudly bearing my spoils.

Dad was in the kitchen, melting lard in the pan to make us a big Ulster fry and it smelt delicious. I was able to add my potato farls as a contribution to the feast. I felt like a caveman coming home from the hunt with a dead, hairy pig on a broom handle.

Big T was playing 'Una Paloma Blanca' on Downtown and I sang along as the fat spat from the cooker across the kitchen.

'Much did yer man McGregor pay ye, son?' asked Daddy, as he slapped the streaky bacon into the bubbling pan.

'Thee fifty, Daddy,' I replied.

My father rolled his eyes and shook his head. Without so much as a word I was able to translate these gestures as saying that if yer man Leslie was that good livin' you would think he could pay a wee lad better than that!

Mammy was in the living room sewing a halterneck dress for a swanky woman from Glengormley to wear to a dinner dance for guide dogs in the boarded-up Europa Hotel.

'How'd ya get on with your bread, love?' she called from the next room.

'Aye, dead on!' I replied, as my mouth began to water for my fried potato farls.

'Was any of them oul' dolls bad to you?' she enquired.

'No Mammy, just Mr Black, but sure he's an oul' blurt to everyone.' I answered, as the smell of crispy bacon began to permeate the entire house.

'Aye, pay no attention to that oul' git, love. All he cares about is them bloody greyhounds!' she added supportively.

'Is everybody still distracted about Elvis, love?' she added.

'Aye, Mammy!' I replied.

'Fry's ready!' shouted Dad.

My two brothers appeared from the garden shed where my big brother had just won my wee brother's pocket money in a game of poker. We all sat down together as a family around the Formica picnic table that just about fitted into the living room. Our Ulster fry was served, complete with the potato farls I had contributed to the house. It was a perfect Saturday morning. The King may have been dead, but my new career as a breadboy had just been born, so it had.

3

SATURDAY NIGHT FEVER AT THE WESTY DISCO

'Them Bee Gees sing quare and high, so they do!' said Titch McCracken with a genuine look of amazement on his freckled face, as he sucked on a shoplifted Curly Wurly.

'Fruits,' said Phillip Ferris.

Saturday Night Fever had exploded on to the Upper Shankill.

The Bee Gees were shrieking 'Stayin' Alive' at the Westy Disco. My da, who was the oldest DJ in town, even turned the volume down a little in case we got too close to the two enormous speakers on either side of his rickety double-decks. Dad got scared after he watched a long documentary on BBC2 about loudspeakers making young people at pop concerts go deaf. He worried that if the high pitch of the Bee Gees' falsetto did any permanent damage to our tender teenage ears then the school nurse would pin the blame on him.

The old Nissen hut on the West Circular Road was throbbing to the amazing new disco beats from America. There were dangers from bombs and bullets outside but we were safe with bubblegum and boogie inside. Everyone was talking about *Saturday Night Fever* and disco dancing and John Travolta. Mrs Piper said my father was leading us all to hell because disco dancing was a sin, as it made you want sex. My da told her to catch herself on.

'Night Fever' was sweeping away the Rollers and the Osmonds and was even keeping ABBA off the number one spot, even though Benny and Bjorn had tried very hard to copy the Bee Gees with 'Summer Night City'. The hit parade in the Westy Disco was changing too. 'Night Fever' made old dances like the Slush look very old fashioned and only middle-aged women did it now to Elton John and Kiki Dee at dinner dances and weddings. No one requested 'The Hucklebuck' anymore either, much to my father's disappointment, because it reminded him of the showbands and the dance halls in Belfast where he had fallen in love with my mother in the olden days in the 1950s.

'But all the wee girls love them there Bee Gees and they're millionaires and all,' continued Titch. 'I wish I was a Bee Gee.'

This was ridiculous! I couldn't imagine anyone in the world who was less suitable Bee Gee material than Titch McCracken.

'Like, are you thick as champ, wee lad?' interjected Heather Mateer, as she took a break from snogging an accordionist from Rathcoole. 'You can't be ginger and wee and a Bee Gee!'

We were all sitting around an old wooden table beside the tuck shop at the Westy Disco. The words UVF, UDA, ABBA and AC/DC were carved, one on top of the other, each acronym darker and deeper into the grain of the wood. The tabletop was a battlefield for both paramilitary and pop dominance. Our weapon of choice was the penknife, if Uncle Henry hadn't confiscated it when he searched us for drink at the door. I had declined to participate, not just because I was the only teenage pacifist in

West Belfast, but in case Leslie recognised my writing and I got sacked. Leslie helped my parents and Uncle Henry and Auntie Emma to clean up the mess at the end of the Westy Disco every Saturday night so the floor would be clean for Sunday School the next morning. He didn't want the wee children to get their good clothes dirty when they were sitting on the floor colouring in Jesus feeding the five thousand. This clean-up was a major task because the spat-out chewing gum of four hundred teenagers would stick very stubbornly to the old wooden floor of the Nissen hut. Compacted Wrigley's was almost impossible to remove, like the glue from my Airfix Spitfire model I had spilled on my mother's good Formica table. The wooden floor of the Westy Disco was covered in thousands of blobs of bubblegum. Some of the gum had hardened like Polyfilla but other blobs remained sticky and clung to your platforms on contact. Every week, after Leslie had scraped chewing gum from the floor, he also inspected the premises for the slightest evidence of any new graffiti. On several occasions he was able successfully to identify the culprit, like when Billy Cooper foolishly scratched 'Scoop Rools OK' on the toilet door. It was his nickname and the limited spelling ability that gave him away. I realised that vandalism was incompatible with Leslie's expectations of a good breadboy so I resisted a persistent urge to express my love for Agnetha in carved form on any wall, door or table in the Westy Disco. I used the back of my school exercise books as my canvas instead, apart from my chemistry book because when I was chemistry class I had a much more immediately available object of affection.

'Aye, themuns' white trousers in the Bee Gees is even tighter than yours, Ginger Bap,' my big brother replied to Titch, and then added unnecessarily, 'Cause yer oul' ma can't even afford to buy ye a new pair!'

Titch hit a reddener instantly and, with him being pale and ginger, this was very red indeed. Poor Titch blushed more brightly than anyone else I knew. I usually only blushed when Judy Carlton smiled at me or when Clint Eastwood had sex with a woman with her breasts out in front of my parents in the living room in a late film on BBC2. But Titch McCracken hit a reddener at almost anything. Of course, let's face it, he did have an awful lot to be embarrassed about. Getting caught stealing sweetie mice from the Mace and setting fire to our street's telephone box were just the tip of the iceberg. However on this occasion I was on Titch's side because I understood the devastating impact of a public put-down from my big brother. It was at times such as this I was tempted to reveal to the whole world that my hard-man brother was the same seventeen-year-old who cried when Mary Ingalls went blind in *Little House on the Prairie*. And yet I realised if I dared to expose this shameful fact he would knock my melt in every day for the next three weeks.

We had just emptied several packets of Tayto cheese and onion crisps and we were washing away the debris from our teeth and braces with brown lemonade from a big, big C&C bottle. The Bee Gees were now screaming 'night fever' in the Nissen hut and everyone was up dancing and doing that up-and-down diagonal pointing. It seemed that everyone in the Westy Disco had Night Fever. Well, nearly everyone.

'Bee Gees ballicks!' grunted Philip Ferris, predictably.

I wanted to be John Travolta in a white suit, dancing in the middle of the floor with all the girls admiring my moves, but they didn't sell any white suits in my size in the *Great Universal Club Book*. So I had to improvise with my old flared jeans that had been washed so many times they were nearly white. I also sported a white cap-sleeved T-shirt from John Frazer's in Gresham Street, even though it exposed the fact that I still had no discernible upper arm muscles, in spite of lifting hundreds of loaves every Saturday morning.

'I heard that the thee of themuns sing up high like that the whole way through the movie, so they do,' Irene Maxwell added, with her usual air of authority on matters of art and culture. Irene got *Jackie* magazine.

'Fuckin' fruits!' was my big brother's musical critique. He was now competing with Philip Ferris for biggest-hard-man-in-the-group status.

Philip responded by taking out his penknife and carving a new word beginning with a P into the much-abused tuck shop table.

'I wanna go and see it, cause the music's brilliant and yer man John Travolta's lovely, so he is,' announced Irene. 'Everyone in my class is goin'. Are yousens goin'?' she enquired.

I was a little concerned because as far as I knew *Saturday Night Fever* was X-rated and I was worried that I might not get in.

'Heather Mateer's already been to see it five times in the ABC!' added Irene.

'Aye,' confirmed Heather proudly as she skilfully wound pink chewing gum around her forefinger. The wee lad from Rathcoole was agog at her tongue and finger skills.

This movie was becoming a major cultural phenomenon on the Upper Shankill. I had never heard of so many people wanting to go and see a movie since *Jaws* and as far as I could tell no one even got their head bitten off in *Saturday Night Fever*. I couldn't imagine going to the same movie five times, although I had gone to see *Jaws* twice because it was better when you knew in advance which severed body parts were about to appear under the water.

Irene proceeded to provide us with all of the vital information she had gleaned from *Jackie* magazine.

'John Travolta's dead gorgeous, so he is. He dances in a big disco with flashin' lights under the floor in a white suit and a big sparkly mirror ball hangin' from the ceiling and all,' she explained.

'Is that it?' I enquired. 'Is there no story?'

I thought this was a reasonable question, now that I was studying *The Merchant of Venice* for my English GCE.

'Wise up, wee lad. It's a musical,' was Irene's knowledgeable response. 'Musicals don't have to have stories.'

At this point I was tempted to argue with Irene as I remembered watching *White Christmas* and it was a very famous musical and it definitely had a story. Miss Baron at BRA had promised we would be doing *West Side Story* as the school play next year and I was certain it had a story about gangs and fighting like in Belfast.

'Well are yousens all goin' to see the bloody filum or nat?' asked my big brother.

'Aye,' said Irene. 'My Uncle Sparky says he'll give us a lift to the ABC some Friday night as long as there's no bombs and we give him 50p for petrol.'

This was an offer too generous to refuse and so it was agreed. We would finally get to see the whole film rather than wee bits on *Top of the Pops*. My big brother and I, Irene Maxell, Heather Mateer, Titch and Philip Ferris were going to see the greatest movie of all time, apart from *Star Wars*, of course. I would have preferred to go to the cinema with Judy Carlton but I had yet to initiate verbal communication with her and I assumed her father wouldn't allow her to go to the ABC to see an X-rated movie with a wee lad from up the Shankill. It was *Star Wars* that I really wanted to see because I was coming to the conclusion that, in spite of *Night Fever*, I probably wanted to be Luke Skywalker more than I wanted to be John Travolta. All the girls loved John Travolta but Luke had Princess Leia who was lovely apart from her funny hairstyle that no one ever got done in His 'n' Hers beside the Shankill graveyard.

Once we had decided we were going to see *Saturday Night Fever* I had an urge to get up on the dance floor in my nearly white flared jeans and my white T-shirt and dance like John Travolta himself. I jumped up from the tuck shop table and walked across to the middle of the dance floor. I tried to walk dead sexy like John Travolta. I had never before seen anyone march down a street less like an Orangeman. I tried to strut all cool and swagger like Travolta but it was difficult to pull it off because the chewing gum kept sticking to my platform soles. In my enthusiasm to hit the dance floor I bumped into my wee brother, causing him to spill his sherbet dip all over the floor. Whenever sherbet made contact with freshly spat-out chewing gum on the floor of the Westy Disco it fizzled like an experiment in chemistry class.

I had been secretly practising the dance moves from 'Night Fever' in front of the big mirror in my parents' built-in wardrobe in their bedroom. These rehearsals had improved my dancing immensely, but one day my pointing hand knocked over the Spanish donkey my Uncle Freddie had brought us from the Costa Brava. The stuffed donkey flew across the bedroom and when it collided with the woodchip wall its head snapped off. I hid the damaged donkey at the back of the wardrobe, underneath old plastic handbags that smelt of perfume.

For some time now I had been trying to slick my hair back like John Travolta. I made use of my baldy father's redundant, ten-year-old jar of Brylcreem from the back of the bathroom cupboard, but I still looked more like Fonzie than Travolta. Spurred on by the exciting prospect of my forthcoming trip to the ABC, I flicked my hair and strutted onto the Westy Disco dance floor, imagining I was John Travolta himself. Everyone except Titch and Philip followed me. My great moment was spoiled somewhat when my father stupidly put on Boney M singing 'Hooray, hooray, it's a holi-holiday'. I was too embarrassed to sit down again so soon after my big entrance, so I danced through the song half-heartedly and with a sneer on my face in case anyone watching suspected I was a Boney M fan. I ended up dancing in a circle beside Lynn McQuiston with the buck teeth, Sammy Reeves who didn't wash much, Irene Maxwell, my big brother and Irene's white handbag. My big brother did not attempt any Travolta moves at all. He just did his usual boot-boy stomp in his Dr Martens to show how hard he was. Lynn McQuiston had recently transferred her affections from Les McKeown from the Bay City Rollers to John

Travolta. This was a good barometer – indicating that John was officially the new pop idol for teenage girls. As she boogied down to Boney M, I was amazed that not one article of Lyn's clothing was tartan. This would have been unthinkable even a year ago. Irene was dancing much too enthusiastically beside me in her sequinned boob tube, but she still had no boobs even though she was old enough to grow some. Thankfully my father eventually noticed his error with the playlist and put on 'Night Fever' again, for the sixth time that night. Within seconds the dance floor was full, just like when he put on 'Dancing Queen'.

I imagined I was John Travolta at a big disco in New York and all the girls were about to gather round me in an adoring circle. But as I began to try to dance like Travolta, I noticed with great surprise that Sammy Reeves was doing all the moves much better than me or anyone else on the dance floor. Sammy was wearing a proper white suit, but it must have been his granda's because it was too big on him and it didn't have flares. He must have been to see the movie already or he must have got the dance instructions from the *Jackie* pull-out special because he was brilliant. A circle of girls began to gather around him just like with John Travolta in the clip from the movie, except the girls didn't dance too close to Sammy because of his BO and all. I was jealous of his dancing but I wasn't too worried because I knew Sammy would never be real competition for girls until he started to have a bath or at least began to use Denim aftershave to cover up the fact he was mingin'. I refused to give up and as the Bee Gees screeched their way towards the chorus I began to do my diagonal pointy thingummys in time with the music. This got me some welcome female attention. Two of the girls from Sammy's circle began to dance towards me and one of them wasn't wearing pink National Health glasses. Then Irene Maxwell started to dance right in front of me and gaze up at me lovingly, like the blonde lady gazed up at the blind one with the UDA sunglasses in Peters & Lee. Irene was smiling right at me with her whole brace. She had never showed this much interest in me before, even when I had delivered her precious *Jackie* when I was a paperboy. My Travolta pointy diagonals had obviously been so impressive that she now looked upon me in a completely different way. If only Judy Carlton could see me now, I thought, she would be similarly captivated. As the last refrain of 'Night Fever' approached, I was determined to win more girls from Sammy Reeves. He was sweating now and stinking even more and consequently the circumference of his circle of girls was ever widening. I thrust myself into my most determined moves yet, when all of a sudden my legs disappeared from beneath me.

Suddenly and with a crash I found myself lying flat on my back on the sticky wooden floor while 'Night Fever' continued above me. In the midst of my initial disorientation I tried to work out what had happened. I couldn't possibly have slipped. The large clumps of chewing gum on which I now rested made slipping almost impossible. As I began to get up I caught a brief glimpse, between Irene Maxell's legs, of Titch McCracken and Philip Ferris running towards the boys' toilets in hysterical fits of laughter. As I got up to chase after the two wee bastards who had deliberately destroyed my performance, I noticed large quantities of warm and sticky, grey chewing gum now attached to the backside of my jeans. My father put on Demis Roussos and the floor cleared. He should have known better. As I rushed towards the boys' toilets, attempting to pull the chewing gum from my rear end, my big brother followed close behind shouting, 'Why are you feelin' your own bum, ya wee pervert?'

I was grateful to Demis Roussos for blocking out the sound of these humiliating taunts. When I arrived at the door of the toilets it was locked and from the inside I could hear Titch and Philip shouting and laughing uncontrollably, like the Martian robots in the Smash advert.

'Tony Travolta landed on his arse!' guffawed Titch.

'Saturday Night Ballicks,' laughed Philip.

I stomped back to the tuck shop table and sat down alone. This was typical of Belfast. If you were even nearly good at something everyone tried to knock you down. Even if you were brilliant at something nobody really liked it. They always said, 'Ah, but...'. If you got your eleven-plus, like very few of us on the Shankill, then they said, 'Ah, but he'll never survive in a grammar school.' If someone got a brand new Ford Cortina people would say, 'Ah, but he couldn't afford a Ford Capri', and if someone got a good job in the bank they said, 'Ah, but he wasn't smart enough to be a doctor.' When I told Titch that my family was going to Butlin's in Mosney for Easter he said, 'Ah, but can youse not afford Disneyland?' When I told Timothy Longsley at BRA that the Westy Disco might be going to London to get away from the Troubles for a week he said, 'Ah, but if you weren't wee deprived plebs from up the Shankill, you wouldn't be going anywhere!'

These negative attitudes surrounded me like an army cordon

in a riot. No one was ever allowed to become a big-head in Belfast. You weren't allowed to be too good at anything. Nobody would let you. If you dared to excel at anything then someone would slap you down sooner or later. My father called this behaviour 'begrudgery'. He once said, 'This country is full of nothin' but a shower of begrudgers!' and I agreed with him. But then he went and did it too! At the remotest indication of self-congratulation my father would always remind me, 'No son of mine is gonna turn into no big-head.' Maybe this was why all the big-heads left Belfast and never came back. Why would they want to come back to live in a place where you had to hide your talents? Sometimes I hated this city. It was a strange feeling because I loved the place, but these harsh attitudes squashed you down. I sometimes wondered if I should get out and join all the big-heads across the water.

I tried to get up from the table to go home early in the huffs and watch *The Two Ronnies*, but I found I couldn't move. The chewing gum on the backside of my jeans had glued me to the chair. As I began to extricate myself from the sticky seat, I could just see the chewing gum on the back of my jeans stretching like stringy cheese on a pizza in an American movie. Just then Irene Maxwell ran over, beaming with her newfound interest in me.

'Never worry about themuns, they're just jealous wee shites,' she said.

I appreciated the beauty of these words of consolation but I didn't fancy her back. Irene got so close to my face I could actually smell the Tayto cheese and onion on her breath. She looked deeply into my eyes and said, 'I thought you were brilliant, so I did. You've got lovely John Travolta hair and all.'

As she spoke, Irene began to give me an affectionate pat on the back and I let her because I knew she was starting to adore me. But then she stopped suddenly and looked in horror at the palm of her hand. Warm sticky chewing gum from the floor of the Westy Disco had made its way from my back to her hand and she was horrified.

'Disgustin'!' she squealed and ran off in the direction of the girls' toilets.

Auntie Emma stopped selling sweetie mice at the tuck shop for a second and looked at me questioningly, as if I had done something on Irene to provoke this unfortunate reaction.

'Never touched her!' I said, holding up both hands to everyone who was now staring at me. I went redder than Titch McCracken.

I looked down and momentarily noticed the word Philip Ferris had just carved into the tuck shop table. It said 'PUNK'. I was surprised because Philip had never before expressed an affiliation with any musical movement. I got up and left the Westy Disco, sadly and alone, to the strains of Kate Bush's 'Wuthering Heights'. I was scundered and nobody cared. It wasn't fair! I was stuck in Belfast where you weren't allowed to be a good dancer or be a big-head or be brilliant at anything. I was stuck in this hateful city as firmly as the chewing gum to the floor of the Westy Disco. I was fed up, so I was.

4

BOY MEETS WONDER GIRL

Judy Carlton was lovely, so she was. She had vivid blue eyes and silky black hair like a lovely model in a commercial for Harmony hairspray. Judy looked like Lynda Carter who was Wonder Woman. According to *Look In* magazine, Lynda Carter had been a Miss America or something before she started to spin around and around on TV every week to turn into a gorgeous superhero. Wonder Woman wore sexy American-flag hot pants and bullet-deflecting bracelets. I wanted Judy Carlton to be my own personal Wonder Woman, in any colour of hot pants, and I thought that every woman in Belfast deserved to have a pair of bullet-deflecting bracelets.

Even though I was all grown up now, I had only experienced one true love. Sharon Burgess had been my first sweetheart. She had beautiful brown eyes and lovely brown hair, flicked like the blonde one in Pan's People on *Top of the Pops*. During the course of our relationship I had taken Sharon in a black taxi down the Shankill to see the Bay City Rollers in concert at the Ulster Hall. I was a very romantic person. Sharon displayed more interest in me than in Les McKeown that night. But sadly it had all gone terribly wrong when she started asking me for too much commitment. Sharon expected me to be present with her at the Westy Disco every single Saturday night, even when it clashed with the *Eurovision Song Contest* or a repeat of the *Morecambe and Wise Christmas Show*. To be perfectly honest, in the end I had to dump poor Sharon. No matter what Titch McCracken told everyone, I chucked Sharon. She definitely did not do the chucking. All right?

Later, to prove she still hadn't got over me, I heard through the grapevine that she may have fallen in love with my big brother. But he wasn't interested in her because he preferred girls who did gymnastics. Sharon ended up with a wee lad that stacked shelves in the Co-op. I realised I had broken her heart. It was very sad and tragic, like that *Love Story* movie on TV, except nobody died. Poor Sharon thought we were going to be a forever couple like Bjorn and Agnetha in ABBA. It must have been very hard for her, but I hope she got over me.

After Sharon, I had contented myself with weekly episodes of *Charlie's Angels* for a while, as an alternative to a real-life girlfriend. But even Farrah Fawcett-Majors up on my bedroom wall in a swimsuit wasn't the same as having a real girlfriend who would hold your hand and kiss you like she meant it, the way Sharon Burgess had during Donny Osmond songs on the dance floor of the Westy Disco. When Farrah left *Charlie's Angels* I redirected my affections to Lyndsay Wagner, the Bionic Woman, for a short while. But this relationship didn't work out either. I enjoyed watching Lyndsay run in slow motion, but the Bionic Woman and I simply weren't compatible. Inevitably, the very first time I set my eyes on Wonder

Woman I knew that my relationship with Lyndsay Wagner was over. My love life was becoming more complicated than the trials of Sandy in the wheelchair in *Crossroads*, but I realised this was just a part of being all grown up now.

Fate had placed Judy Carlton and me in the same chemistry class. On the momentous morning of our first lesson together, Judy sat directly opposite me on the other side of the classroom. I had never noticed her before this because, even though we had been in the same form for three years, we had never been in the same class. I didn't even know her name until Miss Kelly, the chemistry teacher, started to do the roll call and I heard Judy whisper a shy 'present Miss' after the name 'Miss Carlton'. Even though I learnt the name of every element on the periodic table that term, none of these names – not even the more interesting ones like neon and mercury – caught my interest like Judy Carlton's. All that separated me from her was Frankie Jones' spotty face, sitting right in front of me, and the back of Timothy Longsley's rather large head, sitting right in front of Judy. Every time I glanced up from my chemistry books I caught a glimpse of her pretty face, concentrating earnestly on an acid or an alkaline. Sometimes her porcelain forehead wrinkled as she struggled with the complexities of oxidization, but even then she remained perfect in my eyes. Whenever I lifted my head from the challenges of analysing a chemical reaction I could always detect her sweet smile across the classroom. As I gazed upon her loveliness my safety goggles steamed up and I couldn't see the blackboard properly and so sometimes copied down formulae incorrectly and lost marks in my homework. But I didn't care. Judy was worth every fogged-up goggle and every dropped mark. I could sense from her occasional glances and smiles in my direction that we were starting to develop a beautiful relationship, although we hadn't actually spoken to one another yet. So I made use of every opportunity to make first contact, like the aliens in *Close Encounters of the Third Kind*. When our chemistry teacher called the roll I said 'present Miss' firmly, in my deepest most broken voice. I tried to sound more Antrim Road than Shankill Road. I was sure this would capture Judy's attention. Miss Kelly was a very old and tiny teacher with wrinkles from Dublin. Frankie Jones said she was probably a Catholic because you weren't allowed to be a Protestant in Dublin. Miss Kelly had never married and Frankie asserted that this was the reason why she was grumpy most of the time. I wasn't so sure of this cause and effect hypothesis because my granda had been married to my granny for years and this seemed to make him grumpy most of the time. However even Miss Kelly's gloomy countenance could not smother the flames of love that were igniting right under her wrinkled nose, like a belligerent Bunsen burner refusing to extinguish even after you tried turning off the faulty gas tap.

Unfortunately there was one major barrier to my blossoming relationship with Judy Carlton and it was sitting right in front of her. It was Timothy Longsley. He was literally getting in the way. I had never met a real Timothy before I went to grammar school. There were no Timothys whatsoever on the Shankill and it wasn't even a Catholic name. I read about Timmys who drank lashings of ginger beer in Enid Blyton books. I watched plenty of posh English Timothys on sitcoms on BBC1 who called their parents mamaaa and papaaa. But I had no idea that we had real live Timothys right here in Northern Ireland. When I first went to BRA I discovered that there were at least a couple of Timothys in every class. They did all their homework and pronounced all their ings. The Timothys in books and on television were usually English twits to laugh at, but Timothy Longsley was no laughing matter. He was smart and rich and tall and good at rugby. He had been recruited into the Medallion Rugby Team even though he wasn't in fifth form yet. He was always being called up on to the stage during assembly to receive medals, applause and adoration for his great sporting achievements. When the PE teacher got us to pick teams for football, Timothy always got picked first and I got picked almost last, although mercifully before the boys with lisps and asthma. Of course Timothy had proper sideburns and he had already started shaving. He smelt of Mandate aftershave, which was Denim for rich people. The first form girls giggled when Timothy swaggered past them in the playground because they all fancied him. I couldn't understand why he impressed everyone because I had never met anyone so arrogant in my life. Timothy enjoyed exposing people's weaknesses in public acts of humiliation, usually in the playground. He looked down his nose at most people but he was particularly snotty with me when he discovered that I came from up the Shankill.

'Burnt any buses this weekend, van boy?' he asked sneeringly one Monday morning in front of Judy in the playground.

'Don't show your ignorance, Longsley. Sure you know I'm a pacifist, so I am,' I responded firmly.

'Fucking stupid as well as poor!' he retorted. Several members of the Form 1 hockey squad passed by giggling irritatingly behind their hands. Timothy was a true test to my peace-loving values. I know I was supposed to be the only teenage pacifist from West Belfast, but I often had the urge to attempt some violence on Timothy. However, I restrained myself because I knew I had my principles to keep – and, apart from that, he was bigger than me and I knew I would only get decked.

Timothy Longsley lived up the Antrim Road in a big house with a million bedrooms and a swimming pool in the back garden surrounded by flowering cherry trees. His papaaa was a lawyer and his mamaaa always wore a fur coat and too much make-up at the school prize-giving. His brother played in the Glorious First XV rugby team and always got a prize for Latin. At school concerts, when his parents politely applauded off-tune Gilbert and Sullivan operetta, I noticed how clean their hands were. The Longsleys owned a cottage in La Someplace-or-Other-Sur-Mer in France. As a result of this unfair advantage he always came top of the class in French. We used to have a family holiday home too, but our caravan in Millisle-Sur-La-County-Down-Coast could never compete with what Timothy regularly referred to as 'ma petite gite'. I hated Timothy Longsley. He was a git with a gite.

However, it was his proximity to Judy Carlton that concerned me more than anything else. He got to sit opposite Judy in chemistry class, purely as a result of alphabetical seating. This privileged position ensured that he got to speak to Judy and do experiments with her. I watched from a distance with growing jealousy as I observed Judy sharing test tubes with Timothy. My envy grew when I noticed Timothy helpfully screwing Judy's retort stand.

'What's the matter, Tony?' asked Frankie Jones insensitively. 'Is Timmy experimenting with Juicy Judy again?'

He followed this remark with a laugh that was as filthy as the magazine hidden underneath his chemistry textbooks. Frankie's obsession with sex seemed to get worse with every fresh eruption of spots on his cheeks.

'Is she givin' his test tube a wee shake?' he added, with a deep and filthy cackle.

All of sudden everyone wanted to talk about sex and make jokes about sex all the time. Our teacher in RE said it was because we were going through puberty, which I thought sounded like going through purgatory and only Catholics did that. Frankie Jones knew more about sex than anyone else my age. He brought smutty magazines into school in his school bag and he told dirty jokes that I didn't fully understand. Frankie laughed hysterically every time I asked him to lend me his rubber. I soon learned to join in and laugh loudly at any dirty-sounding joke, just in case anyone noticed that I didn't understand everything there was to know about sex. In fact sex was turning out to be rather like chemistry. There was a lot of talk about the theory but very little practical experience. At the beginning of term it became clear that Frankie Jones had become the class expert in a new hobby called masturbation. He seemed to practise it an awful lot. I wondered if this was why he had so many spots.

'It's class!' he enthused to the uninitiated. 'It's like the real thing, except without a woman!'

This sounded fairly pleasurable to me, so I assumed it was a sin. I earnestly searched the Bible, but to my relief I could not find a relevant 'Thou Shalt Not'. At the beginning of term all the other boys in chemistry class made fun of Frankie Jones and called him a wanker. By the end of term we were all wankers (except Martin Patterson who said Jesus wouldn't let him).

With all of these teenage hormones rampaging around our chemistry class it was hard to concentrate on the actual task in hand. In spite of valiant efforts by Miss Kelly to teach me about elements and compounds, I used the precious hours in her classroom to analyse the extent to which there was chemistry between Judy Carlton and me. Eventually I realised I would have to speak to Judy and so I wondered how to set up some experiment to be the litmus test of our relationship. I had learned many years ago at the Westy Disco that if you wanted to let someone know you fancied them, you had to persuade a friend to check out the level of reciprocated interest first. The purpose of this was to reduce embarrassment, to save any unnecessary direct rejection, and also to avoid the scenario of your big brother shouting 'Turned down, sickener!' to the assembled crowd if the response happened to be negative. I had often been on the receiving end of such enquiries from the more available girls at the Westy Disco, who tended to be millies, who said 'fuck' a lot, and smoked, and twirled their chewing gum around their fingers between chews.

'Here, wee lad! Will you see my friend?' was the typical request.

I was determined to find some more sophisticated way of giving Judy the opportunity to respond to my advances, such as asking her to a disco. Judy lived in a posh house on the Antrim

Road so I assumed the Westy Disco up the Shankill would be out of the question. In chemistry I had a very limited pool of friends I could persuade to approach Judy for me. But I was also aware that if I didn't get a move on, Timothy Longsley would get in there first, and in no time at all, Judy would be cheering for him on the touchline at rugger games. It was this sense of urgency that led me to make my first big mistake with Judy. The nearest, most obvious person to make the initial enquiry was Frankie Jones. He was in the same class, sat opposite me and knew everything there was to know about girls and sex.

'Once a month they don't do PE in case they're pregnant,' he explained knowledgeably.

So I foolishly asked Frankie to find out if Judy liked me back.

'Will you ask her if she fancies me, Frankie?'

'Aye, no probs!' replied Frankie, as he preened a little on his stool at my recognition of his masterful way with women.

'Don't tell her I fancy her and don't make me sound like a hornball,' I instructed him.

Later that afternoon, as we left chemistry class, Frankie caught up with Judy on the stairs.

'Here, Judy!' called Frankie, much too loudly, as every pupil on the packed stairway seemed to fall silent.

'Hiya Frankie!' replied Judy sweetly.

'Whad'ya think of Macaulay?' he asked even more loudly.

'Who?' replied Judy.

'Yer man over there with the Leeds United school bag and the big spots on his chin!' said Frankie, pointing me out to Judy and the whole of the school.

'Dunno,' replied Judy, looking at me curiously, as if I had hitherto been the Invisible Man.

This was probably good news. It was all very embarrassing and I was hitting a serious reddener but this reply gave me great hope. It wasn't a no. But then Frankie destroyed the romantic moment with one devastating remark.

'He wants to snog you like he sucks a Cadbury's Creme Egg!'

Judy blushed, lowered her eyes and walked on briskly while several disgusted female classmates pointed in my direction shouting 'pervert'.

Frankie had no idea how inappropriate he had been with my sweetheart. I wanted to kick him so hard between the legs that he would have to abstain from masturbation for at least a day or two. But I realised a teenage pacifist should not even consider such violence so I went into the boys' toilets and kicked a urinal instead.

One day Judy Carlton would notice me, I was sure of it. It had to happen. Sooner or later, I imagined, we would become a proper couple like Paul and Linda McCartney. We would meet outside chemistry and I would bring her buns from the Ormo Mini Shop and she would accept an invitation to the Westy Disco, even though it was up the Shankill. We would dance and she would let me snog her. One day Judy Carlton would be my girl and everything would be brilliant. I was in love, so I was.

5

PARALLEL UNIVERSES

I was a Jedi Knight, so I was. I finally got to see *Star Wars* – the greatest movie of all time. When I sat down on the greasy, red-velvet tip-down seat that fateful night in the ABC Cinema I was unprepared for the magnitude of the thrill that ensued. I had never before seen anything so completely astonishing! It felt like you were right there on the spaceships with Luke Skywalker, Han Solo, Princess Leia, and the big hairy thing that honked. I could detect no strings holding up any of the spaceships, none of the walls wobbled and the monsters weren't just men in rubber suits. In fact *Star Wars* was barely a proper science-fiction movie at all! It made *Doctor Who* look wick. Luke's spaceship travelled so fast and so realistically that I kept ducking down in my seat in case I crashed into the side of the Death Star. It was like being on the roller coaster at Barry's Amusements on Bangor pier surrounded by alien enemies instead of hostile skinheads. I became obsessed with *Star Wars* in an instant. I wanted to acquire my very own lightsaber. I planned to hide the space-age weapon behind the Veda loaves in the Mini Shop. If there were any attempted hijackings I could extract it and protect Leslie from all the wee hoods. I imagined having my own wee R2-D2 and a posh English C-3PO robot to walk beside me and help to carry all the extra loaves to the Rosbottoms' house in the estate. I longed for The Force To Be With Me in case breadboys were made legitimate targets by the provos from the Dark Side. I began dreaming more about *Star Wars* than Olivia Newton-John and Wonder Woman put together. One Saturday morning Leslie caught me on in the back of the van using a long crusty bap as an improvised light saber. I had been imagining I was Luke Skywalker and Leslie was Obi-Wan Kenobi. Big Duff was Darth Vader and he had captured Judy Carlton, who was Princess Leia, and he was hiding her in the Death Star in the derelict flats on the estate. Leslie looked at me and cocked his head to one side in confusion at the sound of the strange 'voom' noise I made as I swung the bap. He obviously had no idea what a Jedi Knight looked like.

'C'mere til a tell ye, son,' said Leslie. 'Catch yourself on!'

'May the Force be with you!' I replied with a cheeky smile.

'Yes, brother! God bless you too. Praise the Lord!' replied Leslie, with no trace of irony.

As a Jedi Knight I could travel to a whole new universe a long time ago and far, far away. It seemed that all my heroes travelled to parallel universes. Captain James T. Kirk and Mr Spock with the pointy ears had ventured to parallel universes even more times than I had boldly gone to the caravan site in Millisle. *The Tomorrow People* on UTV were always jaunting to one parallel universe or another with their amazing teleporting belts and the Doctor slipped in and out of parallel worlds in the TARDIS as niftily as my big brother sneaked in and out of the bookies on the Woodvale Road.

Now that I was all grown up I was aware that I too frequented parallel universes, and without the use of dilithium crystals. On weekdays I went to school at Belfast Royal Academy with middle-class mates who got chauffeured in their daddys' new Rovers to discos at the rugby club, where they served chicken vol-au-vents and cheese cubes on cocktail sticks. But at weekends I inhabited a different world – the Ormo Mini Shop whose customers went down the Shankill in a black taxi to purchase pastie suppers and pickled eggs in Beattie's Fish and Chip Shop. Then – as if this wasn't enough to contend with – I had to deal with another two parallel universes, Planet Protestant and Planet Catholic. I lived on the Shankill and on the other side of the peace wall was the enemy territory of the Falls. Inhabitants of these two alien worlds rarely crossed the divide. We were like Romulans and Klingons but with normal heads and Belfast accents. Catholics and Protestants learnt two different histories in separate schools. We played different sports and supported opposite teams. We were taught to love our neighbours (but not necessarily our enemies) in separate churches and we got five-minute bomb warnings to evacuate different pubs.

I myself had very little idea about the shape of the world on the other side of the peace wall, although I was very curious about what it was really like over there. I sometimes wondered if they had a Catholic Ormo Mini Shop on the other side and if the breadboy was called Seamus. I wondered if Seamus was allowed to sell potato bread and soda bread for an Ulster fry because the

'Ulster' part made it sound much too Protestant for the provos to allow it on the Falls Road.

Now and again I caught a glimpse of life on Planet Catholic. My mother took all three of her sons to a big barber shop in Castle Street at the very bottom of the Falls Road and we got our hair cut with Catholics. She never articulated the words but it was clear that she trusted these barbers to get very close to our Protestant necks with scissors and razors. On one occasion a careless young barber nicked my ear with his scissors and drew blood, but there was no suggestion that this had been a sectarian attack. As I sat in the barber's chair and watched my shorn locks hit the floor I noticed how my Protestant hair was then swept up and mixed with the Catholic hair of the other customers. Black and brown hair, ginger and blond hair, Catholic and Protestant hair – all were brushed together into great ecumenical piles in the corner. At one such shearing we bumped into wee Theresa from the Falls Road with her three sons who were about the same age as us. Mammy had sewed trousers with wee Theresa in a suit factory before the Troubles. The six boys examined each other inquisitively as if we were looking into some cross-community mirror. Meanwhile wee Theresa whispered to my mother that sure half the women on the Falls Road still bought all their knitting wool in Mrs Quinn's wool shop on the Shankill. My mother nodded knowingly and added that it was terrible all that was going on, so it was, and sure it was a minority on both sides that was causing all the trouble, so it was. It occurred to me that perhaps the women of the Falls and the Shankill were secretly crossing these forbidden boundaries for wool and haircuts all the time, as if they were *The Tomorrow People*.

It may have been impossible for me to visit the alien world on the other side of the peace wall, but I was able to compare the parallel universes of grammar school and the Shankill Road at will.

In one universe I was an insignificant schoolboy who couldn't even play rugby. In another world, several black-taxi stops away, I was an exceptional breadboy with much-admired customer service competencies. It was like being Clark Kent one day and Superman the next, although I didn't own a pair of red underpants and, even if did, I would never have worn them over the top of my flared jeans because my big brother would have slagged me forever. From Monday to Friday I was a mild-mannered swot at BRA, but on Saturday mornings I was transformed into an Ormo superhero. One minute I was at grammar school with middle-class kids who loved rugby and learned classical piano and the next minute I was back home with customers who loved Linfield and learned the accordion. When the BRA rugger boys beat Methody in the Schools' Cup they crowed, 'Hurray! We were bloody amazing!' When Rangers beat Celtic, wee hoods on the Shankill yelled, 'Yo! We bate the Taigs!'

Most of the children at my primary school had failed the eleven-plus or didn't bother with it because grammar schools weren't really for us. Most kids just went to the secondary school round the corner, although quite a few didn't actually go there either as mitching was very popular. It was rumoured the boys' secondary school had the highest level of truancy in Europe. It was as if they had won the Eurovision Mitchin' Contest. There had never been a grammar school round the corner on the Shankill but no one seemed to mind. In spite of all of the requisite sacrifices, my parents were determined that their three sons would go to a grammar school no matter what. It was more important than new carpets or a holiday to a swimming pool in Torremolinos. In fact, I had never seen my parents more determined about anything. I suspected they might even have allowed a United Ireland if it meant their children got to grammar school, and there was no bigger sacrifice than that!

'No son of mine is going to end up working in no filthy foundry!' was my father's mantra.

I began to appreciate that Dad was prepared to work in a filthy foundry so that he could afford to buy his sons grammar school blazers every year.

On the Shankill I was rich because I lived in a semi-detached house with central heating and a rose bush in the front garden. My father was a respected foreman in the foundry and he could afford a car. In BRA I was poor because I didn't live in a detached house with an avocado bidet and a flowering cherry tree in the side garden. My father was a mere factory worker who drove a rusty respray. On the Shankill wee hoods called me 'a fuckin' college snob' while at BRA the rugger boys called me 'a bloody Shankill pleb'. As a breadboy I was rich because I could afford to buy cassettes with my bread tips, but as a schoolboy I was poor because I couldn't afford to go on ski trips. Of course ABBA were correct as usual when they said 'Money, money, money ... It's a rich man's world'. Benny and Bjorn didn't just write good tunes, they understood the social and economic problems of the world as well. It must have been a Swedish thing.

There were some advantages to living in two different worlds when you had expert knowledge of both. It was as if I could travel freely through a time-and-space vortex and have brave adventures across the galaxies. At BRA I took great pleasure in explaining to an ignorant Timothy Longsley the engineering for building a brilliant bonfire. On the other hand, during a Westy Disco trip to a chippy in Donaghadee, I tried to educate Titch McCracken on how to hold a fork properly. He threw it at me. You see, one universe was well ordered, with plenty of rules and resources, while the other universe was slightly chaotic, with more fun and fighting. Now that I was nearly shaving I began to feel torn between these two worlds. It reminded me of yer woman on *Top of the Pops* singing about being 'Torn Between Two Lovers'. I wondered if one day I would have to choose between the two universes. Should I stay on the Upper Shankill or should I leave and come up in the world? I loved home but if you went to university or got a good job in the bank you were supposed to leave the Shankill to go and live in posh Glengormley or swanky Bangor because it showed everyone how well you were doing. Mrs Grant's son had definitely chosen to leave. Some Saturday mornings she ordered extra potato bread to post to him at university in England along with a box of Tayto cheese and onion crisps. Apparently this unique Ulster fare was not immediately available in England. Mrs Grant sometimes cried when telling anyone who would listen about her Samuel being at university in England. She said she was crying with pride, but I think she was just missing him. Mrs Dunne's husband had disappeared to England with his cravat and his Shirley Bassey records and he never came back. Mrs Dunne said people accepted Mr Dunne better in England. This confused me because I thought Shirley Bassey was from Wales. At BRA our headmaster recommended that we all go to university in England or Scotland to broaden our horizons, but I noticed that of all the big brothers and sisters of my classmates who went to university across the water, very few ever came back.

Sometimes I felt like I belonged more in one universe than the other but as I got older there were times I felt I didn't belong in either. Thankfully one phenomenon was breaking through all barriers dividing these parallel universes. It was, of course, *Saturday Night Fever*. Nobody asked if John Travolta wanted a united Ireland or not and discos were taking off everywhere in Belfast. All of a sudden, out of nowhere, like a brick appearing over the peace wall, there was even talk of a school disco at BRA. This was unheard of! There had never been a disco at our prestigious grammar school before. One year the school choir was allowed to sing a Simon and Garfunkel song but that was about as rock and roll as we were permitted. This dipping of the music department's toe into the water of popular music proved controversial. Martin Patterson's parents complained that 'Bridge Over Troubled Water' was a song about taking heroine and claimed we were all going to turn into drug addicts. When I informed my father of the Pattersons' concerns about the addictive evils of Simon and Garfunkel he said, cryptically, 'Just goes to show you, son. Money people aren't always clever people.'

Our school had hitherto been much too clever for pop music, but now the Bee Gees had single-handedly smashed the ban in the same way I was certain their high-pitched voices could smash a glass tumbler. Thomas O'Hara whispered the startling news of the disco to me one day in chemistry class during litmus tests. Frankie Jones was still reeling from hearing Thomas talk about 'pHaitch' balance instead of pH balance. Evidently he had never sat beside a Catholic before.

My mind and my eyes turned immediately to Judy Carlton. She was sitting across the classroom, dipping litmus paper into a test tube with the utmost grace. I could never have invited Judy to the Westy, but a respectable school disco in the dinner hall with no smuggled vodka would be the perfect setting for our relationship to blossom.

With Miss Kelly's stooped back still turned, Frankie whispered across the classroom to Timothy Longsley, 'There's gonna be a school disco, so there is! Proper lumberin' in the dinner hall and all!'

'So what?' snorted Timothy.

'You not goin'?' enquired Frankie.

'Wise up, Jones!' replied Timothy.

This was very good news. I didn't like the way Judy was now helping Timothy to spell chemical compounds. I resented it when she pointed across the desk at his errors with her elegant fingers. Timothy did not deserve to have his exercise book touched by such loveliness. His typically arrogant rejection of the disco was most welcome. No Timothy meant no competition. I would have Judy all to myself. I just had to work out how to speak to her first.

I was on very solid ground with a disco. After all, I had been going to the Westy every Saturday night for years now. I could dance almost like Travolta, even on top of chewing gum and I knew all the rules about fast dances and slow dances. I instinctively knew to ask a wee girl up for a fast dance two records before the next slow dance. She would stay up on the dance floor and fall into my arms as soon as the DJ introduced 'How Deep Is Your Love'. No one else in my class had such experience in the dos and don'ts of disco. Just like my superior knowledge of freshly baked Ormo produce, no one in my whole form could possibly be my equal in the art of disco. Frankie Jones had never been to a disco in his life.

'Can you give a wee girl a feel on the dance floor?' he asked.

I did not dignify this question with an answer. I was too busy dreaming of being crowned the Disco King. I would show those rugger boys a thing or two about how to be real man without the use of balls and tackles.

Just as my daydream began the fire alarm went off! It wasn't a fire drill. This was the real thing. Either someone in the classroom next door had placed a school scarf too close to a Bunsen burner or this was another bomb scare. We had bomb scares in school all the time but fortunately they were usually hoaxes. I wasn't sure whether it was the IRA or an unsuccessful O-level pupil phoning in all the bomb warnings, but this was Belfast and the teachers weren't taking any chances. Everyone knew the drill. We had to leave everything immediately and proceed 'briskly', as the headmaster always said, to the evacuation point in the playground. Miss Kelly halted mid formula, dropped her chalk and immediately opened the classroom door. We quickly formed an orderly line in pairs and began to file out of the classroom. I always had a surge of excitement and genuine fear during a school bomb scare. When we reached the bottom of the staircase the headmaster ushered us along: 'Briskly, boys, briskly!'

As we gathered in our appointed space in the playground I felt sorry for the freezing fourth formers who had been evacuated from PE in their shorts. I was also concerned for Thomas O'Hara who was very anxious about the expensive new electric calculator he had just been given for his birthday. This technological instrument was a marvel! When you put in the right numbers it said 'HELLO' upside down, or 'HELL' when Frankie Jones borrowed it. Thomas was afraid that someone was going to sneak into the empty classroom and steal his calculator.

'If someone nicks my Casio, my da'll kill me!' he whimpered.

The next stage in the traditional bomb scare was to administer a roll call to make sure nobody was left behind in a toilet or a domestic science storeroom. Miss Kelly began calling out the roll and, to my immense relief, when she got to the Cs it was clear that Judy Carlton was safe. When Judy answered 'present Miss' in her sweet voice I turned around and found she was standing right behind me. Frankie Jones noticed too and gave me an exaggerated dig in the ribs. This was my chance. There was a school disco next week and thanks to the good offices of a terrorist I was standing right beside Judy. What would I say? How would I ask her? I blushed and started to panic. If only I had splashed on some Denim that morning.

'Go on ya fruit!' said Frankie, before becoming completely distracted by the girls in the PE class shivering in their gymslips on the other side of the playground.

'Hiya Judy,' I said shyly.

'Hiya Tommy,' said Judy shyly.

'It's Tony,' I gently corrected.

Judy blushed.

'Are you coming to the school disco next week?' I asked.

'Yes,' responded Judy. Then she smiled.

I couldn't believe it. Judy had said 'yes' to me.

'Back to class now, briskly!' interrupted the headmaster, signaling the end of the hoax.

As the bomb scare ended and Miss Kelly began to shoo us back up to chemistry I was floating on air. It was clear from her smile, that Judy had accepted my invitation to come to the school disco with me. She had agreed to go on our first date. As Judy returned to the classroom in front of me I imagined slow dancing with her to the sound of the Bee Gees singing 'Too Much Heaven'.

'You'll never guess what you missed when you were pervin' at them wee girls, Frankie,' I said proudly.

'Wha?' said Frankie, still preoccupied and now fiddling in his pockets with both hands.

'I asked Judy to go with me to the school disco and she said "Yes"!' I boasted.

'Wise up! No way!' he exclaimed, plainly impressed.

As we returned to the classroom I had to pass Judy's desk en route to my interrupted litmus test.

'See you at the disco then?' I said.

Strangely Judy did not reply and I assumed she was just very committed to completing her chemistry experiment before break-time. But I was too delighted to fret. My new girlfriend was going to a disco with me next week for the first time. This was more exciting than my plans to go and see *Saturday Night Fever*. This was better than a 50p tip from Miss Adams on a Saturday morning. This was more significant than any parallel universe. It was almost as thrilling as driving the *Millennium Falcon* with Luke Skywalker and Han Solo into the heart of the Death Star to destroy the Galactic Empire's ultimate weapon. It was clear that Judy Carlton desired me. This would be the beginning of a beautiful relationship. I was landed, so I was.

6

LUNCH & JUDY

The day of the school disco had come, so it had. It was just over a week since Judy had accepted my invitation to a date in the dinner hall. There was no telling whether the bomb scare or the prospect of our date had set Judy's heart racing the most that day. As the school disco drew closer it was my heart that began to flutter with the expectation of a proper date with a real live girl from the Antrim Road. When I was a wee kid I discovered I had a disturbing medical condition called a heart murmur and I was always concerned that a heart flutter might result in a cardiac arrest. So I tried to reassure myself that Jesus would not allow anything as pure as my love for Judy to kill me. The disco was all set for a Saturday afternoon and this meant an exceptionally busy day for me. I had to deliver the bread with Leslie in the morning, tackle my father's mammoth Ulster fry for lunch, take Judy to the disco in the afternoon, return home for my mother's fish fingers and Smash and then head out once again to the Westy Disco in the evening. Two discos in one day may have seemed like a lot for an ordinary boy, but I was up for the challenge. John Travolta had to be going to at least two discos a day, I thought, although probably not in a grammar school dinner hall and a Presbyterian Nissen hut. More importantly, this was to be my first date with the lovely Judy and I was prepared to go to as many discos a day as necessary for the slightest chance of a slow dance to the Bee Gees. There was a song on the soundtrack of *Saturday Night Fever* called 'More than a Woman' but I wasn't demanding that Judy be 'more than a woman' – I wanted her just to be my girl.

The day started well. My wonderful plastic alarm clock served its purpose and I woke up in time for the Downtown Radio news and *Eamonn Mallie's Farming Round-Up*. The IRA had burnt down a Protestant sweetie shop on the Springfield Road and heifers in Ballymena were the same price as last week. As I jumped out of bed I had a vague recollection of a dream where I was the star of the school play and forgot all my lines on the opening night and everyone laughed at me until Wonder Woman came to my rescue with a lasso.

Leslie was in particularly good form that morning because he had just received a personal security briefing from an RUC chief inspector regarding the current level of terrorist threat. He was visibly delighted to be privy to such classified security intelligence. He must have felt like James Bond but with a Mini Shop instead of an Aston Martin.

'C'mere til a tell ye! Them Comanches is turning the Falls Road into a no-go area,' he explained, 'and the cowboys round here are just as bad.'

Leslie often drew upon the premise of a good John Wayne movie to enhance my understanding of the latest security situation.

The bread round went almost without a hitch that morning. There were only two incidents worthy of note. The first of these involved a sudden and mysterious increase in the appetite of Mrs Dunne, who sold lipstick and Lemsip in the chemists. A note had been Sellotaped to her windowsill requesting a double order of soda farls, potato bread and plain loaves. This appeared to confirm the suspicion I had heard my mother express to my Auntie Hetty the previous week: 'Yer man with the ferrets from the brickworks has moved in with yer woman with the make-up from the chemists.'

'C'mere til a tell ye son,' whispered Leslie, as he dutifully fulfilled Mrs Dunne's increased order, 'you need to watch women like her, ya know.'

I normally appreciated Leslie's sage advice about matters beyond bread. I had no idea how my boss knew that I did indeed have an urge to watch Mrs Dunne on Saturday mornings. She was one of very few customers who wore make-up so early in the morning and when she smiled at me in her dressing gown over her wee pink nightie with her blonde hair in a bob, like Jill in *Crossroads*, she was lovely, so she was. Mrs Dunne was very popular with most of the men who made door-to-door deliveries in the Upper Shankill. She often invited the various service providers into her house for a wee cuppa tea and they must have talked for ages because sometimes they would be hours with her. My mother said poor Mrs Dunne was lonely because Mr Dunne with the cravat had moved across the water without her. I noticed that Mrs Dunne never invited Leslie inside to sample her hospitality. She must have realised that even the warmth of her welcome could not shake Leslie's unwavering commitment to top-class bread delivery for the Ormo Bakery.

As I carefully used my chin to help balance an armload of extra loaves for Mrs Dunne and the brick man, who should appear in the street beside me but Irene Maxwell. This came as something of a surprise as it was very unusual for other people of my age to be awake so early on a Saturday morning.

'Hiya!' she said sweetly.

Irene was wearing blue eyeshadow like Agnetha from ABBA and a blue satin jacket over her unoccupied boob tube. She must have got up very early that morning to apply the eyeshadow, I thought, possibly in the dark, as the make-up was very smudged. Sometimes girls were very hard to understand.

'Hiya!' I replied, while keeping my chin firmly planted on a plain loaf at the top of my pile of bread for Mrs Dunne. Whenever I did this the smell of fresh bread was overwhelming and I was tempted to puncture a hole in the packaging with my chin and devour fresh bread. Irene was less of a temptation.

'Are you still comin' with me to see *Saturday Night Fever* at the ABC?' she enquired earnestly.

'Aye,' I replied.

Irene smiled as if I was John Travolta himself. I did not reciprocate because, in spite of her early morning efforts, Irene was no Agnetha.

'See ya!' she gushed, and off she went.

As I left Mrs Dunne's order on her windowsill and returned to the Ormo Mini Shop I reflected on this strange early morning encounter. It was the first time I had spoken to Irene since the unfortunate chewing gum incident at the Westy Disco. I was relieved that she no longer found me completely disgusting, but I was concerned that Irene was misconstruing the nature of our trip to see *Saturday Night Fever*. In my eyes, I was going to the movies with a bunch of mates but I got the distinct impression from Irene that she regarded this rendezvous as a personal date with me.

'She's fond!' I thought. 'Wishful thinking on her part.'

I was pleased that Irene couldn't resist my sex appeal but she simply wasn't my type. Judy Carlton was pure Wonder Woman; Irene Maxwell was more like the annoying wee girl with the glasses in *Scooby Doo*.

Big Duff's new glasses were the main talking point when we got to the big estate that morning.

'Did you hear Big Duff's got a pair of them photo-chronic glasses,' whispered Mrs Rosbottom, as she carried an armful of muffins and gravy rings down the steps of the Mini Shop.

'The same boy doesn't like no one to see what's goin' on behind them there eyes of his,' added enormous Mr Rosbottom in an even quieter whisper, as he dismounted from the Mini Shop with twelve plain loaves to see him through the weekend.

I was always fascinated by the fashionable eyewear of paramilitaries. They wore sunglasses during the day as if they were pop stars or film stars from Hollywood, where at least it was sunny. And it was incredible that paramilitaries on both sides wore the same sunglasses. This was one thing they had in common, apart from killing people. Maybe this shared appreciation for the darkened lens would provide some chink of light for peace in the future. Apparently the lenses in Big Duff's new glasses went magically dark in daylight. Big Duff often wore sunglasses even on the darkest of days, the same as the Fonz. He was taking a risk though. What if he got arrested because the RUC recognised the sunglasses he was wearing over his balaclava?

When Billy Cooper's granny with the curlers arrived into the van, before Leslie could greet her with so much as a 'What about ye, love?' she began, 'Have you heard the latest about our lord and master?'

This was the disrespectful way people in the estate described Big Duff when they weren't in the presence of one of his relatives or foot soldiers.

'He must be doin' very well for himself. He's got himself a pair of pornographic glasses,' explained Billy's granny.

These sounded like the sort of glasses Frankie Jones in Chemistry might like.

'I think they're called photo-chromatic,' intervened Leslie, 'because they change in the light, so they do.'

'And why would yer man want to hide his eyes in the daylight?' asked Billy's granny accusatorily.

This question intrigued me. Why would a paramilitary want to hide his eyes from the sunlight? Was she suggesting that Big Duff was a vampire like Christopher Lee? We did not have to wait long to find out the answer to these questions because suddenly Big Duff himself strode up the steps and into the Mini Shop, wearing the very glasses that had sparked such debate in the estate. No sooner had Big Duff made his entrance than Billy's granny demanded, 'a pan, a plain, two soda and two pataita' and scurried down the steps clutching her bread. Big Duff carried clout into the confines of the Mini Shop. He always talked as if he was in charge. For a moment he just stood there, his glasses slowly turning lighter, as he inspected the fairy cakes and the coconut slices. I knew he was waiting for his swanky spectacles to be acknowledged. I began to fiddle nervously with the ring pull of a 7Up can until at last Leslie bravely broke the ice.

'Is them new glasses you got there, sir?' he enquired.

'Aye. Latest thing!' replied Big Duff proudly. He proceeded to take off his new photomathingy glasses and then said to me, 'C'mere and I'll show ye how they work, son!'

My heart began to beat faster. I was being summoned by a paramilitary. But I was the only pacifist teenager in West Belfast. I should decline this invitation to consort with the devil. This was my opportunity to convince Big Duff that there was a better way. I should speak up for peace like that black preacher in America and that wee Indian man with the round glasses from my history books.

'Aye!' I replied.

Big Duff showed me how his glasses worked by putting his hand over the lenses and then exposing them to daylight again. They went dark and then clear, depending on the light. It was like Paul Daniels doing magic on the TV. Big Duff then went on to explain to me in great detail how the glasses worked. He sounded more like Raymond Baxter on *Tomorrow's World* than a paramilitary.

Once he had completed the scientific explanation he said 'Right, now you try them on, son!'

Although the last thing I wanted to do was to put on his glasses,

I obeyed (of course) but I was very jumpy. What if I dropped them? He would kill me! So that's how I found myself trying on the glasses of the most feared man in the Upper Shankill. I got to see the world through his lenses. The world in front of me was nothing but a dark and unpleasant blur. Then I wondered what horrible scenes had been viewed through these glasses, under Big Duff's command. I was certain a pacifist should not be wearing a paramilitary's glasses and so I quickly took them off and silently asked Jesus to forgive me.

'Thanks, Big Duff. They're class!' I gushed and moved on swiftly by asking, 'Do ya want jam or sugar Paris buns this week?'

'Jam, son,' he said and I obeyed.

By the time I got home for my Ulster fry I was already feeling a little tired. After fried eggs, pancakes, soda and potato bread, sausages and bacon and both black and white pudding I was feeling sleepy. Nevertheless, spurred on by the thought of my imminent first date with Judy Carlton, I claimed the bathroom. I inspected my chin and upper lip and detected a definite darkening of the fluffy hairs, but still not enough to merit an attempt at shaving. So I washed my face with Clearasil and splashed on some Denim. Then I put on my best flared jeans, white cap-sleeve T-shirt and newly polished platforms. I completed the preparations by brushing my hair into a Travolta quiff, held in place with a puff of my mother's Harmony hairspray. When I emerged from the bathroom my big brother was waiting impatiently outside. He immediately sniffed out my weakness.

'Are you wearing women's hairspray, ya big fruit?' he enquired.

I ignored this latest affront to my masculinity because in my mind I was already on the floor of the school dinner hall, dancing with Judy to 'How Deep Is Your Love?'. Judy and I had shared this floor before because we had once sat at the same table for lunch. As I devoured my vegetable roll, I watched from the other end of the table as she delicately sipped pink custard from her spoon. I was certain that following this afternoon's date at the school disco, Judy and I would be sitting together having lunch every day.

The only remaining obstacle was securing an appropriate mode of transport to get me to the school disco on time. BRA was about three miles from home. There was no direct bus route to school so I usually travelled there by taking a red bus or a black taxi into the city centre and then another bus from the City Hall up to the Cliftonville Road. I could have walked there in about half an hour from the City Hall, but the route in question was now being called Murder Mile and I was intent on arriving alive for Judy. I couldn't risk being late in case she thought I had stood her up on our very first date. So I was left with only one viable option. I would have to beg for a lift to school in my father's Ford Escort respray. In the Upper Shankill our car was rather impressive but, beside all the Rovers and Toyotas with plastic bumpers outside BRA, it was an embarrassment. It wasn't that the respray had been a total disaster but, two years on, a few scrapes had revealed the metallic blue hidden beneath the new red paint. As far as I was concerned the car screamed 'poor' and this was the last impression I wanted to give Judy because I knew her father drove a classy Austin Allegro with real wood on the dashboard.

'D'ya wanna lift over to your wee disco?' asked Daddy generously.

'Aye,' I replied, helplessly.

On the journey I could tell my DJ father was a little concerned about the competition put up by this new disco.

'I bet they'll not have as many good records as the Westy. We've got all the best singles going back as far as "Puppet on a String".'

I decided not to point out that Sandie Shaw was unlikely to be in great demand in this era of 'Night Fever' not least because I was worrying about how to hide my shameful mode of transport.

'Sure leave me round the corner, Daddy. We're a bit early, so I can walk the rest,' I said nonchalantly.

My father's reply hit me like a Cyberman's ray gun.

'No son of mine's turnin' into no wee prig!' he barked. He had spotted my snobbery a mile off. As my mother always said, 'He's a very clever man, you know.'

'Never you be ashamed of where you come from, son. You're as good as anybody and nobody's better than you. Don't you ever forget that.'

'When are we gettin' a new car?' was my insensitive response.

'We'll see,' replied my father.

In spite of the scolding, he capitulated and dropped me round the corner, so I walked the distance of the final street, past BMWs and gleaming Chrysler Sunbeams. As I passed my middle-class classmates slamming posh car doors behind them, I imagined that one day my father could afford to 'put a Chrysler Sunbeam in my life' and it would 'put a smile on my face', just like Petula Clark promised in the song on the advert. Maybe that day was coming soon, given my father's remark about the possibility of a new car and then I could arrive with all the others at the school gate.

I entered the school grounds and the gothic granite building of Belfast Royal Academy looked down upon me. This oldest part of our historic grammar school seemed to be scowling at the impertinence of the prospect of this first ever disco on its proud premises. I myself found it hard to believe that the same dinner hall where the senior school orchestra practiced the 'Enigma Variations' would soon be resounding with the Electric Light Orchestra and 'Mr Blue Sky'. The first friend I met was Thomas O'Hara in his Peter Storm anorak, which seemed inappropriate attire for a disco. But it was raining as usual and so he had the hood up and was sucking on the drawstrings.

'Hiya!' said Thomas.

'All right?' I replied.

'Aye. Y'all right?' responded Thomas

'Aye.'

Just as this conversation was really taking off, I spotted Frankie Jones in the queue and noticed that he was a sight for sore eyes. He was wearing a blue plastic bomber jacket from John Frazer's, which was quite cool, but his face was an absolute bloodbath. He had five or six little patches of pink toilet paper attached to an array of bleeding spots. I could smell Brut, an aftershave that brought back painful personal memories for me.

'What happened to you, Frankie?' I asked.

'Cut myself shavin', so I did,' answered Frankie.

Thomas and I winced. I could tell we were both thinking the

same thing. It was better to avoid attempting a premature shave if these were the bloody consequences. Frankie would have no chance of getting a girl at the disco looking like that. Before we had a chance to discuss our shaving routines further, the side door of the school opened and everyone began to stream into the dinner hall. I caught a brief glimpse of Judy at the front of the queue, which I thought just proved how keen she was to be here with me. However I was a little disappointed when she ran inside with her friends rather than waiting outside for me. I would have waited for her if the platform had been on the other foot.

After paying 20p for the African babies, we were allowed into the dinner hall. As Thomas was pulling his Peter Storm off over his head, I just stood in awe, transfixed by the transformation. The windows were covered in coloured paper from the art department and there were flashing spotlights that had been borrowed from above the stage in the assembly hall. At the front of the hall was a brand new set of double decks and speakers with lights built into them. It had never occurred to me that anything could make the Westy look inferior, but this made it look crap. The difference was there were very few of us here, compared to the usual crowd of four hundred at the Westy. No one was dancing, even though the teacher DJ, who was much younger than my father, had just put on 'The Rivers of Babylon'.

But these thoughts were a momentary distraction because my attention was focused now on Judy Carlton. I spotted her sitting in the corner of the dining hall, beside the hatch for slops. She was chatting to several of her friends including Joanne Gault, Helen Burnside and Denise Clyde, who were all rather attractive in their own right and very smart at most subjects. The best-looking girls always seemed to hang around together. Poor Judy still hadn't noticed that her date had arrived so I decided to stride across the dance floor to take her hand. I left Thomas and Frankie standing like wallflowers at the back of the dinner hall where the plastic chairs were stacked. As I made my way towards my girl, the teacher DJ faded out 'Matchstick Men and Matchstick Cats and Dogs' by Brian and Michael, which had unsurprisingly attracted nobody on to the dance floor. My father would never have played such a song to teenagers but the teacher must have thought it was educational because it was about some old painter. As the DJ faded out his unfortunate mistake, I continued to walk in Judy's direction and as I did, as if by design, he faded up 'Night Fever'. I recognised the song from the very first disco beat. This was perfect! As I strode towards my girlfriend I began to imagine I was John Travolta strutting down a street in New York. In fact if it hadn't been for the residual whiff of Friday's fish and chips I would have completely forgotten I was in our school dinner hall. All my years of disco experience, honed in the furnace of the Westy Disco, was proving very useful today. As I drew closer to the circle of girls in the corner I noticed all were smiling and tapping their feet and dancing slightly in their chairs. I understood this was a girl's way of communicating the words 'Please ask me to dance with you'. Just then Judy looked up and I caught her eye. She looked away shyly at first and then returned my gaze, as if to check that I was really heading her way. She looked away again, nervously, which was fair enough for a first date, but disconcertingly enough for me to lose some of my swagger – and I stumbled in my platforms as I arrived in front of her. Regaining my composure I initiated first contact.

'Hiya!' I said.

'Hiya!' Judy replied, with the sweetest of smiles.

'D'ya wanna dance?' I enquired gallantly.

At this point I noticed that Joanne Gault, Helen Burnside and Denise Clyde seemed to be trying to suppress some laughter. I glanced behind me to see if someone was doing a silly impersonation of Travolta on the dance floor, but it remained deserted. When I returned my eyes to Judy she began to giggle. The more she giggled the more her three friends were unable to contain their mirth and within seconds all four girls were giggling around me. I understood well that sometimes girls giggled when they were embarrassed about being very attracted to a boy. The Form 1 hockey girls giggled every time Timothy Longsley walked across the playground. But I was beginning to feel uncomfortable with this developing state of affairs.

'D'ya wanna dance, Judy?' I repeated.

I loved to use her name to her face.

'No, thank you,' replied Judy, looking towards the empty dance floor.

The world stopped turning. She had said 'No'. It was a lovely, soft and polite 'No', but it was a 'No' nonetheless.

'But I thought you ...'

I could not complete the sentence because the giggling around me had now resumed with added vigour. The girls were starting to sound like those bloody Martian robots in the Smash adverts.

How could Judy agree to go on a date with me and then turn me down so publicly? As humiliation began to dawn I hit a reddener but thankfully no one could see my blushes because in the dimmed coloured lights all our faces looked red. I glanced back quickly to see if Frankie and Thomas or anyone else was observing my rejection and I sensed many eyes focused on this corner of the dinner hall. So I made an instant decision, the way Leslie sometimes did when he took an alternative route if he spotted a potential hijacker on a Saturday morning. Partly to punish Judy and partly to save face I turned to Helen Burnside.

'D'ya wanna dance?'

Helen shook her head between giggles. Then I turned to Denise Clyde.

'D'ya wanna dance?'

This request received the same devastating response. Now I was starting to panic. This would be the talk of the school. I would be slagged for weeks. This would be nearly as bad as when the domestic science teacher caught Frankie Jones fiddling with himself in the locker room. In a final act of desperation I looked at Joanne Gault. She must have seen the pleading in my eyes, but I should have known better to even ask the question.

'D'ya wanna dance?'

I could have predicted the response. My fate had been sealed. Joanne also declined. The giggles continued, although I noticed Judy had stopped laughing by now and she was looking a little embarrassed. I tried to figure out what had gone so wrong. Why had she changed her mind? Maybe she couldn't dance because it was her time of the month, like when girls brought in a note to say they couldn't do PE. I was confused. But I had to save face. I had to think on my feet, like Manolito in *The High Chaparral*, except without a cowboy hat on this occasion. As I turned to walk away from my erstwhile mockers, I said in a loud voice, so that as many people in earshot as possible could hear me over the top of the Bee Gees, 'That's ok. If none of yousens want to lend me your chemistry notes that's ok! Sure who cares about homework anyway?'

I shrugged my shoulders like I didn't care, even though I did care a whole lot. It took forever to walk across the deserted dance floor to the sound of screeching Bee Gees. I imagined tumbleweed from a Clint Eastwood western blowing across the floor in my direction. I was sweating with embarrassment. I had never actually perspired with mortification before. After a million years I finally crossed the vacant dance floor and reached the back of the hall. I stood beside Thomas nonchalantly, as if I had just popped out for a sly smoke or something.

'Turned you down then?' he said.

The afternoon did not improve. As we came to the last half hour of the disco there was a shared realisation that if no one got up to dance soon we would have had the very first dance-free disco of all time. It was more Saturday Afternoon Chill than *Saturday Night Fever*. As we entered the final twenty minutes Frankie Jones, complete with butchered face, asked Helen Burnside to dance and unbelievably she agreed and there they were, up on the floor, for 'Dancing Queen'. Suddenly nearly everyone was up dancing with someone. I didn't dare to try again so I remained at the back wall with Thomas who had already put on his Peter Storm anorak again to get ready for going home. As we entered the last five minutes and the teacher DJ put on a slow one by 10cc, I was comforted by the fact that at least Judy hadn't got up to dance with anyone else. But then, as if he had been planning it all along, Timothy Longsley arrived late for the last dance. He was in his school uniform and his face retained some muck from a rugby scrum earlier in the day. He spoke to no one and walked across the floor casually, scattering giggling first formers in his wake. He put out his hand to Judy Carlton, commandingly. I watched with despondency as Judy slowly took Timothy's hand and he led her on to the dance floor for a slow dance to 'I'm Not In Love'. Before the day could deteriorate any further, I decided to leave. The woman in the middle of 'I'm Not In Love' taunted me by whispering, 'Be quiet. Big boys don't cry, big boys don't cry, big boys don't cry'. I hated that song. I departed the humiliation of the dinner hall without being seen. I walked alone into town, down Murder Mile, because I didn't care. Judy had rejected me. Worse than that, she had betrayed me with a rugby-playing Timothy with a gite in France. It wasn't fair! Why did she reject me? Was it because I was so ugly with my spots and all? I bet it was because I was from up the Shankill. Did she really fancy Timothy? When I got home that night, I didn't even bother to go to the Westy Disco because now I knew it was crap. I stayed in alone and watched TV. I didn't laugh once when Mike Yarwood did impressions of Frank Spencer saying 'Oh, Betty!' I was scundered, so I was.

7

ESCAPE FROM CAPRI

I needed a break, so I did. I had successfully completed my first dark winter of bread delivery and now, at last, spring was on the way. Leslie seemed very happy with my performance, but I had found bread delivery to be a much more demanding profession than expected. It was a tough vocation in the dark and cold, in the wind and the rain and the snow. I was very relieved that so far there had not been even so much as an attempted robbery, but I had never experienced the deep frost of so many early winter mornings in my life. Furthermore, it was on the coldest and darkest mornings that I was often given extra duties while Leslie remained in the cosy confines of the Mini Shop.

'C'mere til I tell you, son. You do the flats this mornin'. This oul' back of mine's givin' me desperate gip, so it is,' Leslie would say on the coldest and wettest mornings. The customers in the flats were mainly grannies who lived alone on the top floor. The lift was generally vandalised so you had to climb endless stairs that smelt of pee. Maybe this was why the old ladies on the upper floor didn't go out much.

I accepted that the inclement weather was clearly having a

negative effect on Leslie's bones. But my sympathy waned when I returned from a trek through the snow and up and down the smelly stairwell to the flats to find him sitting in the snug driver's cab, tapping his fingers on the steering wheel while munching on a packet of Tunnock's Caramel Wafers. If I'd been spotted, this sort of episode would only have fuelled my big brother's taunts that I was nothing more than Leslie's skivvy.

As Saturday mornings slowly began to lighten and warm, I was relieved that winter was over and satisfied that I had survived in my new-found career. As the daffodils crept up in the neat gardens of the red brick semis in my street and the snowdrops peeked through the scorched earth from last year's bonfire on the green in the estate, I began to look forward to all the excitement of the coming months. Following the minor misunderstanding at the school disco, I had put my relationship with Judy Carlton on hold in order to concentrate on my career. I was also focused on three forthcoming expeditions. The first was the much-anticipated trip to the ABC cinema to see *Saturday Night Fever*. The second adventure was a camping weekend in the Mourne Mountains away from the Troubles with the Westy Disco. Then, shortly after this trip, my father was splashing out with his overtime from the foundry to take our family on our first luxury holiday to Butlin's Holiday Camp, down south in Mosney. These were exciting opportunities to escape from bread and bombs for a while, and I couldn't wait!

When *Saturday Night Fever* day arrived Titch and Philip Ferris called round at our house for my big brother and me. Titch was wearing a second-hand Harrington jacket with a broken zip from the Shankill Methodist jumble sale and old-fashioned parallel trousers from the bargain bucket in John Frazer's. At least there were no obvious stolen goods on his person today, so far. He was simultaneously smoking and chewing gum but neither spearmint nor smoke could compete with Titch's overuse of his da's Old Spice.

'Are you wearin' your da's oul-fashioned aftershave again?' I enquired.

To which Titch replied, 'Aye, yer ma!'

As usual, Philip had made no effort whatsoever and was sporting his customary duffle coat and Rangers scarf. I could not imagine anything less Travolta. He was also smoking a short cigarette butt and it was obvious that this wee feg was a hand-me-down from Titch, who always had more cigarettes than Philip due to his superior shoplifting skills. My big brother was wearing a denim jacket from John Frazer's even though my mother said only 'scruffs down the Road' wore them. I, meanwhile, was looking very cool, like the Fonz in *Happy Days*. I wore my flared jeans and a new, black plastic bomber jacket that was twenty weeks at 69p out of my mother's *Great Universal Club Book*. I had initially struggled with the ethical dilemma over whether the only teenage pacifist in West Belfast should wear a jacket called 'bomber' but I contented myself with the fact that most of the bombers in my city did not actually wear bomber jackets. I wouldn't be seen dead in a balaclava, not even the woolly one my granny had knitted me with smoky-smelling yellow wool from the bomb-damaged wool shop in Sandy Row. I had worked relentlessly at my hair in the bathroom mirror to attempt to look reasonably Travolta. The combination of my father's ageing Brylcreem from before he went baldy and my mother's Harmony hairspray had left an irritating sticky residue across my quiff. I had to remember not to touch my hair at all or the whole construction would fall apart, like one of my Airfix model Spitfires. And I was wearing Denim, of course, in the vain hope of attracting a lovely woman's hand.

We walked round to Irene Maxwell's house and her Uncle Sparky was already there waiting for us in his big red Ford Capri respray. As it turned out the 50p for petrol requested by Uncle Sparky was 50p each, rather than 50p in total, but I was too excited to attempt to communicate my belief that this fare increase was a tad exploitative. Everyone agreed that even though Sparky had failed his eleven-plus he had done very well for himself in windows. He must have been a very smart businessman to realise that replacing shattered glass would become something of a boom industry in Belfast in the 1970s. Sparky had the coolest car I had ever seen and everyone was dead jealous. No one just said Sparky's car was brilliant. Everyone had to put it down.

'Well, he may have flash car, but it's only because he's makin' money out of all them bombs in the town. Sure he probably supports the IRA!' said Mrs Piper.

'Look at yer man Sparky! He's all "I'm me and who's like me?!"' proclaimed my mother when Sparky overtook our car on the West Circular Road, right beside the accident black spot sign.

Even Mrs Dunne pretended to be unimpressed and cryptically commented: 'A car of that size usually means a man is compensating for deficiencies in other departments.'

I had no idea what she was talking about but I assumed this

must be some expert knowledge she had acquired from working in the chemists for so many years.

I didn't care that you weren't supposed to admit you admired Sparky's car, so I ran up to him and said, 'Here, Sparky, you've got the coolest car in the whole Road! It's like Starsky and Hutch's without the white stripe down the side, so it is! Can I sit in the front?'

Sparky wound down the darkened car window and took off his photo-mathingy glasses, which had really taken off since Big Duff had showcased them. But rather than respond to my request, Sparky ignored me and shouted over my head towards Irene Maxwell's front door.

'Will yousens be long?'

'Aye, we're comin' nigh, Uncle Sparky!' an excited Irene shouted back, 'Heather's just had a wee problem with her bell bottoms!'

Eventually Heather Mateer and Irene emerged from the house in full *Night Fever* regalia. Heather was wearing a sequinned boob tube and all of us boys noticed how well she filled it.

My big brother elbowed Philip in genuine wonder and said out of the side of his mouth, 'They're gettin' bigger all the time, so they are!'

All Philip could do was stare and mouth an absent-minded 'Fuck!'

It was only once the power of Heather's breast magnets receded slightly that my eyes were freed up to notice unsightly black stitching around the bottom seam of her white flared trousers. Before anyone could say a word Heather was immediately on the defensive.

'Like, I caught my bell bottoms on her friggin' roller skates!' complained Heather, as if the accident had all been Irene's fault.

Poor Irene looked suitably guilty.

'Ha! That'll harden ye!' laughed Titch, foolishly.

'You shut yer fuckin' bake, Titch McCracken or I'll give you a good boot in the goolies, wee lad!' Heather had a beautiful way with words.

Titch hit a reddener and did indeed shut his bake because Heather was much bigger than him and there was nothing more humiliating than being decked by a girl (apart from being turned down by four girls consecutively in front of everyone at the school disco).

Irene was wearing a red dress like John Travolta's girlfriend in the poster for *Saturday Night Fever*. Irene's mammy had made it from the remnants of red net curtain material she had got cheap in the smoke damage sale in Harry Corry's in Royal Avenue. Irene looked surprisingly pretty – although you could still smell the smoke from the firebomb attack over the scent of her Charlie perfume, and I still didn't fancy her.

'Like, she's been waiting for you for ages, wee lad,' said Heather, looking straight at me. 'That's no way to start a date!'

My big brother turned to me with that look of delight that always came over his face when he had discovered some new rich vein of slagging material with which to torture me.

'So are you seein' wee Irene, ya big fruit?' he asked.

I said nothing and pushed him into the back seat of the car with Titch and Philip. Heather jumped in next and this created a very tight squeeze. Titch had clearly never been in such close proximity to a real boob tube before. I had rarely seen his eyes open so wide but every time Heather turned to look at him he pretended to be looking out the window as if he had just spotted something fascinating on a random lamp post. Meanwhile, it had become clear that there was no further space in the back seat for either Irene or me. And as if she had already given this scenario some consideration, Irene pushed me towards the passenger seat and said, 'S'pose I'm gonna have to sit on your knee then, wee lad!'

If it had been Lynda Carter or Farrah Fawcett-Majors I would have gladly assented to a seat on my knee. In fact, I'm sure I must have dreamt of Olivia Newton-John and/or Agnetha on my knee on several occasions. But the thought of Irene Maxwell on my knee had never crossed my mind – she was Belfast's answer to Laura Ingalls or the annoying wee ginger one from *The Waltons*. Before I could muster any protest we were inside the Capri and she was on top of me and the car door was slammed shut. I now understood how a petrol bomber felt being flung into the back of an army Land Rover. Irene sniffed me.

'Are you wearing Denim?' she asked, coquettishly.

'Aye. I put it on to kill this big cold sore I'm gettin' on my lips, so I did,' I lied resourcefully. Tucker Jenkins had never used that excuse to fend off Tricia Yates in *Grange Hill*.

Irene earnestly searched my lips for any blemish. 'I don't see no cold sores. Just all them there spots,' she diagnosed, after an uncomfortably close inspection of my face.

I could now hear the familiar sound of stifled laughter from the back seat.

'Don't you be takin' advantage of our wee Irene!' warned Sparky, suddenly.

'Never touched her!' I replied indignantly, showing him both of my innocent hands.

'Och, Uncle Sparky you leave my Tony alone. It's our first coort, so it is,' explained Irene.

Now there was unrestrained laughter in the back seat. When I looked in the rear view mirror I could just about see a sequinned boob tube bouncing up and down and Titch's wide eyes following it. As we made our way into the city centre I was sure I could detect one of my big brother's silent but deadly farts begin to dominate the atmosphere in the confines of the Capri. This whole journey was turning into a nightmare. I had been looking forward to going to see the greatest movie of all time, apart from *Star Wars*, of course. But now I was trapped in a Ford Capri respray on a date with Irene Maxwell in a dress on my knee and her Uncle Sparky was about to deck me for feeling her up even though I didn't even fancy her! As if this wasn't bad enough, my big brother and my mates were observing every discomfort with immense glee while at the same being undeservedly spoilt with the delightful pleasures of Heather Mateer's boob tube. This wasn't fair! This was what John Hume called injustice. At one stage I just closed my eyes and imagined I was James Bond, drinking champagne and being chauffeur-driven to a casino in a big fancy limousine with a beautiful Russian spy called Olga on my knee. But I couldn't concentrate on my dream because Irene kept bursting huge bubble-gum bubbles in my face. The shock made me jump and grab her arm, which she interpreted as an embrace. She cuddled me close and the back seat started shouting 'Wooooo!' in a very suggestive manner.

'If you try anything funny with that wee girl of ours I'll break your fuckin' legs, son!' warned Uncle Sparky again.

The only thing I wanted to try was to try to get her off me. It was just as I noticed, with a strange mix of horror and pleasure, one of Irene's hands now stroking my thigh that the Ford Capri finally pulled up outside the ABC. I jumped out of the car like the Bionic Man after a drug dealer.

The cinema was across the road from the Presbyterian bookshop where you spent your Sunday School prize book tokens on pencil sharpeners with John 3:16 embossed in gold. Naturally, it was raining outside and there was a queue right around the block. Fortunately Irene had her Paddington Bear umbrella with her. There was only room underneath for the two of us so I went along with the date charade a little longer to avoid a soaking. There had to be some benefits to being the object of this girl's affections. Philip Ferris actually took off his duffle coat and held it over Heather Mateer's head and kept a close eye to ensure her boob tube remained dry. Meanwhile my big brother and Titch got deservedly drenched along with most of the other teenagers in the queue. The young people of Belfast were prepared to suffer a soaking for *Night Fever*.

We queued up for over an hour in the rain and eventually got into the faded majesty of the ABC foyer. The cinema was typical of many buildings in Belfast – it must have been beautiful years ago, similar to the old Hollywood actresses that Michael Parkinson interviewed on a Saturday night on BBC1. I didn't know my way around this entertainment palace very well. I usually went to the Stadium on the Shankill Road because it was cheaper and smaller but it had too many fights during the interval. The last time I had been at the ABC was to watch Trampas from *The Virginian* fighting dinosaurs in *The Land That Time Forgot* but Philip knew his way around because he had sneaked in through the fire exit to see *The Exorcist* several times.

'It was class!' he enthused. 'The divil takes over a wee girl in her bedroom and her head turns round and round and she bokes up and shouts "fuck" at a priest and all!'

It was the first time I had seen him truly excited about anything in his life and it only proved my suspicions that there was something of the devil about Philip Ferris.

The ABC foyer smelt of Benson & Hedges cigarettes and popcorn, wet hair and damp jeans. All traces of Denim, Old Spice and Charlie had been washed away in the torrential rain outside. We paid our money at the kiosk for wee cardboard tickets that darted out of an amazing steel ticket machine. Then we ran upstairs, elbowing a few popcorn-carrying competitors on the way, to get as good a seat as possible. When we got inside I tried to avoid sitting next to Irene, but the whole gang conspired to make it happen. The seating arrangements seemed to have been preordained the same way Leslie explained that God had preordained who would get saved. The cinema was heaving with damp, eager teenagers. It reminded me of going to see the Bay City Rollers in the Ulster Hall a few years earlier. All my friends remembered the night I had waited at the stage door of the Ulster Hall and ended up having a friendly chat with Woody. Everyone knew my story of how Woody had offered me his autograph. However, every time I told anyone this tale my big brother would sing, 'Jackano-ry, Jackano-ry, Jackano-ry, Dum. Dum.'

Before the film began there was screaming and shouting and 'Sash' and 'Soldier's Song' singing and sectarian name-calling and fighting. But as soon as the lights dimmed and the movie began the children of Belfast were as one, entranced by *Night Fever*. Disco was bringing peace to Belfast, in manageable ninety-minute chunks. The Bee Gees music was electrifying – if a little too high to sing along with if your voice had broken – and the disco dancing was class! As I had predicted, there was no discernible storyline but that didn't seem to matter to Irene. Every time it got even remotely romantic she tried to grab hold of my hand as if I was her own personal John Travolta. I managed to avoid these advances by ensuring my hand was otherwise engaged in popcorn eating, hair fixing and nail biting. It was only when the Bee Gees faded out and they played 'God Save the Queen' and some of the audience stood and some refused to stand and some had a scuffle over who stood and who didn't stand, that I realised I was back from the joy of New York to the tensions of Belfast. With the end of the movie came the spectre of the return journey in the Ford Capri complete with an adoring Irene on my knee and an angry uncle on my case. I had to escape.

'Here, Titch, d'ya wanna get a black taxi back up the Road?' I asked desperately.

'Aye. If you're payin',' he replied.

Fortunately, I had some breadboy tips with me for such an emergency.

'We're gettin' a black taxi back. See youse!' I said swiftly and we left instantly, before Irene could attempt either a protest or a pursuit. As we fled I caught only the briefest glimpse of an incredible poster advertising some new movie with John Travolta dancing with Olivia Newton-John. This must have been his reward for doing so well in *Saturday Night Fever*.

We ran around the corner into Castle Street, past the IRA black taxis that went up the Falls Road and past the barber shop where I got my hair cut with Catholics. I had forgotten that this route would take us through dangerous enemy territory. Maybe this was a terrible mistake. At least Irene wanted to love me. Everyone round here wanted to kill me!

'This is fuckin' provo land!' Titch gasped, with a look of genuine terror in his eyes.

Although we were scared and running, Titch still had time and sufficient breath to add, 'And there's that oul' Fenian barber's where yer ma takes ye!'

Mercifully, within a few seconds we had turned another corner. We ran past Smithfield Market where you bought goldfish and stink bombs until we reached the safety of North Street where Woolworths was still smouldering from a recent incendiary bomb attack. This was the spot where you queued up in the rain to be transported home in a Shankill black taxi, driven by a paramilitary with Ulster tattoos and photo-mathingummy glasses. At first I thought we were out of harm's way but then two skinheads with a cider bottle at the front of the queue kept staring at us, looking for a fight. We pretended not to notice them. At one point I began to sing 'Stayin' Alive' nonchalantly until Titch kicked my chins. I realised the Bee Gees would draw rather than deflect the ire of the skinheads.

We eventually got in a taxi with a lady with gospel tracts and a hat, an old drunk man whose smoke filled our lungs and two women eating a pastie supper out of a newspaper carrying a large Snoopy dog they had just won at the bingo. The lady in the hat recognised a captive audience for evangelism and gradually worked her way around all the passengers asking us the same question 'And are you saved?' The response from the other passengers was negative and so the lady gave each of them a gospel tract with 'Ye Must Be Born Again' on the front and told them politely how they needed to be saved or they would burn in hell forever. Everyone accepted a tract apart from the drunk man who told her to catch herself on. At least when it was my turn I was able to reply yes, I was already saved because I had asked Jesus into my heart on a bin at the caravan in Millisle. I thought she would be delighted that at least one of her fellow passengers would be going to heaven with her, but she responded to me by saying, 'Aye, but are you sure you're really saved, son?' She proceeded to hand me a gospel tract anyway and told me that if I hadn't truly repented and sincerely asked Jesus to be my own and personal Saviour that damnation and not salvation would be mine. I was tempted to get born again, again, right there on the spot, just in case, but it was nearly our stop. When we finally disembarked at the main taxi stop at the steps to the estate, I was very pleased with myself. I had managed to avoid the dangers of skinheads, provos, evangelists and Irene Maxwell on my knee in a Ford Capri.

It was obvious that Titch was secretly impressed too.

'Aye, right, dead on, see ya, big lad!' he said, punching me hard enough to give me a dead arm, before he ran off smiling.

I could be very resourceful when I wanted to be, so I could.

8

THE HILLS ARE ALIVE

We were all dead excited, so we were. We were standing in the rain at the corner of the West Circular Road on a Friday night, waiting for two minibuses to take us away from the Troubles for a weekend of camping in the Mourne Mountains. Some nice people from Holland, who liked windmills and peace, had given the Westy Disco money to take us up the mountain and away from all the fighting. As the only pacifist teenager in West Belfast I felt obliged to accept their generosity. Leslie had kindly granted me a Saturday off work, although he made it very clear that there was no such thing as paid annual leave for part-time teenage professionals. However I was secretly delighted when Leslie informed me that on my Saturday away, he intended to deliver the whole bread round singlehandedly. It was obvious that no satisfactory substitute breadboy of the right calibre could be found. It was good to know I was irreplaceable. However my big brother insisted that Leslie merely saw my forthcoming absence as an opportunity for cost cutting. 'Wise a bap, wee lad!' he declared. 'Sure, yer man's as tight as a duck's arse.'

We all huddled together at the gates of the church – around

thirty teenagers, my parents, Uncle Henry and Auntie Emma. In front of us was a mountain of Man United and Rangers sports bags and a growing pile of sleeping bags. My wee brother was there too because he had now become the small and lively mascot for the Westy Disco. And we couldn't really leave him at home on his own, even with his space hopper for company. We were standing at the exact same spot where, a few years earlier, gunmen had opened fire on my scout troop, so I was quietly praying to myself that the minibuses would arrive soon – and before we all became legitimate targets. Barely standing behind us was the ageing Nissen hut where we danced the night away every Saturday at the Westy. Rev. Lowe disapproved of us calling it this and reminded us regularly that it was, in fact, an activity of Ballygomartin Presbyterian Church Youth Club. I accepted he was technically correct, but it didn't sound quite so exciting and cool. This reminded me of when my music teacher called ABBA, 'a Scandinavian vocal group'. Rev. Lowe didn't understand how important it was to be cool. Using the wrong words made you square, while using the right words made you beezer!

I was relieved to notice that I wasn't the only person who had experienced difficulties packing and carrying a sleeping bag. Although my snake belt had fitted around the rolled-up sleeping bag when I sat on top of it in my bedroom, every time I picked it up, most of the bag fell out on one side. I ended up walking down the street with an unfurled sleeping bag trailing behind me, carefully avoiding a poop recently deposited on the pavement by Petra, our street's favourite Labrador. The rolled-up sleeping bags in the pile before us were tied-up tenuously by an assortment of belts, elastic bands, bin bags, rope and cord. My parents' double sleeping bag (which they had bought specially for the occasion for 20 weeks at 99p out of the *Great Universal Club Book*) was most effectively contained by the last few inches of a roll of very sticky industrial duct tape my father had borrowed from the foundry.

'Your father's a very clever man, you know,' my mother commented when he applied his immense problem-solving skills to sleeping bag containment.

In a threat to all our efforts, Titch McCracken was now smoking dangerously close to the pile.

'Like, thon wee eejit's gonna set all our sleepin' begs on fire!' shrieked Heather Mateer.

Heather's health and safety fears were well founded. I imagined a premature Eleventh of July boney igniting right in front of us.

'Sure he set the telephone box on fire in our street and I couldn't listen to *Dial a Disc* for a year!' added Irene Maxwell. 'He's a wee arsonist, so he is!'

'Aye, he's always arsin' about!' laughed Sammy Reeves.

'At least I'm not a boggin' minger!' retorted Titch.

'You leave Smelly Sammy alone, ya wee gaunch!' intervened Heather.

A short fight ensued, which resulted in both Titch and Sammy getting a final warning from Uncle Henry that they would be sent home if they caused any more trouble. I was certain that the nice people from Holland would be appalled if they ever heard about this outbreak of violence at the very start of a weekend they had sponsored to bring peace to Northern Ireland. Uncle Henry made Titch and Sammy shake hands 'like real men' and went on to remind us all that there should be absolutely no smoking or drinking during the weekend. Titch obediently put out his cigarette on the pavement and then spat aggressively on top of the smouldering stub, but Sammy Reeves kept winking at everyone and smiling, as if he knew what Santa was bringing us all for Christmas.

'Aye. Dead on,' he said.

'Hope we're not stuck in a tent with him the night,' Titch whispered in my ear, with a hint of genuine panic in his voice. 'He's ratten.'

I tried not to join in all the Smelly Sammy slagging because I once overheard my mother telling Auntie Emma that it was 'an awful pity of that wee crater because his mother's bad with her nerves and his da beats the two of them'. However, I could not extend my sympathy for his family problems to tolerance of the idea of sharing a tent with Sammy. Before any further scuffles could develop, two yellow minibuses turned the corner and stopped right in front of us.

'Och, stickin' out!' said a very relieved Auntie Emma. 'Nobody burnt the buses.'

Without any trace of order, we crammed into the minibuses with our bulging sports bags and unravelling sleeping bags. Within two minutes we were en route to Newcastle, County Down, where the Mountains of Mourne sweep down to the amusement arcades and fish and chip shops. We had to stop only twice during the journey. The first time was when Lyn McQuiston with the buck teeth was scolded for shouting 'Kick the Pope' out the window as we passed a Catholic school called St Something's.

The second stop was to allow my wee brother to pee and me to boke in a shuck beside a field of sympathetic-looking cows. Due to my travel sickness and my disdain for sectarian shouting I was relieved when we finally arrived in Newcastle. I had visited this seaside resort once before on a red double-decker bus on the Sunday School excursion. I remembered consuming a particularly vinegary fish supper followed by sticky white candyfloss. I recalled buying a stick of pink peppermint rock that said 'Newcastle' up the middle which I gave to my granny, but it caused havoc with her false teeth. I had not forgotten losing the rest of my pocket money in the 'musies' on a one armed bandit whose cherries never came up. Thankfully this time the minibuses drove past all the amusement arcades and pubs and fish and chip shops, taking us straight into Donard Park and up the dark mountain. The two minibuses cautiously climbed up a steep and narrow twisty lane with more potholes than the Shankill after a riot. I hadn't seen so much darkness since the men at Ballylumford Power Station switched off all the electricity during the Ulster Workers Strike to keep us British. The whole minibus became abnormally quiet. As we noticed the shadows of huge trees looming all around us, it was obvious that most of us were disturbed by this newfound darkness. If it was dark then there must be someone out there who wanted to get you. The whole Westy Disco breathed a sigh of relief when we eventually emerged from the tree-lined lane and arrived at a small triangular concrete building surrounded by tents and a sign on a big stone, which read 'Greenhill YMCA'.

The YMCA Camp was called 'Greenhill' because it was

situated on the side of a very big green hill. In church we sang a hymn about 'a green hill far away outside a city wall' but I assumed that hill was in Israel. This big green hill was called Slieve Donard. It was the highest mountain in the whole of Northern Ireland and it made our Black Mountain in Belfast look wee. Mind you, Slieve Donard was much smaller and less pointy and snowy than Mount Everest, so I doubt if Sir Edmund Thingummy had ever bothered having a go at climbing it, even for practice.

As we disembarked noisily from the minibuses, two friendly men with beards, wearing proper khaki anoraks and big boots, both called Dave, stomped forward and greeted us. As the Upper Shankill exploded on to the side of Slieve Donard and our true nature became apparent, the two Daves smiled nervously. They pronounced all their 'ings' as they explained all the rules about no smok-ing and no drink-ing. My father casually turned around and removed a Hamlet cigar from his lips. A small gang led by Philip Ferris in his duffle coat immediately disappeared behind the building for a smoke, while the Daves coughed apprehensively and explained that we would be climb-ing and canoe-ing and learn-ing about how to work together as a team. I was excited about the outdoor activities but I thought we already worked together well as a team. The Daves had obviously never observed us doing the Slush at the Westy Disco or building a boney for the Eleventh Night.

For our first adventure we were assigned three big green tents in a row, one for the boys, one for the girls, and one for the adults and my wee brother. As soon as I begsied my place at the far side of the boys' tent, Sammy Reeves placed his odorous sleeping bag beside mine. Before I could even attempt to rearrange the sleeping positions, Uncle Henry and my father shooed us out of the tents and back up to the triangular building. Inside Greenhill YMCA there was a hall with a tuck shop on a balcony, a kitchen, toilets, showers, a Coca Cola machine and something called a 'drying room' full of wet khaki anoraks. Auntie Emma gave Titch a clip around the ear for sticking the pin from his Rangers badge into the coin slot in the Coke machine to try to get a free drink. Irene Maxwell began following me around and offering me a share of her Spangles. Did this wee girl really think she could buy my love with a Spangle? The well-booted Daves informed us we were going to go out straight away to climb the mountain. I was surprised at this instant introduction to mountain climbing because it was dark and raining. At least half of us were wearing platform shoes and only a handful had brought our Peter Storm anoraks from John Frazer's, which was definitely not a shop for outdoor wear. A real German girl with no make up called Nina offered us proper khaki anoraks and big boots to wear, from the drying room, but most of us declined because they didn't look cool and we didn't want to be scundered. Within only ten minutes of disembarking from the minibuses we were being marched up Slieve Donard like a junior Orange Lodge on the Twelfth of July, except with girls and no flags.

'This will tire them out,' I overhead one of the Daves whisper to Uncle Henry.

Everyone was unusually quiet for the first half mile, until our eyes started to get used to the darkness and we could see where we were going in this strange environment.

'Oh Mammy!' cried Lyn McQuiston with the buck teeth at every slight noise or apparent movement in the bushes.

I pretended not to be scared at all, but my big brother found it necessary to look at me closely before announcing loudly, 'You're brickin' it aren't ye? Ya big fruit!'

'Leave your wee brother alone for once!' chided my mother. 'He's always been scared of the dark.'

At home this reprimand would have been most welcome, but not here in front of thirty other teenagers. I put up the hood of my Peter Storm and sucked on the drawstrings. My mother's response was not at all helpful. She turned to Auntie Emma and said, much too loudly, 'God love him, he's a very sensitive wee boy, so he is.'

Desperate to save face, I instinctively picked up a stone and threw it at a tree, to display my virility and manly lack of sensitivity. Unfortunately Lynn McQuiston mistook the sound of the impact of the stone on the tree trunk for an imminent attack by a grizzly bear and she began to cry hysterically. It was only when Uncle Henry explained to her that we didn't have bears in Northern Ireland that poor Lynn began to calm down.

'But I saw it on *The Waltons*!' she protested.

As the atmosphere finally relaxed Irene Maxwell started singing 'Climb Every Mountain' from that movie about a nun with a posh English accent running around a mountain singing all the time with a crowd of annoying wee kids. No one joined in.

When we reached a clearing in the forest, one of the Daves explained that we were not going to climb to the very top of the mountain tonight. Instead we were going to walk down a different way to call at the chippy in the town. It was brilliant!

It was now so dark you could see stars in the sky. Uncle Henry pointed to one pattern of stars and said it was called 'the Plough' because it looked like a plough. I had never seen a plough before so I wasn't convinced. I thought the stars concerned looked more like a configuration of Dalek motherships on their way to invade earth again, unless the Doctor intervened, which I knew he would because he always did just in time.

Several offers of a Spangle from Irene Maxwell later, we finally reached the chippy for fish and pastie suppers. We devoured these together on the harbour wall to build our strength for the trek back up the green hill to the tents. I had never seen the members of the Westy Disco look so tired. As you would expect, it was still raining, so we rushed into our tents and got into our sleeping bags as quickly as possible. I was so exhausted I barely had time to notice the unpleasant smell in our tent. However I did notice that Sammy Reeves wore old pyjamas with holes in the knees covered in faded Mickey Mouses that he had grown out of long ago.

I must have fallen asleep very quickly because the next thing I knew it was daylight and I was awake and snug in my sleeping bag and the rain was pattering on the canvas.

Saturday at Greenhill YMCA was simply one amazing adventure after another. It was more exciting than being on a hijacked bus or being evacuated from the top floor of Anderson & McAuley's department store in a bomb scare. One of the highlights was Uncle Henry's canoe capsizing in Castlewellan Lake, caught on camera by my mischievous father. I acquired new skills in archery and imagined I was Robin Hood, stealing from the Sherriff of Nottingham in Sherwood Forest to give bags of coins to the poor. But by far the most memorable outdoor adventure was when Heather Mateer pushed Titch McCracken into the Glen River and laughed at how his wet trousers went all clingy around the region of his jimmy joe.

In the evening, we cooked sausages and burgers outside on a big grill over a fire like American cowboys, except with rain instead of cactuses. The Daves called this mode of outdoor cooking a 'barbecue'. We sang songs around the campfire led by the real German girl. Nina impressed me by playing 'Mull of Kintyre' on the guitar even better than me. I loved it here, so I did! We were happy and free and dirty and having the best time ever! No one would have known we were supposed to be wee potential petrol bombers from West Belfast. If the nice people from Holland who had paid for all this could see us now, I thought, they would be dancing with delight in their clogs up and down the nearest dyke.

However, the perfection was briefly interrupted on the Saturday evening by the YMCA's attempt at a disco. As devotees of our very own Westy every Saturday night, we had very high standards. In fact you could say we were connoisseurs of disco, even before John Travolta. Unfortunately none of the Daves could compete with my father's DJ skills or choice of music. The BRA school disco may have made the Westy look crap but the YMCA only had an ancient set of double decks and one battered speaker that didn't produce much volume. The needle kept jumping off the records if anyone danced too enthusiastically near the turntables. Worst of all they only had about ten records and one of those was an LP by Simon & Garfunkel. The Daves may have been very good at climbing mountains but they had no idea that 'Bridge Over Troubled Water' was not ideal disco dancing material. They did have 'Dancing Queen' but it got so many people on the dance floor that the wooden floor vibrated and the needle just jumped and jumped until eventually ABBA was abandoned. Then they kept putting on Nina's twelve-inch version of 'I Feel Love' by Donna Summer, which was good at first, but it just went on and on and on forever. We were united in our disappointment. One by one we drifted out of the hall towards the tents until only the Daves remained. My father had respectfully remained outside all evening in an attempt not to intimidate the two Daves with his superior disco competence.

As each person left the disco they made passing remarks to my DJ da: 'You could teach themuns in there a thing or two, Eric!'

'That there music's shite, so it is!'

'Couldn't bate the Westy Disco with a big stick!'

I could tell my father was very proud. He was so delighted with this appreciation I sensed that a request for extra pocket money would not be rejected.

Heather Mateer was the last person to leave the failing YMCA disco. 'Like, see yer woman in there on that twelve-inch? She STILL feels fuckin' love!' complained Heather.

As we weren't quite so tired on Saturday night there was a lot more craic in the tents. In the girls' tent Irene Maxwell produced her cassette recorder and proudly played last Sunday's top forty countdown, which she had recorded from Radio 1 especially for the trip. I could hear the muffled sound of Paul

Burnett counting down from number forty to number one and the girls singing Bee Gees songs and laughing into the early hours of the morning. Now and again I could make out my mother's voice imploring them to get some sleep. Once I thought I heard the words 'Irene wants a snog in the Ormo Mini Shop,' followed by guffaws of high-pitched laughter but maybe that was just a nightmare.

Meanwhile in the boys' tent we were no less subdued. I had 'accidentally' spilled some of my Denim aftershave over Sammy's sleeping bag and this made the smell more tolerable. Sammy himself was in great form. I had never seen him in such high spirits. He had brought a big bottle of orangeade with him and he was generously sharing it with everyone. It must have been a new kind because I noticed it wasn't as fizzy as usual and it left an odd warm feeling at the back of your throat. Soon everyone was on brilliant form and the craic was mighty! Titch was in stitches even though his cigarettes still hadn't dried out after being thrown in the river and my big brother was laughing his head off at proper jokes instead of just laughing at me. At one stage I'm sure I even heard Philip Ferris chuckle into his sleeping bag.

'Punk rules the ballicks Bee Gees!' he giggled.

Eventually I was so relaxed I stopped rubbing clean the top of the orangeade bottle when it was my turn for a swig after Sammy. I was so happy I couldn't stop laughing and I giggled so much that when I tried to get up I just kept falling over, which made me laugh even more. I don't remember much more about that night but just as I was drifting off to sleep with my head spinning, Sammy whispered over to me in the darkness, 'I don't wanna go home, Tony.' I remembered this because he sounded dead sad all of a sudden.

I don't know what happened during the night, but the next morning I woke up with the worst headache ever. I concluded that the tent door must have been flapping open all night long and the wind had got in and given me an awful creak in my head and neck. It must have been a faulty tent because all the other boys woke up with the same headache. In fact we all slept in and missed breakfast. Uncle Henry was ragin' and we just had enough time to get up and pack our bags before the minibuses returned to bring us back to Belfast.

The following year I was not at all surprised when I heard a pop group called the Village People on Radio Luxembourg singing a new song with the lyric, 'It's fun to stay at the YMCA'. The Village People were from America so I don't think they had ever stayed in a big green tent in Greenhill on the slopes of Slieve Donard. But their song was true because the kids from the Westy had the best fun ever the weekend we stayed at the YMCA.

On the way home in the minibus, Philip Ferris would not stop slagging Sammy. 'I heard Smelly Sammy cryin' his lamps out last night in his sleepin' beg!' he taunted.

Sammy didn't reply and just gazed out the window looking dead sad again. I too was approaching breaking point because my big brother was inexplicably calling me 'a wee wino'. I was about to announce to the whole bus that he had cried when Mary Ingalls went blind in *Little House on the Prairie* when luckily for him (and probably luckily for me too), we were stopped by the British Army. All the boys had to get out in the rain and turn around and put our hands up against the back of the minibus and get searched for guns and bombs. When we got back inside the minibus, Uncle Henry decided to cheer us up with the announcement that our next trip away from the Troubles would be to London in the summer. The English accents of the soldiers must have reminded him. This was fantastic! We were going to travel to the place where the royal family and James Bond lived! We were going to see Big Ben from *News at Ten* and the Tower of London where they chopped off your head in my school history book. The response was ecstatic and we sang 'The Streets of London' the whole way home in the rain, although no one could remember all the words. Every trip away from Belfast was getting better and better. I couldn't wait to go to Butlin's for Easter and now I could look forward to an incredible journey to London this summer on the biggest Westy Disco trip ever. I was becoming quite a jet-setter, so I was.

9

ALL CREATURES GREAT AND SMALL

I didn't want to be, so I didn't, but I was ragin' again! Everyone in our street had a dog except us and it just wasn't fair! You had to have a dog to be a proper family. It was like having a granny. There were more dogs than soldiers on the streets of Belfast. A gang of wee mongrels ruled every street corner. Sometimes you could tell which street you were in without looking at the houses, just by recognising the pack of dogs that ran up and down. Assorted poodles, Labradors, Jack Russells, Alsatians and their variegated offspring were omnipresent. The howling could be quite exasperating, especially when the whole estate barked for an hour after a bomb or a band parade. Some people bred dogs in their backyard for a hobby but many dogs bred up an entry just for fun. Some dogs tried to breed with your leg at every opportunity.

The dogs in our street weren't just animals, they were personalities. Everyone knew their names and we all became familiar with their individual characters. As a breadboy I became intimately acquainted with every dog in the street. Wee Scotty, the West Highland Terrier, whose mammy got a wheaten bannock and a plain loaf, was a yappy wee glipe but would never bite you. Brandy, whose daddy got a Procea loaf because he was allergic, would have sex with your leg at the very slightest show of affection. Then there was Petra the Labrador, the most well-loved personality in the Upper Shankill, who enjoyed being stroked by the whole street. Petra had a very kind face and loved to play football and lick you. She waited at the end of the road for all the children coming home from school at the same time every afternoon. I was amazed that she knew the difference between weekdays and weekends. Petra was very intelligent and she was possibly more popular than Paisley.

When Mrs Piper was arguing with my father about politics she always said, 'Even the dogs in the street know', to indicate that some point she was making was very obvious. Apparently, even the dogs in the street knew we were being sold out for a United Ireland. Even the dogs in the street knew we were being sold down the river to Dublin. The poor dogs in the street must have been bored to death always knowing the same old stuff. Maybe that's why they barked at the cars and pooped on the pavements so much, just to relieve the boredom. In my opinion the dogs in the streets had no interest whatsoever in the Troubles. I was certain that Catholic dogs and Protestant dogs were just the same underneath their coats, just like us kids underneath our Catholic and Protestant school uniforms. I suspected that even the dogs in the street knew rightly they would still get fed and bred no matter whether Northern Ireland was British or Irish. Then again, I did notice that dogs felt compelled to mark out their territory, the same as Protestants and Catholics. Dogs peed up the same lampposts we put flags on. I hoped for a day when all the dogs in

Belfast would bark across the peace line like those cartoon dogs in *101 Dalmatians*. They would agree, using canine language, to combine the power of their paws to dig a big tunnel under the peace walls so they could be free to run alongside the dogs on the other side.

Of course, the dogs in the street presented certain unwelcome challenges to the bread delivery industry. If you walked into the Ormo Mini Shop with any whiff of dog's dirt on the sole of your Dr Martens, Leslie was furious. All service was postponed until you had completed an extensive decontamination process.

'C'mere til a tell ye!' he would say. 'Watch where you're puttin' your kebs, young fella. This place has to be spotless. What we're sellin' goes in people's mouths, ya know!'

It seemed particularly unfair to me that while I still had no dog, some people had more than one dog. Mr Black had his two yappy greyhounds that he raced at Dunville Park where you placed bets on the fastest dog. The Clarks had two Afghan hounds with long hair that bit me after I delivered two pan and a plain in spite of the fact that Mrs Clark said, 'Never worry, love. They wouldn't touch ye.' I was envious that some families were allowed to have two of something that I was being completely denied. John Hume would undoubtedly call this injustice.

Rev. Lowe said that when you wanted something very badly that belonged to someone else then you were 'coveting'. This was another of the 'Thou shalt nots' that God had written on two big stones for Charlton Heston up a mountain in Sunday School. When Rev. Lowe said in church that God wrote these commandments on tablets of stone, I giggled and got a firm dig in the side from my mother. I thought tablets were what you got on a prescription from the doctor if you were bad with your sinuses. I couldn't imagine even one 'Thou shalt not' fitting on a tablet. There were only ten 'Thou shalt nots' up the mountain in the Bible but I heard about dozens of extra commandments on the slopes of the Black Mountain. Thou shalt not smoke, thou shalt not drink, thou shalt not go to pubs, thou shalt not have a wee swing in Woodvale Park on a Sunday – the list was endless. As a wee good livin' fella I tried to keep all the commandments but I managed some 'Thou shalt nots' better than others. Unlike some people in my city I had no problem with 'Thou shalt not kill'. 'Thou shalt not commit adultery' was easy because I still didn't know how to do it. But I couldn't help myself from coveting Petra.

My mother rigidly forbade dogs in our house. She said they were all 'dirty wee mutts' and would make the place smell like a pigsty. I vaguely remembered our family getting a pup when I was very young, but it peed so much on the shag pile in the good room that it was 'sent away to live on a farm'. I could never extract from my parents any more specific details on the exact location of the said farm. In spite of repeated attempts to persuade her to have another go, my mother was steadfast in her refusal to allow any canine paws anywhere near her carpets. This intransigence was reinforced when Mrs White, who had a yappy wee black poodle called Curly, invited us in for a wee cuppa tea and a ham sandwich one day. This act of kindness was intended to calm my mother's nerves after the provos had blown up the police station on the Springfield Road a few minutes after she had driven past. As Mrs

White comforted her with the idea that someone up there must be looking after her and all, my mother discovered a curly black hair sticking out of her ham sandwich.

'That's why there'll never be no boggin' dogs in our house!' she whispered, pointedly, when Mrs White returned to the kitchen to boil the kettle to give our tea a wee warm.

My father was more pro-canine than my mother although he always described Mr Black's greyhounds as 'nathin' but runnin' and shittin' machines' after the day he observed Mr Black permitting them to poop in Auntie Mabel's nasturtium borders. My brothers and I attempted to garner my father's support in pleading for a dog, but he routinely caved in under pressure when my mother retorted, 'And who's gonna be left to look after the wee crater, as usual? Sure don't I have enough to do, lookin' after my mother and father and the four of youse?!'

I suppose she had a point, but I was offended that she placed the looking after of me in the same category as looking after her mother, as I was convinced that I was much less demanding than my granny. I never once waved a poker in anger at my granda and I would never hide a bottle of whiskey behind the Domestos under the sink in the working kitchen.

For months there was no compromise. It was like politics in Northern Ireland. But eventually we came to an accommodation. It was clear that a dog was completely out of the question. So I gradually lowered my sights to ownership of smaller animals. According to my mother, a cat was nearly as bad as a dog and they didn't even love you back for all your trouble. Anyway, they were always getting squashed on the road. Sadly, a few cats fell victim to the entirely innocent Ormo Mini Shop when the diddledee ding button wasn't working properly and we approached the streets unseen and unheard in the dark on a Saturday morning. I had accepted the dog ban in our house when I was a child, but now I was all grown up I was determined to take on the responsibility of caring for another creature. I wanted to be like a vet in *All Creatures Great and Small*, though I didn't want to stick my hand up a cow's bum. So, next I tried to argue for other smaller furry creatures. There was a precedent here because for many years when I was a child we had an overweight albino rabbit called Snowball, who lived outside in a hutch. We fed Snowball dandelion leaves and horses tails until he nearly burst and finally died – in the snow – one winter.

A pet rat was a definite no-no because, according to my mother, 'there's enough dirty vermin runnin' round this city without bringin' one into your own livin' room!' Even cuddly hamsters were at first dismissed as completely out of the question because, technically, they too were rodents. Before I was born my parents had a budgie called Peter that went blind like Mary Ingalls. My mother never really got over it, just like Ma Ingalls. Another budgie was ruled out because no bird would ever replace 'her wee Peter that had to be put down with gas because he couldn't see his seed no more'.

I accepted that if we could reach agreement on something very small to start with, then I might be able to work my way up to something bigger and eventually I would be allowed a dog. It was like when Mrs Piper said, 'If you give them Papishes an inch then eventually they'll want til take over the whole place!' So I developed a clever strategy for securing a dog. I would start with the smallest, quietest and easiest to clean. I would begin with a goldfish, the cheapest life in the pet shop in Gresham Street. The pet shop was only a short black taxi ride away and opposite John Frazer's where we bought all our clothes. The goldfish hung in plastic bags outside the shop and you could buy two fish for only 50p, the same price as two unsliced wholemeal loaves. It was a real bargain and, if they died, at least you could flush them down the toilet and still afford to buy another two quite soon. I chose my moment very carefully and one day at my granny's house, after successfully lighting her fire with sticks and *Belfast Telegraphs* and a big white firelighter, I sensed that my helpfulness could be rewarded.

'Ach, God love our Tony. He's all grown up now, but he still loves his wee granny,' she announced during the Milk Tray advert in the middle of *Coronation Street*. Of course, I did love my granny but at twenty stone and an even bigger personality she was anything but wee. Rev. Lowe described her as a formidable woman, which I think meant he was scared of her, and this was quite something because Rev. Lowe wasn't scared of the paramilitaries because he shooed them off the streets into the pubs when they were out rioting.

'Aye, he's a good wee boy most of the time, when he's not givin' any of his oul' cheek,' added my mother graciously.

'Will ya let me get a goldfish then?' I replied cunningly, and with sad orphan eyes.

'Ach, go on, love, let the wee crater. Sure he's awful good to his granny and he knows how bad I am with my pains and my nerves and all,' lobbied my doting granny.

The matriarch had spoken and I sensed a victory was at last within reach.

'Aye, all right then,' assented my mother. 'But if you don't change its water the wee crater'll be swimmin' round in its own wee-wee and you'll just be bein' cruel!'

I was permitted to go down the Road and buy two goldfish from the pet shop in Gresham Street. This was to become the beginning of a long relationship with the pet shop owner. I carried home my first two goldfish very carefully in a plastic bag which didn't leak too much over the torn upholstery in the back of the black taxi. The wee girl sitting opposite me on her mammy's knee started to poke at the fish with the liquorice stick from her sherbet dip so I had to protect my new charges from the word go. When I disembarked from the taxi I had to escape from two wee hoods outside the chemist when they threatened to throw my goldfish down a gratin'. I named the first two goldfish Starsky & Hutch and, when they died, I named the next two Morecambe & Wise. After the Two Ronnies, Frida & Agnetha, Luke & Darth, and George & Mildred died, I concluded that either I did not have the required skills for keeping goldfish alive or there was something dodgy in the tap water in West Belfast.

However, once I had been given permission to look after one genus, I successfully used this precedent to move on to new and more exciting species. But unfortunately I struggled to achieve a decent life span for any animal. Each newly acquired creature met a premature and tragic end. It was easy to progress from goldfish to a tank of tropical fish but they needed an electric heater to keep them alive, which was 20 weeks at 69p from the *Great*

Universal Club Book. In weekly trips to the pet shop, financed by my breadboy tips, I gradually built up a thriving community of tropical fish surrounded by beautiful plastic plants rooted in blue and pink pebbles. When I added a plastic underwater diver my tank started to look like under the ocean where Jacques Cousteau went diving on BBC2. I had angelfish and guppies and even an exotic red-tailed black shark like in *Jaws* but smaller and without the teeth. Sadly tragedy was never too far away from my pets and so one catastrophic day, when I returned home from school to feed my tropical fish their daily pinch of flakey food, I came upon a scene of utter carnage. There had been a power cut all day long because the provos had blown up the electricity substation for freedom. Without warmth from the electric heater, all of my poor fish perished at Belfast room temperature. There were no survivors, not even my beautiful red-tailed black shark. I was devastated and angry because now I had no living pets whatsoever again and I still owed twelve weeks at 69p for the electric heater. I held the provos personally responsible for this pet massacre. Were innocent angelfish the latest legitimate targets? Did they think guppies were Protestants? I knew I was a wee good livin' fella and I was supposed to love my enemies and forgive them and all but nobody else in Belfast took that seriously. As I flushed the whole community of tropical fish down the toilet with one sad pull of the chain, I said a prayer to God, who understood because He was on our side anyway, that the provos would never get their United Ireland.

This was not to be my final pet tragedy and the body count of small animals was set to climb higher than dead drug dealers in an episode of *The Sweeney*. To make up for the loss of all my precious fish I was allowed my first small golden hamster with a cage and sunflower seeds and a squeaky wheel from Gresham Street. He was called Benny after the fat funny man that ran after girls in their bras and he peed an awful lot on his sawdust. One Saturday morning after my bread round, I made the tragic mistake of taking Benny out of his cage to show him off to a group of girls in our street. Irene Maxwell's wee friend Sandra Hull, with the permanent parallel snatter tracks under her nose, said Benny was the cuddliest wee dote she had ever seen in her life, so he was. She gave him a big hug and broke his neck. Sandra was only seven and it was clear she had no murderous intent. She simply treated Benny as if he was one of her troll dolls with the long hair, but the outcome for me was yet another fresh grave in the back garden. A small pet cemetery was developing under the holly bush.

My next doomed pet didn't even get a decent burial. He was a gerbil from Gresham Street called Brucie, after yer man with the chin that got Anthea to do a twirl on *The Generation Game*. I made the fatal error of asking Titch McCracken to look after Brucie for just one week when I was away to Butlins. Little did I know that Titch's cousin from Ballymoney, who thought Ulster Protestants were the Lost Tribe of Israel, was visiting him for the Twelfth with his pet snake Rocky. Titch loved the *Rocky* movies and he wanted to look like Sylvester Stallone in spite of the disadvantages of being skinny and ginger. He loved to watch boxing and wrestling and claimed he was keen to find out who would win if Brucie and Rocky were matched in a fight. I was never given the full gory details but suffice to say that neither Brucie nor Rocky survived.

I heard later from Philip Ferris that it had been a brilliant scrap until Rocky choked on Brucie. This must have been a cruelly enjoyable experience for Philip as it was one of the few occasions in his life that he refrained from describing something as 'ballicks'. Instead the slabber stuck out his chin and, in a very bad Bruce Forsythe impersonation, cried 'Nice to eat me, to eat me … nice!'

By this stage my family had noticed my exceptionally poor record in sustaining life and they tried to dissuade me from further acquisitions.

'Why does all your wee animals die?' asked my wee brother.

'Ach, love, don't be buyin' any more of them poor wee craters that'll only go and die on ye!' pleaded my mother.

'No son of mine is gonna waste all his money on no more sick animals from that bloody pet shop!' announced my father.

'Whad'ya gonna murder next?' enquired my big brother.

Of course, I didn't listen. Yes, my animal husbandry was creating more animal tragedies than that cartoon movie with squashed rabbits with 'Bright Eyes'. But I was still determined to find a pet that lived. By this stage when I arrived in the pet shop in Gresham Street I imagined all the animals were cowering in the corners of their cages fearing I would buy them and reduce their life expectancy. The pet shop owner now recognised me as one of his best customers. If all the animals I had purchased from his shop had lived, I would have had enough for a pet shop of my own by now. Following my disastrous flirtations with fish and rodents I decided to set my sights on a new species – reptiles. I read in a fossil book from the Shankill Library that reptiles were descended from the dinosaurs and I recalled my father arguing in the street with Mrs Piper about this. She said there were no such things as dinosaurs because God created the earth in seven days and not that long ago. My atheist father offended her once again by challenging this certainty. Although I still hadn't forgiven Rocky, the murderous snake, I wondered if I should give a less violent reptile a go. One sunny Saturday afternoon, after a particularly happy bread round with no complaints, extra tips and a jolly Leslie, I caught a black taxi down the Road to Gresham Street in search of a tortoise. I named him Steve Austin, the Six Million Dollar Tortoise. He cost me only £2.50 but he moved in very slow motion, just like when Steve was chasing baddies on his bionic leg. My wee brother had a Steve Austin doll with plastic bionic parts you could remove with my mother's eyebrow tweezers. He said it was class! But my big brother disapproved because he said removing Steve Austin's clothes to take his bionic bits out was homo. Unlike the bionic man, Steve Austin the tortoise declined to move very much at all in the first twenty-four hours in my care. From the minute we left Gresham Street he kept his head resolutely in his shell. This was understandable on the journey home because black taxis tended to be quite noisy and smoky and were crammed with small children with snatters. But I became concerned when, back in the relative peace of our house, Steve Austin's head remained steadfastly in his shell. I decided to offer him a fresh lettuce leaf and a tomato but to no avail. My wee brother offered to assist by poking Steve's shell with matchsticks, but I initially declined. However, after five hours of no movement, I decided that a little gentle poking with one of my mother's blunter knitting needles might be required. Again, this produced no discernible response. It seemed as if Steve Austin was either very shy or very scared. He certainly wasn't bionic! After another twenty-four hours of no movement whatsoever, I took Steve back to the pet shop in a shoebox from Tylers with a limp leaf of lettuce and an untouched carrot.

'I wanna bring this tortoise back, Mister,' I explained to the elderly pet-shop owner.

The old man always wore a brown shop coat and smelt of sawdust. I could tell by the raising of one bushy eyebrow that he recognised me from previous pet post-mortems. Up until this point I had always liked the pet-shop owner and I sometimes said a wee prayer for his merchandise when a bomb went off near Gresham Street. I was concerned that, unlike the Wrangler jackets in John Frazer's just across the road, the poor wee pets would never make it to a smoke-damage sale.

'What's the matter with it, son?' he asked, in a reasonably patient tone of voice.

'It doesn't work!' I replied insensitively.

'Maybe you put the batteries in wrong!' he replied in a markedly less patient tone of voice.

'Wha'?' I responded, before realising that the pet-shop man was practising what my English teacher called irony.

'What did you do to the wee crater this time, ya wee hallion?' he barked.

Several puppies behind him yelped in unified disapproval.

'I didn't do nathin', Mister. His head wouldn't come out when I got him home.'

'Well he was perfectly healthy when he left my shop,' interjected the pet shop owner, noticeably too quickly.

I knew my head was often full of sweetie mice and my father regularly said I lived on cloud cuckoo land but there was something in the defensiveness of this remark that created in me the suspicion that perhaps my pet-keeping skills were perfectly fine. Maybe I had just been buying terminally ill animals! The pet shop owner sniffed loudly and rubbed his nose so hard he left a light residue of sawdust above his upper lip. He refused to give me my money back or accept the tortoise corpse but he did give me £2.50 worth of plastic ornaments for goldfish bowls, on the clear – and frankly insulting – condition that if he sold me another pet and it died immediately he would report me to 'the Cruelty'.

I left the shop, dejectedly clutching the shell encased body of my latest victim, and with nothing but a yellow plastic anchor and a red plastic treasure chest in my care. But as I left the shop I noticed on the stall on the pavement outside the front door a sign saying 'New! Terrapins. Small and Easy to Keep'. Beside this sign was a small plastic tray with an island in the middle and a plastic palm tree on top with two tiny turtles swimming around, both with their heads out of their shells and very much alive. It looked like Tracy Island from *Thunderbirds* but with pets instead of international rescue vehicles. This was irresistible! Terrapins were both exotic and 'easy to keep', which was very important to me now. These wee turtles provided both the underwater attraction of goldfish and the dinosaur connection of a tortoise. I resolved that terrapins would be my next pets.

I was still smarting from my most recent experience with

their near-relative from the reptile family but I was determined to sustain life. It was like trying to stop the Troubles. I was never going to give up. No sooner had I buried Steve Austin in the rapidly expanding pet cemetery beneath the holly bush than I was planning my next attempt at successful pet ownership. The only problem was that, due to the serious deterioration of my relationship with the owner of the pet shop in Gresham Street, I would have to identify an alternative vendor. After some enquiries at school, wee Thomas recommended Cobb's Pet Shop on the Crumlin Road, near the gaol and the courthouse with the tunnel under the road to stop the prisoners escaping. Cobb's sold pets and garden tools and saddles. I could never work out who bought the saddles because I never saw anyone on horseback in Belfast, apart from children having a go on Mickey Marley's Roundabout for 10p in Cornmarket. Several weeks of lucrative bread delivery later, I had saved sufficient funds in my plastic Abbey National savings book to go to Cobb's and buy two tiny terrapins and the beautiful habitat of a plastic tray. The tray featured a plastic green palm tree and a small raised platform, on to which the terrapins could climb if their water got too dirty because you hadn't cleaned it that week because you had been given extra biology homework for giggling when the teacher went red while explaining about sperm tadpoles swimming up eggs. Once purchased and safely transported home on my knee in the back of the Ford Escort respray, I continued my tradition of giving my endangered pets novel names from popular culture. Noel Edmonds, who was very funny and extremely clever on *Swap Shop*, had been teaching me the humour of the pun. So I named my two terrapins Amy Turtle and Dick Terrapin – Amy was named after the wee fat woman who cleaned the bedrooms and forgot her lines in *Crossroads* and Dick was named after the highwayman in a book from the Shankill Library. Once my new pets were named all they had to do now was to live. Please live! Even for a little while.

Sadly, within a few weeks, Amy Turtle joined Steve Austin beneath the holly bush. However, to everyone's surprise, not least my own, Dick lived. Not only did he live, but he grew and grew. He had begun with a shell the size of a 50p piece but he kept on growing until he was the size of one of the cake plates Auntie Mabel used for serving an apple sponge to the soldiers. At first I had fed Dick the same fish flakes that goldfish ate but very soon he had graduated to gobbling little scraps of raw bacon and even small shards of cooked ham from my hand. My parents were amazed at the rapidity of Dick's growth and wondered what I was doing so well. I had no idea, but one day I caught my big brother offering Dick a small ball of snot after picking his nose. I was disgusted and shouted at him but I wondered if perhaps snot was the elixir of life that was helping Dick to thrive. My overgrown terrapin survived so long that I even had to relocate him to my vacant fish tank. Then I had to ask Thomas O'Hara to look after Dick when we went away for weekends or holidays. Thomas shared my enthusiasm for reptiles, but one day at school our shared interest led to a most embarrassing incident. Thomas and I were standing chatting in the playground, the morning after I had cleaned out Dick's tank in the bath. On these occasions the normally restricted reptile happily enjoyed the brief freedom of the whole length of the bath. I would hold a piece of cooked ham to his nose and then pull it away as he went to take a bite and he would chase it the whole length of the bath.

'What about your turtle, Tony?' Thomas enquired, naturally enough.

'Oh aye! I was playing with my Dick in the bath last night and it was class!'

Just as I uttered these words, Timothy Longsley brushed past us. He then gathered considerable pace as he traversed the playground, looking back at me every few seconds and shaking his head. He ran up the steps towards the dinner hall very purposefully as if he had just discovered some exciting news. I assumed he had just been picked to captain a Glorious rugger team but it all became clear after break when I arrived slightly late for chemistry. When I opened the door, Timothy was sitting back on his stool smiling even more arrogantly than usual, as if he had just come first in the class again. He pointed at me and started to laugh and within a few seconds the whole class was looking in my direction and joining in the laughter, like those hateful Martian robots in the Smash advert again. The test tubes on the shelves seemed to reverberate to their guffaws. Even the lovely Judy Carlton was giggling and for some reason she couldn't look straight at me. I figured the joke was on me so I sat down very quickly hoping for the mercy of an explanation from someone.

Frankie Jones leaned forward on his stool and whispered, 'Timmy told everyone what you were doin' in the bath last night, you dirty wee baste ye!'

'But I was just playing with my ...' I started and then the penny dropped.

I hated Timothy Longsley! I know I was supposed to be a blessed peacemaker but I sat through the whole of chemistry pondering whether to use a conveniently lit Bunsen burner or some handy hydrochloric acid for revenge. Timothy chose to repeat this whole incident for weeks to anyone who would listen. Apparently it made for great hilarity in the minibus on the way to practice for the remainder of the rugby season. More worryingly, Judy Carlton couldn't look me straight in the eye. I considered trying to explain the whole situation to her but that would have been even more embarrassing. I was learning that although puns could be very clever, just like Noel Edmonds on *Swap Shop*, they could also become very annoying as well, so they could.

10

POLITICAL EDUCATION

Now that I was all grown up I was becoming much more aware of the complexity of politics in Northern Ireland, so I was. I used to think it was all just about Protestants and Catholics wanting to be the boss of each other but now I was nearly shaving I was old enough for a more mature analysis of the situation – I was able to use terms such as 'constitutional status', 'power sharing' and 'no' with great authority. Soon I would be as well informed as yer man Robin Day with the dicky bow who asked politicians hard questions on BBC2.

One Saturday morning I was working in the back of the van gathering together the Rosbottoms' vast array of pans and plains, when Leslie stopped the Ormo Mini Shop abruptly in the middle of the estate. Such was the suddenness of this halt that I was thrown against the crusty baps and squashed a packet of currant squares. I was doubly worried because not only had I just damaged precious merchandise, but I also assumed from the emergency stop that we were about to be hijacked.

'Are you all right in there, son?' enquired Leslie, who had obviously heard a thud from the back.

'Aye, I'm all right, but I've squashed a packet of flies' graveyards!' I replied, deciding that if my career was to survive this incident an immediate confession was the best course of action.

I popped my head into the cab and saw through the windscreen that a small crowd of people was gathering around a tall man wearing a hat in the middle of the street. Belfast men didn't wear hats except for paramilitaries with balaclavas, workers with flat caps and Orangemen with bowler hats. As a man, wearing any other sort of hat attracted the accusation that you were a homo. After Leslie had diddledee-dinged at the crowd several times it became clear that the crowd had no intention of moving, even if it was to clear a pathway for providers of Belfast's best-loved foodstuff. Leslie decided to go outside and investigate and I knew it was my professional responsibility to assist him. It was like being the companion getting out of the TARDIS with the Doctor after landing on a strange and dangerous new planet. As we stood by and listened it became clear that the tall man in the hat was a real live American, like on TV. He was asking lots of questions about the Troubles and everyone in the street wanted to explain the situation to him in great detail. He was nodding his head and scribbling down pages full of words and funny squiggles in his notebook. My customers were interrupting one another in an uncoordinated effort to inform the USA about what was going on and why it was all the other side's fault and why we were being sold down the river and why all the Americans should stop sending money to the IRA to kill us. The American journalist looked very interested, but his expression reminded me of when the Doctor had discovered a mysterious new alien life form and was trying to work out whether it was a goodie or a baddie.

'But, can you guys explain to me why modern people in Europe in the twentieth century are still fighting and killing each other over religion?'

'Sure, son, most of us round here have never been to Europe!' shouted an old man with National Health glasses and a tooth. 'Most of us don't have 2d to rub together, never mind til go til Spain!'

Big Duff's wife, still in her dressing gown and pink fluffy slippers, elbowed the other political commentators aside and took centre stage in the middle of the road.

'Here, I'll explain it all, Mister. No one ever listens to our side!' she began. 'Protestants want to stay part of Britain and Catholics want a United Ireland.'

'But aren't y'all Irish if you live here in Ireland?' asked the journalist.

At this stage I began to fear for his safety. The whole crowd began objecting and raising their voices at once and Leslie joined in.

'There's nathin' Irish about me!' shouted a wee hard man wearing a Union Jack T-shirt. 'This is Northern Ireland. Ulster! British! It's themuns down south that's Irish!'

These assertions drew several appreciative shouts of 'Yeeooo' from the crowd.

'Sorry, can you say that again?' asked the American. 'I can't understand your Irish accent.'

Mrs Big Duff spoke up again. Big Duff was still in bed, but it was clearly accepted by all present that his authority was delegated to his wife in such circumstances.

'We're British. We were born British and we'll die British!' she proclaimed. Several bystanders began to applaud.

'God Save the Queen!' shouted the old man, 'and God bless' – he began to cry – 'our lovely Queen Mother.'

He walked away absentmindedly with his head down.

'His Uncle Jimmy died in the Battle of the Somme, Mister,' whispered Leslie in very respectful tones.

I had never heard of the Battle of the Somme. I knew about the Battle of the Boyne when King Billy beat the Catholics in 1690 because it was painted on all the murals on the gable walls. I knew about every single arrow in the Battle of Hastings in 1066 from my school history book. But no one had ever told me anything about a Battle of the Somme. Maybe they were saving it for A-level history.

'So do you guys support discrimination against the Catholic minority in the North of Ireland?' enquired the American.

Each question seemed to create more anger than the previous one. If he kept asking questions like this he might need to seek refuge in the Ormo Mini Shop and unfortunately he was also getting on the wrong side of Leslie.

'Discrimination my arse!' was Mrs Big Duff's response. 'A lot of themuns over there is better off than usuns over here!'

I knew this might be true because a lot of the Catholics I met at the School of Music had more money than me and could afford to buy, rather than hire, their violins. But I was sure I had seen a documentary on UTV where a family with lots of children from up the country wasn't allowed a house just because they were Catholic. It didn't seem fair to me. When they interviewed John Hume he said it was injustice. I knew it was better not to mention this particular example in the present context, in case I might appear disloyal. This could have serious consequences such as being denied tips or getting beaten with a baseball bat. I didn't dare to admit it there, but I wasn't all that fussed about a United Ireland as long as the IRA wasn't in charge. Having said that I still preferred the BBC to RTÉ so I was worried that in a United Ireland they would replace *Top of the Pops* with *The Angelus*.

'So what do you good folk think will bring peace to Ireland then?' asked the journalist, smiling nervously.

'NORTHERN Ireland!' corrected Mrs Big Duff.

A barrage of conflicting suggestions followed the American's question.

'No Surrender!'

'Both sides stop fightin'!'

'Kill all them IRA bastards!'

'Power sharing!'

'Send all the Taigs down south!'

'Independent Ulster!'

'Not an inch!'

'Receive the Lord Jesus Christ as your own and personal Saviour!'

I didn't even bother to contribute, as I knew I would be shouted down as usual. Unfortunately the divergent set of responses resulted in the crowd breaking up into smaller groups arguing over the way of peace and some of these debates became quite heated.

The one positive outcome was that the road was now clear so Leslie and I could return to the van and get back to our work. The American seemed genuinely shocked by the lack of unanimity in the estate. He must have thought we were all the same.

'Hey kid, what do you think?' he asked me as I was departing.

I was surprised that an adult would be interested in my views. I thought about the question for a second and then I told him.

'My da says it's all about rich men gettin' poor men to fight each other so they stay rich and we stay poor, so it is.'

As soon as I had spoken these words I felt disappointed because I realised I was just repeating my father's view. Maybe it was time for me to start having my own opinions. Nevertheless, the journalist seemed to like what I had said and scribbled it down with a smile.

'Your startin' to sound like yer man Karl Marx,' said Leslie.

I could tell by his tone of voice that this was meant as a criticism, but I had never heard of Karl Marx. Was he one of Groucho's brothers? I was about to engage in a serious political discussion with my boss when Billy Cooper's granny interrupted us.

'A pan, a plain, two soda and two pataita,' she said.

As I delivered the remainder of the bread that morning I decided I was going to become an expert on politics. If tall men with hats from America were prepared to come the whole way across the Atlantic Ocean to try to understand Northern Ireland, then I should at least have a go myself. It seemed to be an important prerequisite for being the only pacifist Protestant on the peace line.

I began to amass political knowledge from watching angry

men arguing on *Scene Around Six* on BBC1 and listening to my father's running commentary on the various politicians who appeared on the TV. He described most of them as bastards of one sort or another but mainly the other sort. I noticed that Northern Ireland's politicians really hated each other. They were always interrupting one another and talking over the top of each other and I always felt embarrassed watching them. It was the same sort of discomfort I felt when my granny fell down the escalator in Robinson & Cleaver's near the City Hall and shouted, 'Bloody hell, the legs went from under me!' so loudly that all the swanky ladies on the make-up counters whispered 'shocking' and other such 'ings' until we left the shop in shame. As I observed the embarrassing spectacle of Northern Ireland politics I learnt that politicians were always right and weren't supposed to listen to each other. If David Dunseith on UTV tried to interrupt them to ask a question, they accused him of being on the other side's side. When I watched Robin Day interviewing posh English politicians on *Panorama* on BBC1 I noticed they didn't abhor each other as much as our politicians. But they still didn't answer the questions. I sometimes watched American politicians on *John Craven's Newsround* and they smiled more than our politicians and had very nice teeth. Politicians in the USA looked good on new colour TVs but I thought our politicians looked much more at home on old black-and-white ones.

As well as scanning the media I expanded my knowledge even further through the debates I heard in the street and in the playground. I gained much insight from the wise conversations I overheard on the bus or in the black taxi on the way home from school. My political ideology was being influenced by many different people such as Leslie (who always had the inside track on the latest thinking of the Grand Orange Lodge of Ireland), Patrick Walsh from Andersonstown at the School of Music (who was the only person I knew who wanted a United Ireland) and Mrs Piper (who was able to prove from the Bible that God was an Ulster Protestant). My father said he used to vote for the Northern Ireland Labour Party because they were 'for the workin' man' but he said they gave up when the Troubles started because being Irish or British was more important. I was shocked when my mother casually confessed that her grandfather had been a Communist who taught her to sing 'The Red Flag' while sitting on his knee as a wee girl. I was very confused by this revelation as no one had ever mentioned that my great-grandfather was a Russian. Communists supported the provos in their frequent attempts to kill us and they had big atomic bombs pointing right at us. I sometimes wondered if the evil Russian president with the eyebrows would decide to take the nuclear bomb aimed at Belfast and point it at another city instead, once he heard we were blowing up most of Belfast for ourselves.

At first I thought there were only two main types of politics in the world – unionist and nationalist. Protestants were unionists and Catholics were nationalists. Unionists were right and wanted to keep Ulster British and nationalists were wrong and wanted a United Ireland. Unionists liked the Queen Mother and Orange parades and nationalists liked the Pope and Irish dancing. Nationalists were winning and unionists were losing. The rest of the world, even English people who sent the soldiers to protect us, were on the side of the nationalists but God was on the side of the unionists. England was rich and didn't want us and down south was poor and didn't want us either. I couldn't understand why we were fighting so hard to be British or Irish when nobody really wanted us because of all our oul' fighting anyway.

However as my political knowledge deepened, I realised there were as many different types of unionists and nationalists as there were flavours of Tayto crisps. First of all, there were the posh unionists who said all their 'ings' and used to run Northern Ireland from a big empty white building called Stormont somewhere over in east Belfast, near where they built the *Titanic* that sank. I never met any posh unionists on the Shankill but my mother fancied one called John Taylor even after the IRA shot him in the face. Then there were Paisleyites, like my granny, who loved Rev. Ian and hated priests and Dublin and didn't let you play on the swings in the park on a Sunday. My granny loved these unionists so much that she would vote for them several times at each election. I could never understand how the people collecting the votes didn't notice the same twenty-stone woman coming into vote more than once.

'Oh my God. She's gonna get arrested for personating!' my mother would fret on election day.

The other unionists were called loyalists and they were poor and dead hard, apart from loving Elvis. They ran drinking clubs down the Road and killed Catholics to save Ulster. They were called loyalists because they were very loyal to the Queen, even though none of them could afford corgis or horses. They said they would die for the sake of the royal family but I couldn't imagine Princess Margaret doing very much for them in return.

Poor unionists loved flags but didn't like the posh unionists they voted for because they never did very much for them. Paisleyites didn't like posh unionists because they said they were watery Protestants who gave in to the IRA. As I tried to come to terms with all these different brands I concluded that unionists simply weren't too good at being in union. They were always arguing over who was the most Protestant and who was the biggest and bestest unionist. My father said they all just wanted to be 'Super Prod'. Sometimes Protestants seemed to hate each other more than they hated Catholics, and that was quite a lot of hatred.

It was much harder for me to come to a full understanding of nationalists because they all lived on the other side of the peace wall. I had only ever spoken to one real live one about politics, Patrick Walsh at the School of Music, who was better than me at the violin but at least his voice hadn't broken yet. Patrick thought all Protestants should go back to Scotland on the Larne–Stranraer ferry. To compensate for my limited contact with nationalists I watched TV news debates and furtively read Catholic newspapers in Central Library. I soon became an expert on this side too. Nationalists wanted a United Ireland because they were fed up with the British for oppressing them for thousands of years. Although there were fewer flavours of nationalists, I soon learned that Titch McCracken was wrong when he said, 'themuns are all the same, ya know'. As far as I could tell, the nationalists who liked John Hume were teachers and social workers who wanted a united Ireland but wouldn't kill you for it. They didn't like injustice or Protestants. They wanted our jobs and our houses but they wouldn't force us out. Meanwhile republicans were poor and dead-hard nationalists who supported the IRA to kill us to get a united Ireland. Republicans hated Protestants, especially policemen, but they hated the British most of all because everything was their fault. Republicans thought the Brits were evil invaders like Daleks and Russians. However, the provos seemed to like Russians because the Soviets were pointing hundreds of atomic bombs at the Brits. I was terrified of republicans in case they made Protestant breadboys legitimate targets in their fight to free Ireland. An armful of bread was not an effective shield in a machine-gun attack.

As my understanding of politics deepened I also became more and more aware of all the contradictions. Patrick Walsh said Catholics were poor and Protestants were rich, but he always had more money than me for the tuck shop. Patrick sometimes lent me 5p for a Puff Candy bar during the break from our crucifixion of a Bach concerto and so he couldn't have been all that poor. There were so many contradictions I didn't know who to believe. Titch McCracken said all the Catholics up in Andersonstown had too many children but Patrick only had two brothers the same as me. Patrick said Protestants had all the best land but most people on the Shankill didn't even have a garden. Mrs Piper said Catholics kept their coal in the bath but that seemed very impractical to me for any religion.

With all of this confusion it came as a great relief to me when I became aware of a political party created with the aim of bringing Protestants and Catholics together. It was called the Alliance Party. Both unionists and nationalists laughed at it and said it was 'middle of the road' and 'wishy-washy' which was exactly what the *NME* said about ABBA. I thought the Alliance Party was a great idea because if we all got together and stopped killing each other then there would be peace. I assumed that when everyone my age was old enough to vote, then we would all vote Alliance and the Troubles would be over. However, I soon discovered that my enthusiasm was not shared by very many of the people around me. Titch McCracken sneered that the Alliance Party was trying to turn us all into 'Protholics and Catestants' and Patrick Walsh said they were all do-gooder unionists from Bangor. Mrs Piper said the members all sat on a big fence somewhere in Cultra and this meant they really supported the IRA. Timothy Longsley at BRA said the Alliance Party was 'nothing but a pack of middle-class wankers'. I thought this was rich coming from Timothy as he was the biggest middle-class wanker of all! But in spite of all of this hostility I decided that perhaps I should join as part of my calling to be a blessed peacemaker. I was certain Jesus would have joined the Alliance Party if he had been in my shoes. But I wasn't sure exactly how you went about joining a political party. They didn't advertise at the back of *Look-in* beside the sea monkeys and stamp clubs and I didn't know anyone at all from the Upper Shankill who was a member.

Then one day, to my great surprise, I found an unexpected ally in the playground at BRA. I was having yet another row with Ian Forrester (who read the *NME* like a Christian read the Bible) about punk rock versus teenybopper sell-outs. He was insisting that The Clash had more to say to the youth of today than 'them bloody Bee Gees'. Of course I won the argument by pointing out which of the two bands had sold most records to the youth of today. At this point Ian rolled his eyes as if to suggest I was too stupid to recognise the foolishness of my argument. It was the same look my father gave me when I tried to convince him that God existed and loved him and wanted him to get saved. Just as I was about to storm off to the locker room in a huff, Ian commented, 'Sure, just because most people in Northern Ireland vote for all the bigots, doesn't mean the Alliance Party has nothing to say.'

At last Ian and I had found common ground and so together we decided we would join the Alliance Party and bring peace to Northern Ireland, as long as our parents would let us. A few days later during break time, Ian borrowed the *Yellow Pages* from the school office and we looked up the Alliance Party telephone number. At lunchtime we sneaked out of the side gate and round the corner to the red telephone box to arrange an appointment. Leaving the school grounds during the day was strictly forbidden in case we got shot, so we were risking a hundred lines and three lunchtime detentions for the sake of peace. Ian did all the talking on the phone because he was more confident than me but I listened down the earpiece to hear what the Alliance Party sounded like. A nice lady who pronounced all her 'ings' seemed very pleased to hear from us and said that a nice man called Seamus would come out to one of our homes to meet us some evening after school. When she asked for the address I pointed at myself furiously and Ian gave her my home address. There were a few perceptible moments of silence when Ian gave the nice lady my Upper Shankill address but she regained her composure and assured us that Seamus would come out to see us the following Wednesday evening after *Scene Around Six.*

When I explained to my parents that Ian was coming round for tea they were delighted that one of my school friends from North Belfast was visiting. But when I added that I had invited the Alliance Party to our house too there was less enthusiasm.

'Oh my God. This wee lad's head's in the clouds!' cried my mother.

'Let him carry on, sure he's young,' said my father.

'But he'll end up gettin' shot!' exclaimed my mother.

I was shocked at this reaction. It wasn't as if I was joining a paramilitary organisation and as a general rule the IRA and the UVF seemed to regard the Alliance Party as too nice to be worth shooting. Of course I was aware that Seamus sounded like a Catholic and there had never been a real, live Catholic in our house before, apart from Val Doonican in a rocking chair and Eamonn Andrews with a big red book on *This is Your Life*. As a result of these concerns I conveniently forgot the name of our political visitor and my family remained in the living room laughing at Frank Spencer falling off a ladder in his beret on *Some Mothers Do 'Ave 'Em*, oblivious to the fact that a Seamus was calling. Ian and I were allowed full use of the good room with the shag-pile carpet for the political negotiations.

When the doorbell rang, I ran to the front door immediately and welcomed a nervous-looking Seamus. He was very nice and pleased to meet us and very friendly but he kept looking out the window towards his car as he spoke. It was as if he was scared of something bad happening. Ian asked him clever political questions and I nodded, pretending I understood everything when Seamus gave long answers about 'constitutional status' and 'democratic deficit' and 'unionist with a small U' and 'power sharing' and all. I recognised the words 'power sharing' because when politicians said those words on the UTV news my granny would lift the poker and shake it at the TV screen. After about an hour Seamus left, giving us nice leaflets and application forms to fill in and he said he looked forward to having us in the party.

'Thanks very much, Seamus. It was very interest-ing,' I said politely, shaking hands.

Unfortunately this farewell exchange coincided with my big brother passing en route to the toilet. Of course he observed everything.

'Snobby Fenian lover!' he whispered in my ear, as I closed the front door on Seamus.

Within seconds my mother had joined us in the hall and was pleading with me not to get involved in politics because it was too dangerous and my father told her to catch herself on.

After that evening, Ian Forrester seemed to tolerate me more in spite of our differing musical tastes. I faithfully sent off my application form to the Alliance Party and waited several weeks for a reply. After a few months I was still waiting. This was taking longer than my Charles Atlas pack and it was posted from America. I assumed the they were being inundated by all the young people in Northern Ireland joining up to help them stop the Troubles and they would get round to me eventually, but my membership card never arrived.

Within a few weeks I was down south at Butlin's holiday

camp in Mosney for a family holiday. My big brother declined the invitation because he was too grown up now for going on holiday with us; instead he organised a poker school in our good room while we were away. In spite of my granny's concerns that we were going to 'give hard-earned money to them Free Staters' my father insisted that his family should experience at least one vacation in a traditional holiday camp before they all closed down. We crossed the border near Newry and my father drove very cautiously through bandit country. Aware of our northern number plate, my parents were silent during this part of the journey, presumably hoping that the hundred of provos hiding in the fields all around us wouldn't consider Protestants invading Butlin's to be legitimate targets. I looked out the windows of our Ford Escort respray to see if all the roads down south were as terrible as everyone said they were and to check if all the people really were very poor. The roads were pretty bad but the people just looked the same as us. Titch McCracken said you weren't allowed to be a Protestant down south and I had worried about this so much that I'd managed to convince myself that we'd have to turn Catholic before they would let us in to Butlin's. Surely you didn't have to know how to say a Hail Mary to be allowed to enter the knobbly knees competition!

When we arrived at the holiday camp we received a warm and friendly welcome from a man with a lisp and a Terry Wogan accent in a red coat. Once we settled into our very small chalet I explored all the delights of Butlin's in the rain with my wee brother. Everywhere looked like it had been brilliant before we were born. It all needed painted but we still had fun in the old-fashioned dodgems and roller-skating in a proper rink for the first time in our lives. It soon became clear from the southern accents and all the Irish-sounding names being called by the mothers that we were the only Protestants in Butlin's. On most of the rainy days that week we went for a swim in one of the Olympic-size swimming pools that needed a good clean. There was a window underneath the pool so you could nip down to see if any of the kids had pooped in the water before you go in. One day it stopped raining and we splashed around in the outdoor pool for hours and I imagined I had a dolphin for a best friend like on *Flipper*. While we were at the outdoor pool enjoying the sun as if we were Judith Chalmers in Spain on UTV, I met two pretty girls about my age who were also on holiday.

When I heard one of the girls shouting 'Here, wee girl, will ya stop scunderin' me in my bikini!' I worked out they must come from Belfast too.

'Wise a bap, Sinead, your heads a marley, so it is!' replied the other.

I was disappointed to discover they were called Siobhan and Sinead and so they were clearly not Presbyterians. I had to reluctantly relinquish my initial desire for Siobhan to become my holiday girlfriend because you weren't allowed to go out with someone from the other side. Although romance was totally out of the question we got on so well together I thought I could at least persuade the girls to join the Alliance Party with me, just to keep the numbers balanced. We could prove that Catholics and Protestants could work together and this would be an act of peace in a time of war. Siobhan was lovely and Sinead lent me her rubber ring so I could discern among us true hope for a more peaceful future across the barricades. On Easter Monday, my last night at Butlin's, I was sitting alone outside our chalet in a white plastic chair reading *Look-in* and finishing off a Yorkie bar Easter egg for real men. The walkway of the second floor chalets above acted as a barrier against the hailstones. My parents were out competing in the ballroom dancing competition and my wee brother was at a Punch and Judy show with Irish accents. I was planning to ask Siobhan for her address so we could stay in touch and join the Alliance Party together and help bring peace to Northern Ireland. As luck would have it, just as the hail stopped hammering on the corrugated roofs of our chalets, who should turn the corner and stride across the muddy grass strip between the chalets but Sinead and Siobhan. They were giggling and singing and it seemed to be the perfect moment to request, if not a snog up an entry, at least an ongoing platonic relationship for the sake of cross-community reconciliation. However, as the two Belfast beauties drew closer I began to hear more distinctly the words of the song they were singing with such glee.

'We are the provies from the Lower Falls,

We are the provies from the Lower Falls!'

I realised immediately that Siobhan did not share my commitment to the way of non-violence and I retreated sadly into the chalet. I was so shocked I had nearly fallen for a terrorist that I lay down on the thin mattress of the very small bed and sulked. I was getting very good at sulking but it was usually better if someone else was around to notice. After coming to terms with the initial shock my mind returned to going back to school and inevitably these thoughts led to Judy Carlton. I had been putting our relationship on hold to concentrate on my career but now the Easter holidays were nearly over maybe it was time to try to work things out with Judy. I was sure this was what Judy would want. In the distance I could hear the melancholy sound of Siobhan and Sinead singing some other song I'd never heard before about 'The Men Behind the Wire'. All thoughts of us joining the Alliance Party together faded into the night.

When my parents and wee brother eventually returned to the chalet I remained in bed and put my head under the sheets pretending to be asleep. This was not a time for conversation about politics or religion or peace and reconciliation. I was getting tired of peacemaking and the more I was learning about politics the more I despaired, so I did.

11

FADS, MUSIC AND SADNESS

I loved gadgets, so I did. This was one thing I had in common with my father. I didn't share his love of going fishing because it involved unnecessary violence against one of God's wee creatures. I couldn't match his proficiency in DIY because I always hammered my thumb. I was unable to join in his zeal for atheism because I was too well saved. And, although I inhaled his Hamlet cigar smoke while laughing at *The Eric Sykes Show* on UTV, I never really shared his chain-smoking habit either. Dad was always up to some new hobby, from growing tomatoes in his rickety greenhouse to cooking tasty Chinese food in the kitchen. One day he was engraving metal with a machine he had borrowed from the foundry and the next day he was brewing his own beer in a bucket beside the nails in the garage. I could barely keep up with every passing craze. My mother described each hobby as 'your father's latest notion' and correctly predicted that all new interests would pass in a matter of months. My granny was less understanding. When Dad brought home a Japanese bonsai tree kit she said, 'Look at Buck Alec! He never knows what to be at! No son-in-law of mine should be supporting the Japs after what they done on us in the war.' I knew the Japanese were cruel to prisoners of war in black-and-white movies and I accepted they had made us drop atomic bombs on two of their cities. But thirty years on I thought my granny should give the Japanese people another chance because now they liked ABBA and made brilliant *Godzilla* cartoons.

Dad's fads were fascinating but I sometimes wondered if all these short-lived hobbies were just a sign that he was bored doing the same job at the foundry every day for thirty years. When his latest interest involved anything electronic with buttons I joined in enthusiastically. My father rarely purchased anything from the *Great Universal Club Book* but he thumbed through the electronic pages nearly as often as my wee brother scoured the toys pages and almost as regularly as I looked at the section with nice ladies in bras. So I was not too surprised when one day a box from the *Club Book* arrived at our house containing a newfangled white plastic metal detector. It cost him 20 weeks at 99p and he promised my mother he would stop chain-smoking to pay for it. Every Sunday afternoon he went up the fields of Divis mountain to look for ancient coins and swords. He used to find old clay pipes and Stone Age arrowheads up there, near an ancient flint quarry and a cave where it was rumoured the UDA had their planning meetings. My father was clearly the foremost archaeologist on the Black Mountain but unfortunately the metal detector rarely buzzed and, even when it did, he only ever found old sixpences and pennies from before we went decimal. One Sunday afternoon I accompanied him to the beach at Millisle to search for ancient coins dropped by careless Vikings and Romans. My school history book mentioned neither of these invaders raping and pillaging in Millisle. Maybe they had heard about the tartan gangs during the Twelfth fortnight. Dad allowed me to hold the metal detector and switch on the buttons so that a little red light came on and it made a buzzing noise like a lightsaber in *Star Wars*. When I told him I felt like a Jedi Knight seeking out hidden treasure on the Death Star he told me to 'stop bein' such an oul' blether'. I wielded the amazing white plastic metal detector along the surface of the beach, over sand and shells, across clumps of smelly seaweed and over the faded yellow plastic of discarded Tayto Cheese and Onion crisp bags. All of a sudden the mild buzzing tone increased to a high-pitched electronic scream like when the Daleks lost their temper and shouted 'Exterminate! Exterminate!' at the Doctor. My father immediately began digging with the garden trowel he had brought along for such a discovery as this. Within seconds he was ten inches down in the sand.

'Is it Roman or Viking?' I asked excitedly.

'I'm not sure yet!' replied Dad.

I was so proud of my archaeologist father. He reminded me of those posh English men in pith helmets that dug up the scary Mummy that lived in the Ulster Museum. But our excitement was short-lived. A disappointed silence fell on the beach as the last few trowelfuls of wet sand revealed a crushed, corroded Harp lager can. The seagulls above us screeched as if they had been watching the whole drama and were mocking us now.

'But maybe it's an old one!' I said, attempting to revive some archaeological interest. However once we had fully retrieved the artifact, a closer archaeological analysis revealed a price sticker from the Wine Lodge indicating that the object was mostly likely buried circa 1977 during a binge on the beach after the bonfire on the Eleventh of July.

Thankfully, there was one other new gadget my father and I both loved that never disappointed. One day he arrived home with a big box in the boot of the Ford Escort respray and I noticed it said 'Handle with Care' on the side. Dad proudly carried the mysterious package into the good room and gathered the whole family around it on the shag-pile.

'I got us a surprise with my overtime!' he announced.

I was instantly excited, although I had to dismiss my initial hope that it might be a puppy because there were no holes in the box to let the wee dog breathe and with my track record I was now very sensitive to animal welfare. My father slowly opened the box to reveal a treasure chest of polystyrene. My wee brother began to play with this crumbling white packaging but he got a clip round the ear because when he scraped Evel Knievel's plastic motorbike against the polystyrene it produced a horrible sound that my mother said would make her nerves bad. The layers of polystyrene were gradually removed to unveil an amazing black plastic record player with a built-in radio and cassette player. This astonishing work of electronic engineering elicited a collective gasp from the gathered family. The wondrous machine had two speakers with black sponge on the front and wires so long that you could place one speaker on either side of the good room, a full 10 feet apart! Yes, the Macaulays now had an amazing black plastic stereo! How many families could say they had a colour TV AND a stereo? Wait until I tell Timothy Longsley! My father smiled delightedly when he saw the wide eyes of his three boys.

'Alice Cooper in stereo! Class!' cried my big brother.

'Cliff Richard in stereo! Lovely!' cried my mother.

'Does Rolf Harris sing "Two Little Boys" in stereo?' asked my wee brother.

'No, son. He's mono,' replied my father.

For a second I glanced sadly at the old 1950s stereogram that had served us so well, realising that it was now heading for the garage and maybe even the Eleventh boney. But then I realised what the arrival of the new stereo really meant. 'ABBA in stereo,' I cried.

'Ya big fruit!' responded my big brother.

Unfortunately this latest insult forced me to drop my pacifist principles momentarily, and I hit my big brother across the head with one of his Rod Stewart LPs. A fight ensued in which my big brother threw me down on the floor very roughly. I was saved from serious injury by the polystyrene packing but I realised the beautiful family moment had ended when my father stood up and shouted, 'You ungrateful wee shites!' My big brother and I got the strap and we were sent to our bedroom for the rest of the night. This was a cruel punishment because we shared a room, and so we had to spend the rest of the night sulking together, with our backs to each other. The stereo sounds of Cliff Richard, Tammy Wynette and Rolf Harris wafted up the stairs from the two speakers in the good room. Not even the woodchip on the walls of the sitting room could dampen this glorious new stereo sound. It wasn't fair! Everyone knew that stereos weren't invented for old-fashioned music! I was so ragin' I nearly said 'fuck' out loud but I resisted because if my big brother ever caught me swearing he would say 'Oh aye! Yer not so good livin' now, so you're not!'

The next day, when I finally got a go on our amazing new black plastic stereo, I was enthralled to hear Agnetha and Frida magically emerging from different speakers at the same time with 'The Name of the Game'. The other exciting feature of this new wonder gadget was being able to record on to a cassette directly from the radio or the record player. The outcome of this innovation was that now I could record the top forty countdown on Radio 1 on a Sunday night without having to hold my old cassette recorder microphone up to the wee speaker on my transistor radio. I could stop worrying about recording my mother walking in and ordering me up the stairs to tidy my room over the top of 'The Rivers of Babylon'. Never again would everyone laugh when I played back the recording without fast forwarding being told off by my mammy.

In spite of the embarrassment my transistor radio had caused me, I loved it. It was small and mustard with a plastic handle. You didn't have to plug it in because it ran on batteries that lasted for ages. It went everywhere with me. I kept it safely in the pocket of my duffle coat on the way to school and listened to Dave Lee Travis playing 'Don't Cry for Me Argentina' on Radio 1 at the bus stop. On Saturday mornings – if I had a lengthy walk up and down the stairs in the flats, and so long as I had one hand free of bread – I could reach into my duffle coat pocket and click the 'on' switch to snatch a brief listen to the new Brotherhood of Man single on Downtown Radio. Under the sheets in bed at night I could listen to Emperor Rosko playing the latest Power Play after the news headlines on Radio Luxembourg.

The problem with constantly listening to my transistor radio was the news. Every station I listened to interrupted the latest hits once an hour with the news headlines. And Northern Ireland was always on the news and it was always bad news. I hated living in the middle of all this fighting and I prayed for all the violence and hatred to end, but it never stopped. And what could I do? Sure nobody would listen to a pacifist breadboy from Ballygomartin. I wanted to leave Belfast and escape from bad news and bombers and gunmen. I wanted to grow up somewhere else with no soldiers or paramilitaries. It was dead scary to walk past a parked car with its lights on, in case it blew up and I hated being searched for bombs at the door of every shop. Unfortunately, I couldn't afford to emigrate because a full year of breadboy tips would barely raise sufficient funds to buy a ticket to the Isle of Man. My father seriously considered moving us away from Belfast to Carrickfergus or Australia. We were very close to leaving a couple of times but he could never see it through.

One terrible day, as I was listening to my mustard transistor radio playing the latest hits, I heard on the news that the IRA had blown up the La Mon House Hotel and killed a lot of people from a dog club. It was horrible! The people were all burned! How did the provos think killing all those poor people would help them get their way? Did they not want dog lovers in a United Ireland?

Then I had to listen to news reports about a gang of men from the Shankill Road who roamed around the streets near my school and picked up people and murdered them just for being

Catholics. They tortured those poor people like in your worst nightmare! Did they really think cutting up Catholics would help us stay British? The newsreaders always called them 'the Shankill Butchers' and this made everyone from the Shankill sound like we were evil murderers from a bloody horror movie.

Then things came much closer to home. One evening as my family was finishing our Smash and fish fingers and *Crossroads* was ending, we heard four loud bangs in the street outside. I had never heard gunfire so close before. Everyone ran out into the street. One of our neighbours, Mr Oliver was slumped over the wheel of his car, parked just outside his house. Another car with men cheering out the windows was speeding off down the street. Mrs Oliver was frozen in the passenger seat, her eyes staring straight ahead. Her husband had just been shot four times in the chest. Mr Oliver was a shopkeeper on the Road and he was still wearing his white shop coat. He liked fishing. There were four small bright red circles across the front of his white coat. Mr Oliver had turned one of the bushes in his front garden into a big rooster with his hedge clippers. No one in our street had ever seen a gardener quite like him. My father helped Mrs Oliver out of the car and went back inside to phone the ambulance and the RUC. Auntie Mabel carried out one of her good dining room chairs and set it on the pavement. Mrs Oliver sat in the chair, rocking backwards and forwards and crying a crescendo of painful wails from the depths of her heart. Mr and Mrs Oliver had grown-up children who lived across town. The red circles on Mr Oliver's shop coat grew wider and wider until they all joined together into one pure red bloody circle. My mother jumped into the back seat of the car. She had turned up the trousers on Mr Oliver's good suit for a dinner dance. My mother put one arm around him and stroked and patted his head gently. Mr Oliver always wore Brylcreem to slick his hair back, like men in the fifties. I could hear my mother telling him he was all right, love, so he was, and Mrs Oliver was okay. I heard her tell him the ambulance would be here very soon and everything would be all right, love, so it would. His eyes were closed. Mr Oliver always wore a vest and braces and a tie under his shop coat. Deep red blood came flowing down his nose and from his mouth. Mr Oliver died in my mother's arms.

Within an hour our street was on the news. We were on Downtown Radio and Radio Ulster. We were even on *News at Ten* after one of Big Ben's dongs. As I lay in bed that night, I tuned my mustard transistor radio to every radio station I could find. From Dublin to London, from Athlone to Brussels, I heard my street on every news bulletin. I listened to the distant clatter of endless cups of tea being prepared by my mother downstairs in the kitchen, in the vain hope that a wee cuppa tea for all the traumatised neighbours would make everything all right. So I turned up the volume of my transistor radio and retreated under the sheets to drown out the desperate muffled conversations below.

'You don't realise how bad it is, 'til it comes to your own door,' was the phrase I heard repeatedly above the whistles and crackles as I switched stations and languages.

I lay there for hours listening to all the radio stations report in different accents the news of a shopkeeper shot dead in the Upper Shankill in Belfast. It was as if by hearing the bad news again and again, confirmed by every radio station, that the reality of what I had just experienced would finally sink in.

I detested this country. All this hatred and fighting was too much to bear. I wanted Mr Oliver to be still alive and serving his customers and loving his family. I longed to hear the sound of Mrs Oliver calling him in from their front garden for his dinner on a summer's day. I didn't want to hear any more about who started it and how it was always the other side's fault. I wanted to leave these shores forever. I wanted to live in a place where they didn't shoot shopkeepers in front of their wives. I longed to move to a country where at least they didn't cheer after they had shot you four times in the chest. I wanted all the DJs on the radio to forget about the news and replace it with an extra track from *Saturday Night Fever* or the theme from *Star Wars*. I would rather live in a country where they played an Elvis medley instead of telling us more and more bad news. I wanted Emperor Rosko and DLT and Big T to drown out all the hatred and all the blood with music about love and adventure and dancing.

When I fell asleep that night I dreamt of moving abroad on a big ship to a very clean city in Canada, surrounded by miles and miles of prairies from my geography book. No one got cut up and tortured because of their religion and dog lovers were not legitimate targets.

The next day at school, I didn't talk about my murdered neighbour. I was too ashamed because the worst things always happened in the worst areas. Nobody noticed, but deep down I was heartbroken.

12

OH MARIA *THIS* LONDON'S A WONDERFUL SIGHT

It was the summer of 1978 when I next escaped from Belfast. This trip was to be the most adventurous so far for the members of the Westy Disco. Some benevolent Americans who liked peace had donated money to give us children of the Troubles a holiday away. We were going to London this time and, because it was so expensive, we had to contribute half the money ourselves. I had been saving most of my breadboy pay and tips for months. Titch had been selling his granny's delft ornaments in Smithfield Market every Saturday afternoon (I think his granny was unaware of this enterprise). Ever since Uncle Henry had announced the forthcoming trip, on the way home from having fun at the YMCA in Newcastle, I had been dreaming of seeing a real live Beefeater. I couldn't wait to see a soldier with a big black furry hat guarding the Queen's house in Buckingham Palace. This latest expedition required only one Saturday away from home and, although Leslie was happy to give me the morning off, he couldn't find a satisfactory substitute for me. I gloried in my indispensability.

It was the summer of John Travolta and Olivia Newton-John in *Grease*. John had obviously kept up his dancing after *Saturday Night*

Fever but my Olivia was a revelation. When she sang 'Summer Nights' on the video on *Top of the Pops* she was dead lovely, skipping along and smiling with her lovely hair and dress and all. But when she permed her hair and changed into tight black Lycra leggings and high heels for 'You're The One That I Want' I was genuinely shocked. Up until this point Olivia Newton-John had been a virgin like me. Our whole relationship had been built on the unspoken understanding that we were saving ourselves for one another. Olivia had entertained other red-blooded males in her life before now, such as Cliff Richard, but he was a wee good livin' pop star so I assumed they had never actually done it. Of course, I was in no position to be judgmental, given my ongoing relationship with Farrah Fawcett-Majors up on my bedroom wall in a swimsuit. But it was still a shock when Olivia came on the screen with a feg in her mouth, flirting suggestively in a tight black boob tube at a fairground. This was a long way from 'Banks of the Ohio'. Up to this point Travolta had been a hero to me. I even defended him when Philip Ferris called him a fruit because he danced. But now Travolta was a love rival. John Travolta was to Olivia Newton-John what Timothy Longsley was to Judy Carlton.

In spite of these romantic complications, no one could deny that the music from *Grease* was brilliant! The tunes took over the Westy Disco completely. On some Saturday evenings there were more songs from *Grease* than Boney M and ABBA put together. Everyone knew all the words and we sang along as we danced. Some wee girls in our street had actually been to see *Grease* twenty times. However this morning as we gathered at the Nissen hut to wait for the minibuses to take us to the Larne–Stranraer ferry, it became clear that another musical phenomenon had taken hold of the Upper Shankill in a most unexpected way.

We were once again gathering at the church hall around an ever-growing mountain of suitcases and canvas sports bags, some in better shape than others. My big brother boasted a brand new Manchester United bag and Irene Maxwell had a new purple suitcase with Bee Gees stickers. Irene got quite upset when Titch McCracken threw his old black leather suitcase (held together with a snake belt because it didn't close properly) on top of her suitcase and dirtied Barry Gibb's teeth but everyone else thought it was hilarious. Irene was so disgruntled she stopped sharing Spangles for the rest of the journey. Heather Mateer had a pink vanity case, which Titch suggested was full of bras and boob tubes, and Sammy Reeves carried a battered old leather suitcase he had borrowed from his granda. Uncle Henry was ticking off the names of everyone who had arrived and my mother and Auntie Emma were busy reminding us that there was no smoking or drinking allowed at any stage on the trip. My father was across the road at the shop stocking up on Hamlet cigars for the week.

Suddenly a strange figure strode around the corner in front of us. He had spiky hair, sticking up on end like when Stan Laurel got electrocuted in a black-and-white movie. This unfamiliar person was wearing a black leather jacket and a dog collar with studs from some bulldog. He was wearing black Dr Martens and tight blue jeans with rips at the knees. He wore metal chains round his waist on top of a belt with studs that looked so sharp they could put your eye out. It was a real live punk rocker walking along the West Circular Road and heading in our direction. The whole Westy Disco looked on in astonishment. We were expecting to see loads of punks in London, so this apparition seemed strangely premature. Punk had been going for ages now and all the proper punks went to clubs in town and stood outside the City Hall between Paisley rallies. But so far we didn't have very many punks in the Upper Shankill.

As the punk rocker drew near, I noticed he was carrying a small canvas bag. It was covered in the names of punk bands such as The Sex Pistols and The Boomtown Rats and Sham 69. He appeared to be coming in our direction, almost as if he was one of us.

'Who's that?' asked Uncle Henry.

'It's one of them there punks that spits and all, so it is!' explained Irene Maxwell.

The punk stopped beside us and threw his bag into the pile of suitcases, strategically striking Barry Gibb between the eyes. He was wearing an earring with a skull and crossbones, which reminded me of the flag on the top of Captain Pugwash's ship. But most shocking of all he had a big safety pin, the size of the one my mother had used for my wee brother's nappies, pierced right through his nose!

'Sorry son, this is the youth club trip to London. You need to have paid your money and all weeks ago,' explained Uncle Henry.

'Wha'?' grunted the punk.

It was only when he spoke that some vague recognition began to break through. I recognised those surly tones! I knew that face from before it was pierced. I couldn't believe it!

'Oh my God. Philip Ferris is a fuckin' punk!' shrieked Heather Mateer.

'Language, Heather, love,' said Auntie Emma.

The whole Westy Disco took a sharp intake of breath. It was true! It really was Philip Ferris. Gone were the duffle coat and the non-descript clothes. What a transformation!

'I'm surprised his mammy let him go out like that,' whispered my mother to Auntie Emma, 'and her that good livin' and all.'

'His da'll not let him play for the BB five-a-side football team if he turns up to a match dressed like that!' replied Auntie Emma.

All the adults seemed to disapprove, except my father, who preferred to retain his disapproval for religious and political leaders rather than teenagers.

'Here, wee lad. When did ye turn punk?' asked Titch.

'Yeah, right,' sneered Philip with just a hint of an English accent.

'But why have you gone all punk and all?' asked Irene.

'Anarkeee in the You Kay!' answered Philip in an English accent, with a defiant clenched fist in the air. He sounded like the skinhead in the *Dick Emery Show* on a Saturday night.

For the next few minutes, as we waited for the minibuses, the whole group gathered in a circle around Philip Ferris the punk, examining his clothes and piercings and bombarding him with questions. It emerged the dog collar had been purchased in the pet shop in Gresham Street, the safety pin had been stolen from his mammy's knitting basket and the chain had previously been used to prevent the theft of his Chopper bike. When we finally boarded the buses, Philip sat in the back seat on his own, rattling his chains and scratching his inflamed nostril. I couldn't take my eyes off him because it was such a shock. I got up on my knees in my seat and turned round to have another look.

'Who you lookin' at?' he shouted at me, now with a London accent sounding not unlike Dick Van Dyke in *Mary Poppins*.

Offended by this aggressive behaviour, I turned around and sat down immediately. Titch McCracken was sitting beside me and had clearly been waiting for an opportunity to share his assessment of Philip's transformation. He looked at me with a sneaky smirk on his face and pointed backwards towards Philip with his thumb.

'Never mind the ballicks!' he said.

I laughed the whole way to Larne. Titch McCracken may have been a wee tea leaf but sometimes he could be very funny.

I had been dreading the ferry crossing to Stranraer as my previous journeys on the ferry had seen me boke copiously into the Irish Sea. In preparation for the journey I had declined all Smash and fish fingers for twenty-four hours. On the day of departure I had also refused the offer of a packed lunch of corned beef and tomato sandwiches, a packet of Tayto cheese and onion and a bar of Caramac. Everyone else was enjoying their packed lunch in the rain on the deck, apart from my big brother, Sammy Reeves and several other rebels who were already breaking the no-alcohol rule over several Harps in the bar below. But I was once again hanging over the edge of the deck contemplating my imminent contribution to the contents of the Irish Sea. At least this time I was wearing my Peter Storm anorak, which could be wiped clean fairly easily should a gust of wind from above the waves decide to return my sick. I was fully prepared for boomerang boke. I tried to divert myself with thoughts that I was yer man in the white suit from *Fantasy Island* and my wee brother was the wee funny man that said 'Yes, boss' with a lisp. I imagined we were transporting the members of the Westy Disco to a wonderful adventure on a tropical island with lovely girls with bikinis, but none of this could suppress the nausea. I once again spent most of the trip being sick into the sea and I ventured below decks only once in three hours, to find the toilets, which smelt of seaweed and pee and made me feel even worse. As I was leaving the gents I noticed Philip Ferris at the mirror unhooking the safety pin from his mammy's knitting basket from his nose.

'My nose is fuckin' killin' me!' confided Philip, desperately.

'Well, I'm sure you'd be allowed to take your safety pin out for a wee while, Philip.' I said sympathetically, 'Sure it won't stop you being a proper punk, so it won't.'

Unfortunately I was unable to hang around for Philip's reply because a large lorry driver with loyalist tattoos emerged from one of the cubicles. This released yet another foul smell into the air to assault my already overloaded nostrils and I had to run to the upper deck.

When the torturous crossing finally ended we had to board a coach to take us from Stranraer to London in what was to be the longest bus ride of my life so far. At the back of the bus Philip took out his cassette recorder and began playing The Sex Pistols at full volume, complete with bad language. Irene Maxwell took this as a personal challenge to her authority on all things musical and immediately trebled the volume of her cassette recorder in an attempt to drown out Sid Vicious with David Soul. Thankfully both sets of batteries ran done around Gretna Green, where you ran away to get married if your girlfriend was pregnant or Catholic.

The journey was made more interesting by several stops at motorway service stations on the way through England which revealed unexpected tensions between the young people of the Upper Shankill and our mainland British compatriots. This came as a shock to me because staying British was the most important thing in the world for us. I had always assumed that us being British would be the most important thing in the world for our fellow countrymen and women in England too. The first challenge to our concept of the United Kingdom of Great Britain and Northern Ireland was when the woman on the till in the first motorway café wouldn't accept a Northern Ireland pound note for my father's sausages and bacon.

'Sorry, we don't take Irish notes,' she announced.

'Look, love,' he said pointing to the writing on the pound note, 'it says "sterling". It's a NORTHERN Ireland note.'

'That's right. We don't take Irish currency here,' she replied.

'Listen, love. It's a sterling note from a British bank in Northern Ireland!'

'You'll have to change it into British pounds at the bank.'

My father continued to argue for several minutes. When he began to raise his voice in frustration at having his British currency denied on English soil, my mother intervened quickly by providing a Bank of England note and pointing out that his sausages and bacon were getting cold. As we ate our meals together the news of this outrage spread from table to table.

'I told ye, Eric, love,' said my mother, 'they don't want us over here. Sure we're nathin' but trouble.'

When we finally arrived in London we had to remove our luggage from the coach and carry it down extremely long escalators. Then we boarded an exciting underground train in a huge tube to take us to Chigwell where the youth hostel was awaiting our arrival. When we arrived at Chigwell station we shared out all our English pound notes so that everyone would have enough money for chips. However, as we ordered our food in the local café, I noticed all the English people looking up when they heard our accents. When we claimed a table and piled our luggage up behind it the other customers kept looking over at our bags with great interest. I couldn't understand why they found our luggage so fascinating. I was beginning to wonder if maybe they didn't sell the latest suitcases in England when my big brother whispered in my ear.

'Themuns all think we're friggin' bombers!'

I was affronted! How could the English nation get me so wrong? I was the only teenage pacifist in West Belfast. How dare they think I was a terrorist just because of my accent! My bag contained pyjamas and socks and Denim aftershave. These English people had nothing to fear from the contents of my luggage. My mustard transistor radio, *Doctor Who Annual 1977* and Good News Bible were a threat to no one! How could they mistake my innocent and godly goods for Semtex? Everyone was shocked because we had expected the English to welcome us with open arms for standing up to the IRA. We had assumed English people were on our side like the soldiers on our streets but they wouldn't take our money and when they heard our accents they assumed we wanted to blow them up! To make matters worse, it was July but not one of the English houses we passed by on the coach journey had put a Union Jack out for the Twelfth! I was having my eyes opened, so I was. For the rest of the week every time I was in a shop, to avoid further suspicion, I attempted to speak with a London accent, like the cops in *The Sweeney*.

I got a very strange look in a bakery when I asked, "Ave you any bleedin' tatey farls, mate?"

Of course Philip Ferris had no problem because punks had to talk with English accents anyway.

Thankfully these shocking revelations about the attitude of our fellow British citizens towards Northern Ireland did not detract from the wonders we were to behold in the days ahead. We travelled around London on the amazing underground railway called the Tube. In Belfast a 'tube' was a gobshite. Here the Tube was like the Belfast to Bangor train but faster, with more passengers and under the ground. Above the sliding doors on the underground trains was a big long map with names of all the famous places from the Monopoly board. We took the Tube to see the sights of London every day and soon became experts in travelling around the metropolis. My mother and Auntie Emma were worried we might get lost but it never happened. Apart from when Sammy Reeves fell asleep and missed his stop the day after sneaking a bottle of gin into the boys' dormitory. Sammy ended up in Wimbledon but he didn't see any famous tennis players or Wombles collecting litter in the train station.

London was nothing like Belfast because it had black people

and sex shops instead of bombs and soldiers. It was a huge city with skyscrapers and famous buildings. We visited the Tower of London, which was as big as Long Kesh, and we saw the Crown Jewels through very thick glass. I stared at these royal treasures imagining I was a diamond thief, staking out the joint for the biggest heist in history. But then my mammy grabbed my arm and told me to hurry up because I had promised to buy my granny a souvenir tea towel. We took pictures of the changing of the guard at Buckingham Palace and Titch McCracken tried unsuccessfully to make a soldier with a big black furry hat laugh. However I was disappointed to learn that the Queen wasn't in because she was away on her summer holidays to Balmoral in Scotland. Balmoral must have been like Millisle for the royal family. Then we went to watch a situation comedy called *Rings on their Fingers* at the BBC Television Centre, beside the *Blue Peter* garden. I laughed extra loud but I couldn't hear myself over the rest of the audience when it came out on BBC1 the following year. We saw Big Ben and the Houses of Parliament where posh people with white hair and very pink faces shouted 'Hear! Hear!' My father had written to an English MP and this gentleman showed us around the ancient stone buildings in a pinstripe suit. My father gave me a good clip round the ear for picking my nose while the posh MP was telling us how Guy Fawkes had invented fireworks and how Westminster was the big mammy of all the parliaments in the whole world.

As we walked through Soho one evening I called into one of the newsagents to see if they had the *Look-in Summer Special*. I was shocked to find only shelves full of magazines with pictures of nudie ladies. These magazines looked like the bra section in the *Great Universal Club Book* but without the bras. I exited immediately, as it was probably a sin, but not soon enough to avoid being noticed by my big brother. He felt compelled to point in my direction and shout 'Pervert!' in front of the whole of the West End of London. As we continued our walk through Soho we saw all sorts of things you would never see in Belfast. We saw real live homosexuals holding hands and lots of cinemas showing films with nothing but diddies. A black man with dreadlocks asked me if I wanted any hash but I politely declined because I wasn't sure what it was.

Surprisingly, the greatest attraction in London was not to be found on the tourist trail, but closer to our temporary home in the youth hostel. We were staying in Chigwell, on the outskirts of London, a nice place with swanky houses, cricket fields and pubs with flower boxes at the windows instead of security grilles. The youth hostel was located in its own grounds near Epping Forest. I knew it was nowhere near Nottingham, but it was the nearest I had ever been to an English forest so I imagined I was Robin Hood in Sherwood, robbing from all the Timothy Longsleys and giving the money to all the Sammy Reeveses. The youth hostel had large dormitories located in rows of two-storey chalets the same as Butlin's in Mosney, but with no chalet maids or red coats. At the centre of the grounds was a football pitch with goal posts where my big brother dazzled the girls every day playing 'keepy-uppy' as if he was Geordie Best. I wasn't jealous at all, even though everyone said how brilliant he was and I couldn't kick back doors. There was a toilet and shower block with a sign saying 'Ablutions' above the door. I didn't know what ablutions were so the first day I couldn't find the toilet and had to pee up a tree at the back of the dormitories. However once my mother explained the meaning of the word I did my ablutions there for the rest of the week. The site also included a large indoor hall containing a table-tennis table with a broken net and squashed ping-pong balls, a snooker table that the big boys would never let you have a go on and a wonderful old-fashioned jukebox with the latest tunes from the Top 40. This trusty music machine was in receipt of dozens of ten pence coins every hour requesting Bee Gees, Grease and ABBA. Philip Ferris interrupted the flow of pop and disco music by pressing buttons for the odd Boomtown Rats single, which I had to admit I quite enjoyed even though they were punks from down south and my father said their scruffy lead singer was a slabber who would be forgotten in a year or two.

On the first day in Chigwell we made an amazing discovery at the back of the youth hostel. Titch and Sammy were looking for a few uncrushed ping-pongs so they could have a go at table tennis when they discovered the storeroom. The door was unlocked so Titch didn't have to break in and when we entered the store I caught a glimpse of something that was so exciting I nearly had to run to the ablutions building. It was a brand new double-deck disco unit with two big speakers and built-in coloured spotlights. This was an English Westy Disco just waiting for us! My father was immediately consulted for his professional DJ assessment of the potential for a disco on Saturday night just like at home and he affirmed with all the authority of a great and wise Emperor Rosko that this could be an excellent disco. It was Heather Mateer who noticed one flaw in the plan: 'Like, sure, we've no records with us to play on the bloody thing, so we haven't!'

This was an important observation and we returned to the storeroom in search of 45s. We eventually discovered a small box of records at the back of the store underneath the badminton racquets but this musical stash consisted of Al Martino's 'Spanish Eyes', 'I Am a Cider Drinker' by The Wurzels and three LPs by James Last and his Orchestra that only grannies liked.

'Here, I've an idea!' said Uncle Henry.

He was very good at problem-solving because he was also a leader in the Scouts.

'Why don't youse all buy singles and LPs with your spending money and bring your favourite song along on Saturday night?'

'Aye!' said Irene Maxwell, 'I'm buying the Bee Gees anyway.'

'Aye!' said Titch McCracken, 'I'm gettin' *Grease* for me ma!'

'Anarkeee in the You Kay!' interrupted Philip Ferris, with a clenched fist and an inflamed nostril.

Uncle Henry looked at Philip with bafflement on his face. Either he wasn't familiar with the concept of anarchy or he was confused by Philip's new English accent. The scene was set and so on our final night in London we were going to have a Chigwell Westy Disco. More importantly the disco would be open to everyone staying at the youth hostel. This prospect became very interesting when the Italians arrived on Wednesday night. The Italian teenagers came from Milan at the top of the boot in my geography book but they didn't speak Latin anymore. I was elated to discover that every single Italian girl was stunning. It was incredible to see with my own eyes that there were no millies in Milan. The Belfast kids soon got to know our new European neighbours as we congregated around the old jukebox every day. Sammy fancied Fontana with the bum and the big earrings and Philip had his eye on Isabella with the spiky hair and the black lipstick. Titch McCracken refused to succumb to the charms of the Italian female because he said they were all Catholics and the Pope was their king so they wanted a united Ireland. My big brother was not interested in the Italian girls either because he had started to go out with Lindsay, a girl in our group who was just as attractive as the Italians but who was also good at gymnastics. My Italian girl was Maria, so she had the same name as the beauty in *West Side Story*. Maria was smaller than me and very beautiful with long straight hair, big brown eyes and an irresistible smile with teeth as white as a Bee Gee. I spotted her in the crowd the very first night the Italians arrived in their coach with the steering wheel on the wrong side and a funny number plate. As Uncle Henry and my father were breaking up a scuffle between Titch and two of the Italian boys who wanted a go on the table-tennis table, I noticed the lovely Maria from a distance. She was standing watching these strange fighting foreigners from Ireland speaking English in an unusual accent with several 'fucks' in every sentence. It was love at first sight. I was still committed to Judy Carlton and I would never have dreamt of two-timing Judy. Well to be honest, I did have regular dreams of two-timing her with Wonder Woman, but that wasn't real life. Strictly speaking, Judy had yet to agree to a full romantic relationship and, to be completely honest, she hadn't seemed all that keen on me at the school disco in the dinner hall. So technically I was young, free and single and so if Maria desired me, I was hers. We had enjoyed several chats about pop music at the jukebox. Maria and I shared a love of ABBA and *Grease* and I pretended I had heard of some singer she adored called Umberto or something. Whenever I entered the hall or passed her chalet or bumped into her after my ablutions, Maria's perfect smile appeared. I'm sure she noticed that she made me smile too even though my teeth were more grey than Bee Gee-white, after they'd been stained by antibiotics when I'd nearly died of pneumonia in 1963.

All the boys saw the Chigwell Westy Disco on Saturday night as the perfect opportunity for a brief but passionate Italian romance or at least a chance to try an Italian snog. Kissing an Italian girl from Milan in a disco in London sounded so much more sexy than kissing a wee girl from Millisle in an entry up the Shankill. We spent our last day with penguins at London Zoo followed by a marathon shopping expedition in Oxford Street and Regent Street. I bought a Shaker Maker in Hamley's, the biggest toyshop in the world, which was so different from Leisureworld, the biggest toyshop in Belfast, not least because they did not insist on body searches for incendiary devices at the front door. I bought a bar of expensive Mandate soap in one of the posh chemist shops in Oxford Street and when we got back to the youth hostel I used my manly soap in my ablutions in preparation for the disco.

As the Chigwell Westy got under way, Northern Ireland lined up one side of the hall while Italy lined the other. It was an international interaction like the World Cup without football and *It's a Knockout* without giant gorilla suits. As soon as my DJ da put on 'Night Fever' all international differences faded away to the throb of a disco beat. The evening was almost ruined when I had to hide in the storeroom behind the folded up table-tennis table because Irene Maxwell was seeking me out for a slow dance as Olivia Newton-John sang 'Hopelessly Devoted To You' from *Grease*. In the end she gave up pursuing me and bribed Titch with a Spangle for a slow dance instead. However, Irene finally moved on to Fabio, a skinny Italian who was only thirteen and wore sunglasses indoors even though he clearly wasn't in the UDA. I assumed Fabio's darkened vision had contributed to his decision to accept a dance with Irene or maybe they didn't have Spangles in Italy and the temptation was overwhelming.

'Bella, bella,' said Fabio as he danced with Irene.

As Irene rubbed up close to Fabio she kept looking over at me with a 'see what you're missin', wee lad' look on her face. I pretended I didn't notice just in case Fabio's da was in the mafia. Another notable moment was Fontana asking Sammy Reeves to dance. She snogged him with her tongue throughout 'How Deep is Your Love'. No Belfast girl had ever shown any sexual interest in Sammy Reeves before this because of his personal hygiene issues. My big brother explained that Fontana must have eaten so much garlic in her Italian food that she didn't notice the whiff. As for me, I grasped my opportunity with Maria when Dad put on 'Take a Chance on Me'. The day before I had given Maria 10p to play this song on the jukebox because she said it was her favourite ABBA single. As soon as Benny and Bjorn started up their 'take a chance, take a chance, take-a-take-a-chance-chance' at the start of the record I made my way across the dance floor towards the beauty of Milan. It was as if the super Swedes were speaking directly to me.

'Do you wanna take a chance on me?' I asked Maria, pointing to the dance floor.

'It's-a my favourite,' she replied with that hypnotising smile.

'You're my favourite, so you are.'

'Oh Antonio!' she laughed and stood up, took my hand and we walked together onto the dance floor. My mother and Auntie Emma smiled and whispered behind the tuck shop and my big brother looked on in disbelief at the idea that any girl so beautiful would be interested in me. Titch McCracken had warned everyone not to snog any Italian Catholics or we would be supporting the IRA but his remonstrations had fallen on deaf ears and so he scowled and stomped out of the hall.

When the slow dances came on I held my Italian beauty very close to my body. She rested her cheek so close to my cheek that I could smell the Wrigley's on her breath and Harmony hairspray in her hair. When the final song was announced we kissed and it was a proper kiss like Big Ruby had taught me in the sand dunes in Millisle. I put my fingers through my Maria's hair because that meant I loved her and she smiled and kissed me some more. When Maria and I parted that night we swapped addresses and promised to write, but deep down I knew I would never see her again. I could never afford to go to Italy and no one would want to come to Belfast. I did have some pangs of guilt about betraying Judy back in Belfast. I remembered that 'Torn Between Two Lovers' song on *Top of the Pops*.

When I arrived back in the boys' dormitory the situation was deteriorating rapidly due to the two bottles of vodka that Sammy had smuggled into the youth hostel in his Hamley's bag. I refused the offers of drink because I was still intoxicated by Maria and I was too good livin' to get drunk. When half the boys' dormitory decided to do a streak around the football pitch I also declined to participate because it was probably a sin and more importantly I was afraid Maria might peek out her window and maybe be disappointed with my jimmy joe.

I wrote to Maria for years afterwards and she wrote back, and I worried about her every time there was an earthquake in Italy. I was afraid she might get buried alive under the ash like in Pompeii. I was all grown up and nearly shaving now. I had kissed a real live beautiful Italian girl and she had kissed me back. I was becoming a man, so I was.

13

MISSIONARY MAN

The summer of *Grease* was slipping away as rapidly as the stock of Veda loaves in the Ormo Mini Shop on a bank holiday weekend. With only two more weeks to go before a return to the oppression of homework, uniforms and PE teachers, my heart was now strangely warming to spiritual matters. So far the summer of 1978 had been dominated by a worldly preoccupation with the delights of London and *Grease* and beautiful Italian girls. Now I believed the time had come to attend to my vast religious responsibilities.

Everyone said I was a wee good livin' fella. Mrs Piper announced it with glee because she spoke on behalf of God; Timothy Longsley sneered about it because he was too clever for God. I got saved at a wee meetin' at the caravan in Millisle in 1972. When it rained the children's mission took place in an old cottage where they stored the bins for the caravan site. All the kids on holiday from the Shankill sat on top of the bins and got evangelised by aunties and uncles from Newry Baptist Church, who I thought were unusually young and happy to be actual Christians. We sang choruses about getting our sins washed away and we learned Bible verses off by heart. We competed in quizzes where the victors won pencils with John 3:16 on the side. And so it came to pass that I got born again on a bin in Millisle. Unlike many of my fellow converts I was so certain of my spiritual transformation that I had no desire to get born again, again and again. Some of my mates put their hand up to get saved at wee meetins every week because they had smoked or lied or said 'fuck' since the last time. But my conversion had been much more assured because as far as I was concerned, once I had asked Jesus into my heart, He would stay there forever. My boss and occasional religious advisor, Leslie, called this 'blessed assurance of salvation from the flames of eternal damnation'. My atheist da referred to it as my 'fire insurance policy'. Every time I talked about being saved my father used the term 'sanctimonious' but I forgave him for this persecution for the sake of the gospel. My granny was so proud she told everyone I was going to become a Presbyterian minister even though I had never expressed such grand ambition. To become a reverend was almost as venerable as becoming a doctor at the Royal Victoria Hospital.

One of the sacred responsibilities of being saved was to get other people saved too. My first experience of sharing the Good News was as a Sunday School teacher for Ballygomartin Presbyterian Church. I was very young for such great responsibility but the church couldn't recruit enough adult Sunday School teachers to go round. So when Leslie spearheaded the campaign to open a brand new Sunday School in Whiterock Orange Hall especially for the lost children of the estate, I was one of several teenage Sunday School teachers recruited for service in this missionary outpost. I was pleased to be entrusted with the salvation of the children of the estate at such a young age and I prepared every Bible lesson diligently. The zealous teenage teachers met Rev. Lowe outside the church every Sunday afternoon and then he drove us round to the Orange hall in his hatchback. Once we got through the security gate and the bombproof front door we taught wee choruses and catechism questions to the children who sat around Formica tables, still sticky with lager from the dinner dance the night before. My mother said Leslie was 'an awful good big crater' for persuading the Orange Order to allow the church to open a new Sunday School in their premises. My father said they were only doing it to get put on the church insurance policy in case the provos burnt down the Orange hall. I was shocked that my father misconstrued every act of faith as relating to an insurance policy of one sort or another. Why could he not distinguish between Presbyterianism and the Prudential?

Rev. Lowe was ever-patient when I arrived late most Sunday afternoons because I had been absorbed in some black-and-white St Trinian's movie on BBC2. However, he showed little patience when the British Army stopped us en route to the Orange hall. One Sunday a young soldier from a regiment that was new to our neighbourhood had the audacity to ask our religious leader for his driving licence as proof of identity. This was sacrilege! I knew no one in the world less terrorist-minded than Rev. Lowe and he was wearing his dog collar and everything. Everyone on the Road knew and respected Rev. Lowe and very few people, apart from my father and granny, dared to argue with him. (My father argued about the existence of God and my granny argued about the persistence of Paisley.)

'Driving licence, please?' demanded the soldier, who looked far too small for his army uniform.

The request evoked an initial shocked silence in the car.

'Listen, boy!' began Rev. Lowe.

You knew you were in trouble when Rev. Lowe called you 'boy'. He even called the paramilitaries 'boy' when he ordered them off the streets in a riot – even Big Duff. I wished I'd seen that.

'You are a guest in my parish, boy, and we have children to teach!' he proclaimed, with all the boldness of St Paul.

'But how do I know it's a real collar, mate?' asked the soldier, inadvisably.

Now I was embarrassed because not only was this naive, gun-carrying teenager accusing Rev. Lowe of impersonating a vicar, but now he was referring to our minister as 'mate', like a Cockney in a Carry On movie. I knew the army was here to stop the IRA from killing us and all and I was very grateful, but they didn't seem to trust anybody, even the goodies. It was as if the soldiers thought we all wanted to kill them.

'You listen to me, boy!' boomed Rev. Lowe. 'Do you want me to take this up with a higher authority?'

I wasn't sure whether he was referring to God or a big army general but this threat seemed to do the job. The young soldier cowered behind his weapon, which looked too heavy for him anyway, and we were ushered through the checkpoint. As we drove off I noticed how sad and confused the soldier looked, even with his gun.

I was certain that colouring in Jesus feeding the five thousand, five thousand times, was pretty tiresome for most children so I did my best to make Sunday School less boring. I made up exciting quizzes and games to make it more engaging – my class was like *Crackerjack* with Jesus. The catechism was full of old words that nobody really understood and so it was very hard for the wee kids to learn it off by heart. They had to have another go at the same answers for weeks on end until I finally gave in and pretended they knew it and put a tick beside the unlearned catechism question. I soon discovered that telling the children they needed to get saved every single week was likely to have the opposite effect. I had been saved for years now but I got told I needed to be born again at every single wee meetin' since. I realised reiteration might be a problem during quizzes with my eager Sunday School class. They were only six years old but they had already learned that the answer to every question was probably 'Jesus'. When I asked 'Who fed the five thousand?', my class would answer in unison, confidently and correctly, 'Jesus!' But when the question was slightly more difficult, I began to notice the problem.

'Who was the first man?' I asked.

'Jesus!' was the reply.

'Who had a coat of many colours?' I quizzed.

'Jesus!'

At first I thought these answers were just innocent mistakes but then I became concerned that the source of such great theological error might be my poor teaching. After all I was only fourteen and nearly shaving and sometimes I didn't prepare very well if I was too busy watching *Wonder Woman* or building a boney. I soon noticed that the problem was getting worse.

'Who cut Samson's hair to take away his strength?'

'Jesus!'

'Who built an ark for all the animals?'

'Jesus!'

I began to fret that my Sunday School pupils weren't even listening and so one Sunday I decided to ask a trick question, just to check. I ensured we were well out of earshot of Rev. Lowe and I lowered my head so close to the table that I could almost taste the Harp lager residue from the night before.

'Who is Luke Skywalker's father?' I asked in a whisper.

'Jesus!' came the reply.

'Oh Jesus!' I prayed.

I was a failure in the service of God. My young disciples didn't know the difference between the son of God and Darth Vader.

My guitar-playing skills proved most useful because Sunday School required good musical accompaniment for singing all the wee choruses and there was no working piano in the Orange hall because Orangemen generally preferred flutes. To my relief most of the Sunday School classics such as 'Running Over', 'Jesus Loves the Little Children' and 'Away Far Beyond Jordan' required only the same three chords as my primary musical masterpiece, 'Hang Down Your Head, Tom Dooley'. However, leading the praises of fifty children in the Upper Shankill was not without its disciplinary challenges. In 'Climb, Climb Up Sunshine Mountain' there was a tradition of allowing the children to sing 'All together now!' at the end of the song before repeating the whole chorus for a second time. This was regarded as a slightly worldly practice, more akin to a singsong at the pub, but Rev. Lowe tolerated it because it made the children very happy. However, one Sunday afternoon, the McLarnon twins with the shaved heads and snatters sang 'All together now!' after the second rendition of the chorus. Everyone, including the Rev. Lowe and myself laughed at this impish rebellion and we sang the chorus for a third time. But at the end the twins and several others added another 'All together now!' and proceeded to sing the whole song through once again.

'Climb, climb up sunshine mountain,

Faces all aglow ...'

I had no idea what the words actually meant but when the twins initiated a fifth repetition of the chorus my own face began to glow with some frustration.

'Boy! That's enough now!' said Rev. Lowe.

I stopped playing my guitar but it was too late. The whole of the Sunday School was united in harmonious rebellion from the smallest toddler with a dummy to the oldest teenager blowing gum. Maybe this was their revenge for all the repetition we had been subjecting them to for months. They were going wild! It reminded me of the wee lads on the island in *Lord of the Flies* in English class and I didn't want to end up like Piggy! The children refused to stop singing 'Climb, Climb Up Sunshine Mountain' as stubbornly as the wee ginger Walton refused to stop wearing dungarees. I knew this was a nice song about going up to heaven or something but after the sixteenth rendition, it was more annoying than the constant replay of 'Father Abraham and the Smurfs' on wee Sandra Hull's cassette recorder. Rev. Lowe was starting to climb, climb up the Orange hall walls and he was going very red in the face.

'You, boy!' he said, pointing to one of the McLarnon twins. 'Enough!'

I had never seen my Sunday School children looking so happy and free. They ignored us with great delight and sang 'All together now!' again. Even the British Army had shrunk under Rev. Lowe's authority but these six-year-olds were now unmistakably in charge. The more times my spiritual charges sang the song the more angry I became, and I had to try to control myself. I was here to tell the children that God loved them and to love their neighbour and even their enemies, even Catholics, but after the eighteenth chorus there were only four words on my mind.

'Shut yer bloody bakes!'

The devil on my shoulder was trying to make me curse at wee children that I wanted to get saved. Fortunately the angel on my other shoulder calmed me down and reminded me that I was the only pacifist teenager in West Belfast. But inevitably, after more than twenty repetitions, I snapped. I broke my pacifist principles and I shamed my Sunday School teacher vocation. I picked up a McLarnon twin by his skinny arm and threw him out the front door of the Orange hall. The hall erupted in cheers and a further 'All together now!' led by the remaining twin. Now Rev. Lowe was pointing at the biggest culprits and I became the bouncer, picking them up and removing them by force. It was like the RUC removing protesters from the Road during the Ulster Workers' Strike. After a short chase around the hall I eventually caught the surviving McLarnon twin behind the beer crates and I ejected him from this place of theological learning in the same rough fashion as I had dispatched his brother. The only difference was that this twin bit me on the arm and – disgracefully for a Sunday School teacher – I impulsively slapped him around the head and shouted, 'Ya cheeky wee shite!'

How had my desire to teach love and forgiveness been reduced to this?

Weeks of steady teaching and singing and catechism repetition were reduced to violence and shouting and swearing in a matter of minutes and all to the tune of 'Climb, Climb Up Sunshine Mountain'! I was ashamed, but thankfully Rev. Lowe had not observed my shocking reaction to the twin bite amid the tumult and chaos now surrounding him. I could tell from the laughter that the McLarnon twins didn't seem to mind and I concluded that they had probably been called much worse.

'Take them home, boy!' commanded Rev. Lowe, across a sea of giggling ponytails and scrapping Bible scholars.

Outside the security gate I grabbed both McLarnon twins firmly by their arms and marched them to the front door of their house at the top of the estate. The boys didn't object or resist because they were still laughing. Their hysterical laughter produced snatters that they rubbed on my good Sunday jacket, insulting the fact that it had cost my mother twenty weeks at 99p.

'Why's Sunday School nat like this every week?' asked one twin, as their front door eventually opened.

Mrs McLarnon was standing in her dressing gown looking somewhat flushed, as if she had just finished running a big long race like Mary Peters.

'Oh sorry, love, I was just having a wee lie-down,' she said in a strangely flustered manner.

'They always have a wee lie-down while we're at Sunday School, so they do,' added one of the twins, pointing at his father coming down the stairs in his Y-fronts.

Within seconds the twins were taken inside for retribution. I was offended by the realisation that, rather then sending their children to Sunday School to benefit from my spiritual instruction, parents were actually using my childcare services so they could have 'a wee rest' every Sunday afternoon.

The following Saturday, between armfuls of loaves, I reported the whole sorry story to Leslie. He couldn't help chuckling but I knew he took these matters very seriously. Leslie shared my concerns for the spiritual welfare of the lost children of the Upper Shankill. As we delivered the bread together that Saturday morning I imagined we were providing our customers with Holy Communion like missionaries in a jungle up the Amazon. The communion bread was a plain Ormo loaf and the sacred wine was Fanta, unlike in the Presbyterian Church where the bread was shortbread tray bakes and the wine was Ribena (because alcohol was a sin). Leslie and I prayed fervently as we delivered the bread that the whole Road would be saved – and that was quare a lot of saving, but we believed God could do it.

All of this experience of providing for the spiritual needs of the Upper Shankill was good preparation for going to Dublin as a summer missionary. Leslie seemed only too happy to grant me further unpaid leave for this religious adventure. Earlier in the year I had applied to be a teenage evangelist to save the children of the south of Ireland. Everyone was Catholic down south and apparently the Pope was coming to visit them all soon, so I was led to believe there was an awful lot of saving to be done down there before he arrived. I had been to a training weekend in Kilkeel with the other summer missionaries, mostly teenagers from Ballymena who were much more good livin' than me. They didn't go to sinful discos like me because dancing made you have sex and they didn't watch television on Sundays like me because God didn't allow fun, especially on the Sabbath. Several of my holiest peers were Baptists who talked inexplicably about the dangers of 'marrying outside of the denomination'. I was taken aback when the girls had to wear hats and weren't allowed to wear jeans when they were talking about God. Apparently there was some bit in the Old Testament that forbade girls from doing most things, but when I read these sections of the Bible I noticed it commanded lots of weird things about wearing tassels and killing people for no good reason, so I wasn't convinced. I was certain God loved girls just the same as boys no matter what all the important men said. Of course I dared not argue with the leaders in case my worldliness should be exposed and I would not be allowed to become a summer missionary like all the others. In spite of the abundance of 'Thou shalt nots', I made new friends and enjoyed learning how to teach Bible stories to children.

When I finally arrived in Dublin in August I met Uncle Samuel who was the main man in charge of getting all the children in Dublin saved. He had a big beard and he spoke with all the spiritual authority of Charlton Heston in the Bible. Nearly everyone in Dublin was a Catholic so Uncle Samuel taught us all the main Roman Catholic doctrines like Mass and Mary and then showed us where the Bible said they were all wrong. Every day we went out into the wild estates of Dublin with a Good News caravan and throngs of children with Irish accents crammed into our sanctuary. The young Dubliners listened to our Bible stories and joined in singing happy songs about getting born again. None of the children seemed to know any of the Catholic doctrines so we didn't have to go to the trouble of pointing out they were all wrong, although in one estate a mother removed her children in the middle of the story of blind Bartimaeus getting healed because her priest had told her we were heretics. This worried me because heretics always got burnt alive in my history books. In another estate a very pretty teenager asked me to go behind the flats with her but I declined and explained that we could talk about God just as easily in front of the flats.

One day in a huge estate with horses and bricked up flats like Belfast we were happily telling the children an exciting story about a missionary saving the natives in Africa when suddenly the Good News caravan came under attack. Uncle Samuel had only just been explaining that missionaries got beaten and eaten because they were so saved. He said that only the best Christians got persecuted because when you loved God with all your heart you didn't care about annoying people. As if to demonstrate this Biblical truth projectiles began landing on the roof of the caravan. Wee hard men from Dublin were throwing stones at us. At first we didn't know what to do. My training as a summer missionary had been very thorough but it had not prepared me for this because throwing stones wasn't a Catholic doctrine, as far as I was aware. Fortunately, coming from Belfast, I had a lot of experience of wee hoods and of avoiding stone throwing, so I put my experience to good use and told the children not to worry. I asked them to see if they could sing 'Jesus Loves Me' so loud that they couldn't hear the stones hitting the caravan. As we sang at the top of our voices, Uncle Samuel ran outside to confront the wee hoods.

'Yer talkin' a load a shite Mister!' I could hear the wee hoods shouting over 'Yes, Jesus loves me'.

I ran to the door of the caravan and watched Uncle Samuel sprint towards our persecutors shaking his fist and waving his King James. With his big beard he looked like Charlton Heston chasing the Egyptians into the Red Sea. The wee hoods turned and began to run away but I genuinely didn't want them to run into the Liffey and get drowned like godless Egyptians. It wasn't clear whether it was the fist or the Bible that scared them off but they weren't so hard now. To my amazement, even after they had scarpered, Uncle Samuel kept on running after them, the whole way up the road. In the distance I could see him waving his big black King James Bible and shouting after them, 'You can't run away from God!' This was extraordinary! We had just been persecuted like Daniel in the Bible, although not with lions. We had been stoned like St Stephen except they hadn't killed us this time. I accepted piously that this was all part of the life of sacrifice and persecution that came with being a real missionary man.

When the time came to return to Belfast and to go back to school, I felt more grown up than ever. As my thoughts turned once again from spiritual matters to more corporeal concerns, I hoped and even prayed that when I went back to school in September, Judy Carlton would notice and embrace my newfound confidence and manliness. How could she possibly resist me now? I had spent a week abroad in a foreign country as a missionary and I had been persecuted for my faith. I wasn't just some wee good livin' fella who played choruses on a guitar in an Orange hall up the Shankill. I had been like an assistant to Charlton Heston himself. I was a strong and courageous man of God now, so I was.

14

NEVER MIND THE BALLICKS

'Macaulay! Bring that piece of paper to the front of this classroom now!'

Mr Jackson was very angry, so he was. He scanned my handwritten letter with a dark scowl on his face. A vein on the side of his head began to throb and he started to press his ballpoint pen into the desk with sufficient pressure to create a crevice in the wood. I could feel my heart thumping beneath my blazer.

'Is this some new quadratic equation, sonny?'

'No, Sir,' I growled in my newly broken voice, that made me sound more surly than I intended.

'Read it out!'

'But …'

'No buts, sonny, read it out!' he repeated, accentuating every syllable with the rap of his knuckles on my skull.

It was dead sore, so it was, and I wanted to cry and call him a cruel oul' bastard but I knew I had to try to be a man in front of a class with both Judy Carlton and Timothy Longsley present. So I began to read.

'Dear Jim,

Please will you fix it for me to be lassoed by Wonder Woman? If she is too busy, please could you fix it for me to have a ride in the TARDIS with Doctor Who to the year 2000?

Yours sincerely
Tony Macaulay
Aged 15'

The class fell silent apart from a stifled mucky chuckle from behind Frankie Jones's slide ruler.

'Who is Jim?' demanded Mr Jackson.

'He's yer man from *Top of the Pops* with the cigar and the big chair that makes your dreams come true on BBC1, so he is,' I ventured to explain.

'And who is this woman?' he interrogated, tapping his ballpoint pen so aggressively on my letter that he rendered the words 'Wonder Woman' illegible.

'She's a superhero that twirls round in a telephone box and saves you from the baddies in her hot pants, Sir,' I replied. Well he did ask!

The ensuing eruption of laughter among my classmates made Mr Jackson even angrier. No one ever laughed or smiled in Mr Jackson's class. He made it as clear as a decimal fraction that mathematics was no laughing matter. Although the class was mainly laughing at me there was a high factor of probability that Mr Jackson assumed they were laughing at his obvious ignorance of popular culture. I feared the ugly pulsing vein on his red temple was going to burst.

'De – ten – tion!' he shouted, with three syllabically synchronised full-fisted blows to my head.

The summer of 1978 seemed so far away now. All too soon I was back to school homework and bread delivery and darkness. At least 'Summer Nights' was still number one and in the video on *Top of the Pops* Olivia Newton-John was back to being a virgin in a dress again. But everything else was changing, including me. My voice had finally completed the process of breaking. For a long time now it had been jumping between octaves. For years, when I prayed out loud for no more killing in Northern Ireland I sounded like a man, but when I shouted at my big brother for switching over to the football during *Star Trek* I sounded like a wee girl. Now at last my vocal cords had settled down and on the first day back at school when I spoke to Joanne Gault she rewarded me with a look of surprise on her pretty face and said, 'Oh, lovely new, deep voice, Tony!' I was so delighted I almost returned the compliment because I had noticed her lovely new breasts, but with my newfound maturity I realised that this would be inappropriate. Joanne's breast magnets were particularly powerful but I was learning self-control. It was such a relief to be developing properly at long last. Now my voice had broken it was only a matter of time before I would have to start shaving. I monitored my chin for emergent bristles on a daily basis in the bathroom mirror but I could detect no new growth reflected in the spot-splattered glass. However it was the darkening of the down above my upper lip that demonstrated that manhood was just around the corner. I invested some of my breadboy tips in a plastic disposable Wilkinson's Sword razor and waited patiently for the moustache hairs to harden. I already had sufficient supplies of Denim aftershave and I longed for the day when I could apply its stinging effects to a freshly shaved upper lip. I wondered if Judy would notice my new deep voice and so once again I began to practise saying 'present Miss' in as low a voice as possible in readiness for roll call in chemistry. I tried to position myself to stand right behind Judy in school assembly so she could hear me singing 'Glorious Things of Thee Are Spoken' an octave lower than Thomas O'Hara. Heather Mateer confirmed my new appeal to the opposite sex when I offered her a share of my Revels during a break from 'Night Fever' at the tuck shop at the Westy Disco.

'Like, you'll be lovely when you grow up, so you will,' she said, looking at me as if I was not entirely without promise. This was the nicest thing a girl had ever said to me.

But it was the announcement by Miss Adams one Saturday morning on my bread round that made it official.

'You're turning into quite a young man,' she confirmed across the fairy cakes.

Miss Adams said all her 'ings' like Angela Rippon on the news on BBC1, so when she spoke it had authority. I slipped her an extra fancy pastry when Leslie wasn't looking and she gave me a wee wink.

I was growing in confidence as well as physical and emotional maturity. There were many opportunities coming up when I could show off my new voice and my emergent moustache. The English department was holding auditions for the annual school play and the RE department was participating in a Belfast schools' charity fair for African babies that included a Mr Belfast Schools. I was determined to take advantage of each and every opportunity to prove myself to Judy, apart from when the PE Department was running trials for the medallion rugby team, because I was crap.

Music was changing too. Suddenly punk wasn't just for serious punk rockers with safety pins like Philip Ferris any more. Proper punks went to punk rock concerts and shouted 'fuck' in English accents and boked up and spat at everyone and all. Real punks went to nightclubs with drink and record shops with limited editions in the city centre. It didn't matter whether you were a Protestant punk or a Catholic punk, they were all just punks together. I thought this was very good even though punks weren't allowed to be good. I noticed that some of the adults who disapproved of punks the most were the same people that didn't like Protestants and Catholics mixing together either. Cross-community anarchy must have been very scary for them. Now other teenagers like me, who were either too young or whose mammies wouldn't let us turn full punk, were starting to love punk bands as much as we adored the Bee Gees. In fact I had to admit that I was starting to enjoy the Boomtown Rats more than the Bee Gees. Uncle Samuel in Dublin would have been horrified at my corruption by evil punk rock. I never admitted to him that I owned ABBA's *Greatest Hits* never mind *Rat Trap* by the Boomtown Rats!

When we returned to school that September the change in musical preferences was evident in the names scrawled on most of the school bags. Status Quo and Deep Purple and even Smokie had disappeared to be replaced in thick black marker by the Sex Pistols, the Ramones and the Buzzcocks. My favourite punks were the Undertones because they sang with Northern Ireland accents about being a teenager and wanting to a hold a wee girl like Judy Carlton tight right through the night. The Undertones had a lead singer called Feargal and they got to sing on *Top of the Pops* even though they were from Derry (which was Catholic for Londonderry). I tried to play my acoustic Spanish guitar like an Undertone but the strings kept snapping. I finally persuaded my father to buy 'Teenage Kicks' for the Westy Disco and he relented because he said 'that there wee lad Feargal's a quare good singer, so he is'. And so it came to pass that 'Teenage Kicks' became the first punk anthem ever to be played in the Nissen hut of Ballygomartin Presbyterian Church. Mrs Piper was even more outraged at my father playing The Undertones on 'hallowed ground' than she had been when he first played Dana at the disco. Of course, once Feargal Sharkey had opened the floodgates, the Rats and The Stranglers soon followed. The soundtrack of the Westy Disco became an eclectic mix of pop, punk and disco. One minute I was bopping like Rod Stewart in tight trousers to 'Da Ya Think I'm Sexy?' and the next minute I was trying to pogo like a hard man to The Jam. But it was one artist in particular who transformed my relationship with punk music more than any other. Her name was Debbie Harry. She was small and blonde and gorgeous and sexy and she sang about 'Hanging on the Telephone' in a band called Blondie that was named after her hair. She was the first woman to take over punk the same way that other blonde lady had taken over the Conservative party in England. Mrs Thatcher told Valerie Singleton on *Val Meets the VIPs* that she never wanted to be prime minister but Debbie

Harry screamed from the rooftops that she wanted to be the Queen of New Wave. When Blondie came on *Top of the Pops* I was transfixed. If I was still eating my Smash and fish fingers on the picnic table in the living room when Debbie started singing '(I'm Always Touched By Your) Presence, Dear', the whole plate of food would be cold by the time the song was over. I was very touched by her presence, so I was. Because Blondie was performing live I even watched *The Old Grey Whistle Test* for the first time. This was usually a boring programme on BBC2 for people with beards who were dead serious about music – the *NME* with moving pictures. A clear indication of the establishment of Debbie Harry's place in my heart came when I finally took down Farrah Fawcett-Majors from my bedroom wall and replaced her with Debbie. Farrah had been up there for so long that the Blu-tack pulled chunks of woodchip off the wall. I couldn't bring myself to put Farrah in the bin because I was too grateful for the all pleasure she had brought me in her swimsuit. So instead I folded her up and hid her inside my Form 2 Biology notebook in my wardrobe.

Everyone was talking about Debbie Harry. Philip Ferris discovered her first and thought he owned her. Heather Mateer dyed her hair blonde to try to be just like her. The effect was spoiled only when Heather opened her mouth. Mrs Piper referred to Debbie Harry as 'that wee blondie hussy from America' but Titch McCracken was every bit as entranced as me.

'See her. See Blondie! See yer woman! See me! See her! Fuck!' he panted with understandable excitement and incoherence every time Debbie Harry came on *Top of the Pops*.

Frankie Jones made everyone laugh at school orchestra practice when he said that Debbie Harry could blow his trumpet any day. I wasn't sure what was so funny but I joined in laughing anyway in case it was some reference to sex I should know about. I suppose the idea of a punk goddess playing a traditional brass instrument was quite amusing but I didn't think it deserved quite so much laughter.

'Yeah, Debbie Harry can play my violin too, any day!' I added, expecting further hysterics at my similarly manly witticism. A confused silence ensued and I hit a massive reddener and quickly excused myself from my seat by pretending I had to fetch some rosin for my squeaky bow.

Such was the impact of punk that during lunch break in the playground I even found myself asking a shocked Ian Forrester to lend me his *NME* when Debbie Harry was on the front cover. This scenario would have been inconceivable even six months before. It was like Patrick Walsh at the School of Music asking to borrow my Presbyterian hymn book. Of course, I had certain religious and ethical difficulties with the punk movement. Could a wee good livin' fella really support punk with all its filth and vomit? Could the only pacifist teenager in West Belfast be reconciled to punk's clear clash with the philosophy of non-violence? Even if my mother let me become a full punk, I was sure Jesus wouldn't let me, so I came to a moral and cultural compromise. I decided to call into Oul' Mac's newsagent to cancel my *Look-in* magazine. My former employer was devouring a large bag of KP nuts between drags on his cigarette. He was so surprised at my cancellation that he sprayed the entire shop with peanut particles. I couldn't go the whole way and order the *NME* because it sneered too much at ABBA and I could never be disloyal to Agnetha. So I chose

Record Mirror instead because it reported positively on both pop and punk. For me it was the perfect compromise, like joining the Alliance Party. Even my big brother approved of my new weekly magazine in spite of the fact that it contained no football coverage whatsoever.

'Maybe you're nat such a big fruit after all,' he said, in a rare moment of sibling affection.

Now that I was back at school I was once again giving Judy Carlton all the attention she deserved. She was even prettier in September than she had been last June and she sometimes said hello to me in the corridor outside of the confines of chemistry class. Unfortunately the summer had also been kind to Timothy Longsley because he had grown by several inches and his voice had almost broken. He was taller than me but at least my voice was deeper. On Saturday mornings he was a glorious rugger boy lauded by teenagers and I was nothing but a humble breadboy praised by pensioners.

I noticed with increasing irritation how Timothy flirted with Judy in every chemistry class and I observed how she giggled to humour him. I sometimes scanned the bottles of powdered chemicals marked dangerous lined up on the top shelf in the chemistry store and wondered if I could render Timothy inert by sprinkling some toxic particles on his Tayto cheese and onion crisps. Then I remembered my pacifist commitments and realised I must win Judy's heart through true love and not by murder.

A rare opportunity to interact more intimately with Judy could be coming up soon during the annual school play. Judy had volunteered to be one of the team of girls who did the make up for what Miss Baron called 'the budding thespians'. For some reason every time she said 'thespians' Frankie Jones laughed dirtily. I wanted to be one of the finest actors like Roger Moore and I dreamed of being interviewed by Michael Parkinson on BBC1 on a Saturday night when he would introduce me coming down the stairs as 'One of the Greats!' So the prospect of the school play was doubly appealing. Every year I auditioned for the school play in the hope that I would be cast as the romantic lead, just like Roger Moore in the James Bond movies. For the past few years I had been cast as an old man with a stick and the older boys who could act in posh English accents got all the big parts. I wanted to be the Saint but I always ended up as Steptoe. Of course this could be an indication that Miss Baron recognised the exceptional acting skills required to play a person six times my age. Perhaps Miss Baron saw me as a great character actor like yer man who played Alf Garnett, who wasn't really that old at all. The one advantage of being given the role of a septuagenarian was that it required a lot of make up. While the romantic leads got a quick dusting of make up another old-man role would require detailed hair whitening and added wrinkles and a beard. If Miss Baron awarded me yet another aged part this year then at least Judy Carlton would have to spend half an hour on my face every night of the dress rehearsals and the week of performances.

I imagined sitting compliantly in the chair as Judy gently patted foundation on my face and then added years of wrinkles with a mascara pen. This would be a private moment just between the two of us. Judy would never once complain about my newly erupted spots interfering with her craft and I would not let my eyes water when she applied glue for my beard on top of a recently squeezed zit. I daydreamed about Judy touching my cheek and forehead endlessly with cotton wool and dabbing my nose with a wee sponge in spite of all the blackheads. Judy would lean forward and paint my lips and it would tickle as if before a kiss. I imagined as she applied the pressure on my lips I would look at her lips up close and I would be able to smell Charlie on her neck and Wrigley's on her breath. In this reverie we were real boyfriend and girlfriend and I expressed my gratitude by kissing her sweet lips. However I awoke from this daydream when I started to worry that my beard glue might not have dried out yet and I would end up giving Judy a beard instead of a kiss.

Mind you, the big news was that this year's school play would not be yet another Shakespeare comedy or tragedy full of old people's parts. This year's production was going to be a musical called *West Side Story* about gangs on two sides of a city who were fighting all the time. This was more like real life in Belfast than *A Midsummer Night's Dream* would ever be. I assumed there would be no old men required and when I heard that the lead role was called 'Tony' I knew it was made for me. The auditions were coming up soon and I was so determined to prove myself as the next Roger Moore that I started to practise moving my eyebrows up and down in the bathroom mirror.

However, even before the auditions for the school play came up, another exciting opportunity to impress Judy emerged. We were all standing in the assembly hall after singing 'Glorious Things of Thee Are Spoken' to a German tune for the fortieth time that month. David Pritchard had kept his eyes open the whole way through the school prayer to prove that God didn't exist and the Head of RE was still scowling at him because he had kept his eyes open too, to see who was keeping their eyes open. Our headmaster was making the announcements and it was the usual thing; stop running in the corridor, wear your ties properly, no cheeking the dinner ladies and aren't the Glorious First XV Rugby Team truly wonderful. It was all very routine until this announcement: 'The school charity committee are holding a talent contest at Christmas to raise money for the Save the Children fund.'

I dropped my school hymn book in shocked delight. This was another opportunity to do two of my favourite things at the same time, just like acting and getting my face done by Judy. I could display my impressive musical talents in front of the whole school and save lots of wee children in Africa simultaneously. This was the most exciting thing that had happened to me since Leslie had forgotten to put on the handbrake in the Mini Shop and we had travelled backwards down the hill at speed towards the paramilitaries' community centre and Leslie had jumped back into the cabin and stopped us just in time. I began to hatch a plan of how I was going to win the talent contest. The pupils would be asked to vote for their favourite act with a clapometer like on *Opportunity Knocks* with yer man Hughie Green with the funny eye. From my experiences at the Westy Disco and my weekly reading of *Record Mirror* I knew exactly which musical genre would attract the most votes from my fellow pupils. I knew immediately that if I was to be a winner and if Judy was to see me as the coolest boy in the whole school, there was only one option for me at the school talent contest. It had to be punk, so it had!

15

SANTA CLAUS IS COMING TO TOWN

'It's Christmaaaaàaaaaaaas!!!' screamed Noddy Holder.

It was a very familiar yell. My father's decision to unleash Slade's 'Merry Christmas Everybody' at the Westy Disco officially announced the beginning of the Christmas season even though it was only the end of November.

'It's Christmaaaaaaaaaaaaas!!!' echoed Titch McCracken with a manly stomp and an aggressive spit of additional chewing gum on to the sticky dance floor.

'An-aaw-keee in the You-Kay!' interrupted Philip Ferris with a revolutionary pogo and a clatter of chains. His English accent was getting better but his pierced nose had a scab now.

'Wise up wee lad! Your head's cut!' said Heather Mateer dismissively from the middle of a circle of girls dancing around a hill of handbags. Heather remained steadfastly unconvinced of the musical merits of punk.

'Alrighty, guys and gals. Here's my hot hit pick for the Christmas number one!' announced my da in the mid-Atlantic accent he always used when he was DJ-ing. I listened intently because my father's predictions were usually very good. He always knew what would go to number one, he predicted correctly who would get elected and he said the Troubles would never end. With every fulfilled prophecy my mother would remind me, 'Your father's a very clever man, you know.'

'It's the new 45 from Boney M, so it is. It's a liddle number called "Mary's Boy Child" and it goes a liddle bit something like…' – he pressed the start button on the battered double decks – '…this!'

'Mary's boy child, Jesus Christ, was born on Christmas Day …' began Boney M. 'And man will live for ever more, because of Christmas Day,' they sparkled in stunning a cappella harmony.

'Boney M ballicks!' huffed Philip as he departed the dance floor defiantly. He stormed into the tuck shop and, in an act of pure rebellion, bought a packet of sweetie cigarettes and a lemonade shandy. Every time I saw Philip Ferris he seemed to be becoming more and more of a hard man. His own father had thrown him off the Boys' Brigade football team for refusing to take the safety pin out of his nose during matches.

Meanwhile the dance floor filled with practically every remaining member of the Westy. Of course my big brother was another of the few who remained stubbornly seated and and he uttered just one word at any boy who was enjoying the song: 'Fruit!'

In contrast, I was delighted to experience this unusual enthusiasm for a peace-loving hymn of such deep spirituality.

'People shouted, "Let everyone know, there is hope for all to find peace",' sang yer man with the hair that danced funny.

'Mary's Boy Child' became the biggest instant dance floor hit since 'Disco Duck'. I prayed that this would be the beginning of the religious revival all the old born-again men on the Shankill had been hoping for. Maybe Boney M would be just the catalyst they had been praying for and everyone was going to get saved in tents again like back in eighteen-something. I was convinced of the evangelistic potential of Boney M but I was certain Uncle Samuel would not have allowed this song in the repertoire of the wee meetins in Dublin because it mentioned Mary far too much and she was a Roman Catholic.

Christmas was a time for music. Every year Uncle Henry organised a series of rehearsals for the Westy Disco choir and we prepared to sing our hearts out at the carol services in Ballygomartin Presbyterian Church. We did a respectable 'First Noel' and an admirable 'Bleak Midwinter'. We practised very hard to get our 'glorias' the right length in 'Ding Dong Merrily on High' but unfortunately the smokers always ran out of breath long before we got anywhere close to 'hosanna in excelsis'. By popular demand we revived 'When a Child is Born' every Christmas because the Presbyterian pensioners of the Upper Shankill loved our choral interpretation of Johnny Mathis. When the time came for our performances we were joined on stage at the front of the church by a wooden sheep with a cotton wool coat and several pre-school shepherds with snatters and tea towels held around their heads by snake belts. A Tiny Tears doll from the *Great Universal Club Book* was dressed up as the baby Jesus and placed in a manger with straw from my late gerbil's cage. I had to hold my tongue at the many theological errors contained within this nativity scene and I knew that Uncle Samuel would have been horrified. Yet it wasn't often teenagers were interested in Jesus so I decided to hold my theological counsel. After one of our triumphant performances, as I stroked the coat of the wooden animal, Rev. Lowe said I was 'making love' to the sheep. I was shocked at this remark because it sounded like a man of the cloth was accusing me of doing something disgusting from one of my big brother's dirty rugby songs.

If the lead up to Christmas was an important time of the year for music and religion, it was an even more critical period for bread. From the end of November our customers began to place additional orders to ensure they had adequate bread, cakes and pastries for the Christmas season. Many of our customers requested a dozen mince pies every single Saturday in December. In spite of this great demand I was not a fan of the mince pie – to me, they were simply flies' graveyards with sides. This felt similar to not liking Elvis. But I understood I had to keep my personal tastes separate from my professional duties and so I took every order for mince pies with all the enthusiasm of an elf receiving a letter for Santa. Another typical seasonal order was a slightly stale unsliced plain loaf for making stuffing. It was strange how Christmas reversed my customers' expectations of the plain loaf. For the rest of the year its level of freshness determined its quality, but in December it was more desirable if slightly stale.

But by far the most popular Christmas order in the Mini Shop was a big box of Tunnock's Tea Cakes. We sold these mouthwatering mallows individually and in boxes of six all year round, but at Christmas time everyone bought boxes of thirty-six to give as Christmas presents to friends and relatives. They easily outsold mince pies in the Mini Shop. Each of these delicacies was wrapped in red and silver striped foil that made them look very Christmassy. If you hung a Tunnock's Tea Cake on your Christmas tree no one would even notice it wasn't a proper shiny bauble unless you put it too close to the fairy lights and the chocolate melted and it ruined the tinsel garlands and your mother sent you to your room for being 'as thick as champ'.

On the first Saturday morning in December there were snowflakes falling as we made our initial seasonal deliveries in the darkness. In fact, snow was universal over the Shankill, so it was. The freezing temperatures and the drifting snowflakes urged my customers into full Christmas preparation mode. Leslie arrived outside our house earlier than usual, seconds after my amazing snow-white plastic radio alarm clock had gone off and interrupted a warm and comforting dream involving Debbie Harry and a bubble bath. The Downtown Radio News reported the roads being blocked by snow instead of barricades. Leslie had been monitoring the weather forecast overnight and he decided to leave an hour earlier than usual to ensure that neither ice nor snow would come between Ormo and its customers. He was sporting a woolly hat like Benny in *Crossroads* to keep his ears and baldy head warm. Leslie was also wearing Wellington boots and a very determined look on his face. No one could look as determined as an Orangeman. Leslie regarded inclement weather as a personal challenge to his professionalism. I realised that nothing short of burial in a snowdrift would prevent him from completing the traditional route of his bread round that morning. The Mini Shop was very good in the snow because it had so many tyres to get a grip. This was in contrast to our Ford Escort respray which slid down the icy roads like Bambi on a frozen lake. Leslie sprinkled salt on the Mini Shop steps to stop them freezing over and to avert customer falls, and then we set off on our Arctic adventure. I was wearing my duffle coat and my grammar school scarf wrapped around my neck and mouth up to my nostrils. I breathed warm air from my lungs into the scarf but my breath turned damp and froze on the wool. I wore my Dr Martens to stop me from slipping because my mother insisted that if I didn't wear proper boots in the snow I would slip on the ice and fall into a hedge and put my eye out. In spite of the danger I managed to have a few surreptitious slides down some of the hilly streets just for the craic. When Leslie sent me forth with an armful of loaves I imagined I was Captain Scott from my history book, bravely leaving the safety of the Mini Shop to go out and deliver potato farls knowing that wolves or polar bears might eat me. With every delivery I wanted to say to Leslie 'I may be some time' in a posh English accent.

The first customer of the day was Mrs Grant who ordered a Yule log to cheer up her Richard with his throat and all. A Yule log was an oversized Swiss roll with sprig of plastic holly on top that you weren't supposed to try to eat. Nobody explained this to Titch McCracken and he nearly ended up in the Royal. Mrs Grant shouted this order from her front door because she dared not tackle the ice hazards between her front step and the Mini Shop. At this point I realised my skill and courage were going to be in great demand on this most hazardous of mornings. Mr Black was even more awkward than usual and I had to run in and out of the van three times to meet his demands for Christmas confectionery. Even his yappy greyhounds didn't want to come out in the snow. I was sure Mr Black was doing this on purpose just to make me work harder. I had to calm my temper by reminding myself that this was the season of peace and goodwill to all men, even curnaptious oul' bastards like Mr Black. When we came to Mrs Dunne's house I was surprised to see her arriving up the steps of the van as usual in her dressing gown. She had put two Stewarts supermarket plastic bags over the top of her furry pink slippers and attached them with elastic bands.

'C'mere til a tell ye, love,' said Leslie, 'the wee fella could've taken your order in the house this morning.'

This was true. Mrs Dunne regularly invited a variety of service providers into her home to take an order.

'Och, sure I'm not long home from the Christmas dinner dance at the Chimney Corner, love,' she replied.

Mrs Dunne's make up was smudged around the eyes and I could smell perfume and alcohol. She wore a strand of tinsel from her Christmas tree around her neck. Mrs Dunne was always the first person in our street to put up her Christmas tree, even though she had no children. She had invested in an impressive modern plastic tree from Woolworths in North Street and her shiny baubles were the envy of all the women in our street.

'Does yer woman think she's opening a Santa's Grotto like the Co-op?' asked Big Aggie resentfully.

I felt protective of Mrs Dunne, not least because she gave me a good Christmas tip. As she balanced her Tunnock's Tea Cakes on top of her plain loaves with one hand she managed to produce a droopy sprig of mistletoe from her dressing gown pocket with the other hand. Both Leslie and I declined her offer of a Christmas kiss although she hadn't actually offered to kiss Leslie. Then she retrieved a Christmas present from the other dressing gown pocket and handed it to me.

'Thanks very much, Mrs Dunne!' I said delightedly. 'Can I open it now?'

'No, love, you keep it for Christmas Day,' she advised.

As soon as she left the Mini Shop I ripped off the Christmas wrapping paper to reveal a bottle of Scooby Doo bubble bath with Scooby's head as a lid. I was very happy with this unexpected present but slightly concerned that Mrs Dunne might be suggesting I needed a bath before delivering the bread on a Saturday morning rather than leaving it to Sunday night every week. I sniffed under my arms but I could detect no unpleasant whiff emanating from under my duffle coat. I kept my precious gift behind the wheaten loaves on the bottom shelf at the back of the van for the rest of the morning. When I got home I couldn't unscrew Scooby's head for ages because the bubble bath had frozen.

As Leslie and I continued on our wintry trek on that cold December morn other customers put in their orders for Christmas goodies. Miss Adams ordered a large Christmas cake full of dried fruit and whiskey which came in a tartan tin. We could never afford to consume such an extravagant cake in our house at Christmas so I assumed this was posh yuletide food.

'Seasons greetings!' called Miss Adams, waving from her front door with a proper wreath hanging from the knocker.

When we reached the snow-covered peace line it looked

almost soft and attractive in pure snowy white. Mrs McAllister
had ordered a dozen sweetie selection boxes for all her neighbours'
children and when I deposited the stocking-shaped gifts in the
kitchen her daughter in the wheelchair laughed and clapped her
hands excitedly. Leslie allowed me to spend a few minutes with her
every Saturday morning while he enjoyed a good gossip with Mrs
McAllister about the current security situation around the peace
line. With great sensitivity he explained to me that 'the wee dote in
the wheelchair isn't the full shillin', so she's not'. Eventually I found
out that the girl in the wheelchair was called Naomi, like a woman
in the Bible. It seemed unfair to me that Naomi had to live in a
house on the peace line where rioters tried to break her bedroom
window to bring a united Ireland. Everyone said it was terrible
about poor Naomi, so it was, and it was an awful pity of the wee
crater, so it was, but Naomi seemed happier and friendlier than
most people. She always gave me a beautiful smile and big hug even
though I had forgotten to splash on extra Denim. I brought Naomi
a free can of Coke every Saturday morning and Mrs McAllister
returned my generosity with a good tip. I sometimes wished there
were more people like Naomi who got excited at lollipops and
dogs and cream buns and who didn't care about Protestants and
Catholics. One Saturday morning Mrs McAllister asked me if we
sold toilet roll in the Ormo Mini Shop. Not fully concentrating
and operating on automatic pilot, I answered her enquiry with the
question 'Pan or plain?' Mrs McAllister laughed so hard that she
began to cry and Naomi pointed and laughed too. When she had
composed herself Mrs McAllister called me 'a grand wee fella' and
gave me an extra tip. Although she was kind enough not to share

my error with anyone else, unfortunately Leslie had overheard the conversation and he retold the incident with glee to any other customer who would listen for the next year.

By the time we arrived in the estate the snow had deepened and, apart from army Saracens, the Mini Shop was the only moving vehicle remaining on the road. This proved that we were almost as essential as soldiers. The estate always looked much better at Christmas with a touch of sparkle and flashing lights in every window and a covering of pure white snow over the neglected grey pavements. There was a reassuring smell of coal smoke from the chimneys hanging heavily in the air. This pleasant Christmas card scene was ruined only by the tattered remains of the flags that had being flying on every lamppost since the Twelfth of July. The paramilitaries didn't allow any flags to be taken down ever, even when the Union Jacks became so dirty and bedraggled that the Queen Mother herself would have been affronted.

'No one touches them flegs!' dictated Big Duff.

This made no sense to me. I couldn't understand why the men who said they wanted to be British the most, enforced shredded Union Jacks flying above their streets at Christmas. You had to wait for the weather to take down the flags each year. The wind could not be accused of being an IRA sympathiser and the rain could never be burnt out of the estate.

As we struggled along the icy streets I noticed there was an unusually big security presence in the estate.

'Look's like there's a situation,' said Leslie.

When we arrived at the Rosbottoms only Mr Rosbottom attempted to make the hazardous journey from their front door to the Mini Shop. In his huge dressing gown he looked like a great walrus trudging over a frozen lake in Greenland in a David Attenborough documentary. When he clambered on board, and once the van had regained its equilibrium, Mr Rosbottom doubled his order of everything from now until Christmas. Their bread order was now so expansive that I wondered if I should ask to borrow my father's wheelbarrow (which he had borrowed from the foundry) to carry the whole load for the next few weeks.

'I think there's a situation,' said Mr Rosbottom, pointing out the back window towards a dozen RUC land rovers and army vehicles which were surrounding a bricked-up house at the end of the street.

Just then Mrs Big Duff arrived in the van, looking very animated in Wellington boots and a heavy woollen Union Jack cardigan.

'I've heard there's a situation,' said Leslie, hoping for inside information.

'Yes, there is a situation, so there is,' confirmed Mrs Big Duff, with some authority. 'There was an attempted attack on certain individuals by a certain organisation.'

'Where are they now?' asked Leslie.

'There, they're there!' said Mrs Big Duff inexplicably pointing towards one of the flats.

I assumed this meant the UDA and the UVF were fighting amongst themselves again. I could never understand why the two Protestant paramilitary groups were always feuding because I couldn't see any difference between them. To me they were as indistinguishable as Stork margarine and butter on a Belfast bap. Mrs Big Duff ordered three additional pan loaves to make extra sandwiches for Big Duff. She said that her Big Duff had to do so much overtime commanding operations from the drinking club during the Christmas party season that he didn't have time to get home for his dinner. I tried to imagine what a paramilitary Christmas party would look like. I was certain the UDA were far too hard to pull Christmas crackers and read silly jokes. I was sure the UVF would never play charades and I had never seen a paper balaclava, even an orange one. But then I remembered reading in my history book about the truce at the battlefront on Christmas Day during the First World War. It happened in a place called 'No Man's Land' which sounded like the part of the Springfield Road between the security gates at Springmartin. I wondered if perhaps this Christmas Day the IRA and the UDA would meet there on the peace line and share cigarettes and cans of Harp for a few hours before going back to killing each other on Boxing Day. I imagined Big Duff and a provo wiping snowflakes off their photomathingummy glasses and shaking hands. As I imagined Johnny Mathis sitting on top of a snowy peace wall singing 'When a Child is Born', my peace-loving reverie was interrupted by the sound of Mrs Big Duff's voice as she left the Mini Shop.

'All I know is themuns involved in thon carry-on over thonder need to watch themselves!' she said and marched determinedly towards her front garden where her small children were building a snowman with a carrot for a nose and pieces of coal for his eyes. The snowman was also sporting a Milky Bar Kid gun and holster and was carrying an Ulster flag on the end of a broom handle.

As we continued with our deliveries in the estate Leslie explained to every customer that there was a situation and added with a wink that 'certain organisations' were involved and the RUC were 'diggin' for footprints in the snow'. I still had no idea what the situation was all about but it had certainly got everyone very excited and in the mood for Christmas. The only person who seemed disinterested in the situation was Billy Cooper's granny with the curlers.

'C'mere til a tell ye,' said Leslie. 'Have you heard about the situation and the carry-on with the organisations in the estate this mornin'?'

'A pan, a plain, two soda and two pataita,' replied Billy Cooper's granny.

As we finished the bread round Leslie gave me an extra 50p, a packet of Tayto cheese and onion crisps and a can of totally tropical Lilt as a token of his appreciation for my additional labours in the snow. However just as I was about to leap down the steps of the van to help my wee brother to dig his space hopper out of the snow, Leslie asked me an unexpected question.

'Will you be Santa's little helper with me next week?' he asked.

'Wha'?' I replied.

'I'm doin' Santa next Saturday afternoon for the Sunday School party up in the estate,' explained Leslie. 'The rag-and-bone man is lending me his horse and cart but I need an elf to help me give out the presents.'

'Er …,' I stumbled.

I got a big enough slagging from my big brother for being a

breadboy and I knew that he would have a field day if I agreed to be Leslie's little helper on the back of a sleigh in the estate.

'Sure, it's for the kids in your wee Sunday School class,' added Leslie, recognising that I was going to require some persuasion.

'Do I have to dress up?' I asked.

'C'mere til a tell ye, young lad,' he said, 'not if you don't want to. Sure as long as I'm dressed as Santa nobody'll be lookin' next nor near ye.'

A short silence ensued wherein I was expected to say 'yes'.

'Aye, all right,' I agreed even though I didn't want to do it.

As I paced towards the front door of our house I noticed Mr Oliver's hedge rooster, now highlighted by silver frost, had lost its definition and needed clipped back into shape.

When the dreaded day came I decided not to turn up. This was a big decision for me as I was renowned throughout the Upper Shankill for my reliability. I tried to think of an excuse like being sick but when my mother found me in the bathroom sticking my fingers down my throat and retching she immediately recognised what I was up to and insisted I run over to the estate immediately and carry out my elf duties as I had promised.

'I cant believe you've left that big crater to do Santa all on his own in that there estate,' she said, making me feel instantly guilty. 'He's awful good to them wee children, you know.'

'But mammy I don't wanna be scundered!' I protested.

'Stop your oul' nonsense and get yerself over there to Santa right now!' she insisted.

I reluctantly trudged over to the estate. Within ten minutes

I spotted Santa in the snow. In the distance, at the top of the hill, I could see the outline of Father Christmas on the back of the rag-and-bone cart with tinsel round the sides being pulled by an old horse with a red nose attached. At first it seemed to be a joyous scene of happy children skipping alongside Santa Claus and singing sweet carols. As I made my way up the slippy footpath I could recognise the faces of some of my Sunday School class and I could hear the sound of children singing. But what was the tune? Thankfully it wasn't an abuse of 'Climb, Climb Up Sunshine Mountain' but it wasn't 'Jingle Bells' either. As I arrived into earshot I could hear the children join together in harmony and sing:

> Leslie McGregor's bread,
> Sticks to your belly like lead.
> Leslie McGregor's bread,
> Sticks to your belly like lead.

As if this wasn't disturbing enough I then noticed the scene surrounding Santa Claus was more like a riot than a celebration. As I drew closer I could hear Leslie shouting: 'If one more of you wee Comanches do that again there'll be nathin' but cinders for youse all this Christmas, so there won't!'

I spotted the McLarnon twins from my Sunday School class and several other fans of 'Climb, Climb Up Sunshine Mountain'. These rebellious choristers now began singing a Christmas ditty of their own, which they certainly hadn't learnt at Sunday School.

Jingle Bells,
Santa Smells,
A million miles away.
He done a fart
Behind a cart
And blew up the IRA!

It was only when I got within a few feet of Rudolph that I noticed what else was happening: the Sunday School was stoning Santa! I was shocked to notice two of the younger girls with pigtails from my Sunday School class joining in the attack enthusiastically.

'Girls, girls!' I intervened. 'Don't you know who brings you presents every Christmas morning?'

'Jesus!' they replied in unison, obviously thinking it was a Sunday School question.

My attempts to bring peace and goodwill were shattered when Santa was hit on the nose by a snowball with a large piece of coal inside.

'C'mere til a tell ye, young McLarnon!' shouted Santa, 'If I tell yer da about this you'll get the hidin' of yer life!'

I wrestled with what I should do to save Santa from this contemptible onslaught. I was also aware that if Santa was a target then an elf could also be attacked. Leslie had not yet spotted me among the riotous crowd so I made a principled decision. If Santa was being stoned and I was supposed to be his little helper there was only one thing I could do. I ran away. As I scarpered I could hear the sound of Santa calling my Sunday

School class 'a bunch of ungrateful wee glipes' but I did not turn back.

When I arrived back at the house my father was lying on the kitchen floor fixing a leak in the washing machine.

'Those children over there are wee hallions, Daddy!' I said.

My father sat up and set down the monkey wrench he had borrowed from the foundry.

'You remember this, son,' he said, 'you're better than no one and no one is better than you.'

This sounded like something Jesus would have said. As he returned to the tubes under the washing machine I felt guilty for condemning my own Sunday School class. My father was very Christian for an atheist. He was a very clever man, you know. I felt guilty for the rest of day. I even lost my excitement that ABBA was going to be on the *Mike Yarwood Christmas Special*. I didn't get up on the sticky dance floor with all the others and boogie to Wizzard at the Westy Disco that night even though I too wished it could be Christmas every day. I tried to amuse myself by making a Christmassy thing they had shown on *Blue Peter*. I borrowed a couple of coat hangers from my mother's wardrobe, stuck them together with sticky back plastic and covered them in tinsel. It was only as I attempted to add some of the candles we had used to light the house during the Ulster Workers' Strike that my mother confiscated the whole shiny creation and accused me of building a fire hazard. She had been very highly strung ever since Mr Oliver had died in her arms and Auntie Emma was always asking her about her nerves.

The following Saturday morning I had to listen to Leslie

describing the whole Santa assault in detail to every outraged customer. I felt even guiltier when he added, 'And the young fella here couldn't even help me because he was in bed with a migraine.' My lie was spread throughout the Upper Shankill like runny margarine on a hot Ormo pancake. I would never admit to my cowardice for fear of losing my job so I asked God to forgive me and prayed extra hard for my Sunday School class to get saved before next Christmas. As I was leaving the Mini Shop after our final Christmas delivery, Leslie wished me a Merry Christmas and gave me a big box of Tunnock's mallows. I gave the whole box to my granny as penance for letting down Leslie and Santa and Jesus and my father all on the one day. I genuinely didn't want to be a selfish wee bastard, so I didn't. All I ever wanted was to do the right thing.

16

PUNK FOR PEACE

The last week of term before Christmas at BRA was magic, so it was. The exams were over and the familiar obsession with the twin priorities of GCE and rugby results was replaced with three more exciting prospects. The highlights of this week would be the Christmas carol service, the long awaited auditions for *West Side Story* and – most exciting of all – the opportunity to shine before the whole school in the charity talent contest.

To contribute to the generous atmosphere some of my middle-class classmates brought in Christmas presents for every single teacher, even the Latin teacher with the bad skin. I interpreted this behaviour as either showing off or being a lick. At primary school everyone gave their teacher a bottle of green shampoo for Christmas except for Titch McCracken, who opened his teacher's gift on the way to school and tried to sell it to wee girls in the playground for 10p or a Curly Wurly. Inevitably the shampoo leaked out over the Santa wrapping paper and on to your *Peter and Jane* reading book but our primary school teachers welcomed this annual display of generosity and they always had very clean hair in January. However, now that I was all grown up and at big school,

I only gave Christmas presents to the teachers I actually liked. Several students at BRA opted out of the tradition of Christmas gifts altogether. David Pritchard, being dead clever and all, proclaimed that the nativity was a big fairy story like Santa Claus and said he wouldn't be buying anyone a Christmas present in case they thought he was 'one of those pathetic little weak people who believes in God'. David's credibility as the school's leading atheist was slightly undermined when he agreed to read the Bible passage about the shepherds and the angels at the Christmas carol service. I was ragin'! Why did Shankill breadboys never get picked to do the readings at the BRA carol service? I believed every single word of the Bible, even the ones I didn't understand, and I had spent all summer sharing the gospel with the children of Dublin! David Pritchard defended himself against all accusations of hypocrisy by saying that if he had been chosen out of the whole school to read 'Goldilocks and the Three Bears', he would have agreed to read that too, whether it was true or not. It wasn't fair!

Miss Kelly opened the presents from her most generous or most fawning pupils during chemistry class in between separating and purifying experiments. I was distracted from all this chromatography by my own separation from the purity of Judy Carlton on the other side of the classroom. I assumed Miss Kelly didn't keep her presents to open on Christmas Day because she wasn't married and that meant she would be all alone and sad on Christmas morning. The poor woman seemed fairly pleased when she opened my Christmas gift because it was an appealing jam jar of blue bath salts covered with a knitted ballerina lady. It was only when Miss Kelly removed the woollen dancer to peek at the scented salts that I noticed the similarity in appearance of the perfumed granules inside this jar with the contents of bottles of poisonous chemicals on her top shelf. I prayed Miss Kelly wouldn't get the jars mixed up in all the Christmas rush as I didn't want to be responsible for a tragic Christmas Day bath for my chemistry teacher. Of course, Timothy Longsley gave all the teachers expensive presents just to show how rich he was and to try to impress Judy. When Miss Kelly removed all the silver bows and ribbons and gold wrapping paper from his gift, a box with the words 'Fondue Set' was revealed. I didn't really know what a fondue set was because no one in my street had one – I'd only ever seen one on the conveyor belt of *The Generation Game* after the cuddly toy. We didn't have fondue parties at the top of the Shankill, even on the Eleventh Night. When Miss Kelly was clearly genuinely delighted with this present, Timothy grinned across the test tubes at me as if to confirm another victory. For a moment I imagined Timothy being lowered into a bath of boiling acid like in the *Carry On Screaming* movie and yer woman with the big eyelashes and the sexy voice saying 'Frying tonight!' Then I remembered I was a blessed peacemaker.

The joy of Christmas was temporarily suspended in Mr Jackson's class when someone left a Christmas present on his desk, which turned out to be a pair of Izal medicated toilet rolls.

'And what is the meaning of this?' roared Mr Jackson.

I assumed this was not a philosophical question. The sticky-out veins at Mr Jackson's temples began to throb dangerously. His face went redder than the time he caught Frankie Jones with a smutty picture of a Page 3 girl underneath his probability revision notes. In the inevitable interrogation that followed, the guilty gift giver did not own up and eventually Garvin Wilson pretended he'd done it to save the whole class from a Christmas holiday of detention and extra homework.

During rehearsals for the Christmas carol services it became clear that the repertoire of the school choir at Belfast Royal Academy was much more sophisticated than that of the only youth club choir in the Upper Shankill. The school choir was so sophisticated that we sang Christmas carols no one had even heard of. Throughout December we performed four-part harmony beautifully in services of nine lessons and carols in cold old churches where everyone wore fur coats and said all their 'ings'. Our sopranos soared spectacularly in the descant over the last verse of 'Hark the Herald Angels Sing'. Afterwards there was tea and mince pies in the freezing church halls and not a Tunnock's mallow in sight! The school choir also learned to sing 'Silent Night' in German and when we were invited to sing carols in a hut in front of the City Hall our music teacher got us special permission to go inside the historic building to chant our harmonies in German under the big green dome. It was enchanting, standing under the dome listening to the echo of our voices. When I told my granny of my joy at the German vespers resounding around the marbled walls of the City Hall she was fuming because the Germans had dropped bombs on Belfast's most famous building during the war.

'That's what that oul' brute Hitler wanted!'

I wasn't so sure that singing 'Stille Nacht' in Belfast City Hall had been a significant goal of the Nazi master plan. I was always shocked at how much my granny still hated the Germans even though we had beaten them more than thirty years ago now and we still beat them regularly in the *Eurovision Song Contest*, *It's A Knockout* and *Miss World*. Big Isobel hated Hitler more than she hated Gerry Adams. I wondered how long it would take for my generation to stop hating the IRA if we ever beat them too.

Of course, there were more attractions in the school choir at BRA than the musical catalogue. Judy Carlton was a leading soprano, like Olivia Newton-John in *Grease*. I had started out in the choir as a tenor, along with Garvin Wilson who was good at singing and Irish dancing even though he was a Protestant with glasses. But as my voice just kept on getting lower, I ended up as a small and insignificant bass among a group of tall six formers with acne. The basses stood at the back and the sopranos graced the front row of the choir, but from a distance I could still catch sight of the silky sheen of Judy's black hair on the back of her perfect head as we repeated dull Latin chants until they were in tune. Although I was bored by classical music I pretended to appreciate every single semiquaver because it made you sound clever. It was after one particularly draining rehearsal of Benjamin Britten that Joanne Gault stopped me as I was leaving the music room to ask me a very surprising question.

'Are you going to enter Mr BRA for the Schools' Charity Fair this year?' she enquired, almost as if I was not too physically repulsive to have a chance.

'Me?' I asked.

Garvin Wilson giggled, which was a cheek given he was ginger.

'Yes,' replied Joanne. 'Sure you're gonna be lovely when you grow up and wise up a bit.'

For a moment I was so flattered I wondered if this was Joanne's way of telling me that she fancied me. Then I remembered that she only went out with boys who played in the Glorious First XV rugby team and she had been working her way through the forwards this term. In spite of this disappointment I took her evaluation of my looks seriously because I realised that if I was to be crowned Mr BRA this would make me irresistible to most girls, including Judy Carlton. I simply had to enter the competition. So with the forthcoming beauty and talent contests, on top of the imminent auditions for *West Side Story* this December was turning out to be an exceptionally busy time for a working breadboy.

The auditions for the school play came first. I had always been frustrated that Miss Baron, our drama teacher, had failed to spot my acting talent and give me the sort of starring role I deserved. In recent years I had been overlooked for Tom Sawyer and Huckleberry Finn and ended up with small parts as old men in *The Crucible* and *Much Ado About Nothing*. It was like auditioning to be James Bond and being given the part of the sidekick of the evil genius who had no lines and got eaten by sharks in the first ten minutes. This year I was determined to achieve a starring role. As luck would have it there were no old men in *West Side Story* because it was all about young people in gangs stabbing each other, like on the peace line in West Belfast on a Saturday night. I was perfect for it!

The other advantage I had this year was that *West Side Story* was a musical and I could sing. Providentially, the main character was called Tony. If justice was to be done and I was cast as the leading man then it would be easy for all my supporting actors to learn their lines. They called me Tony every day anyway, apart from Timothy Longsley who called me 'gippo'. Another omen that I was meant to be Tony was my discovery of an old 45 in my parents' record collection. As I was sorting out the groovy records from the square discs for our amazing new stereo in the sitting room I stumbled upon a P.J. Proby single of 'Maria' from *West Side Story*. From the minute I discovered this treasure I began singing along with P.J. I had been learning all the words and practising the high notes and acting all the emotions for months. As I rehearsed 'the most beautiful sound I ever heard, Maria' my mind wandered back to the disco at Chigwell where I slow danced with my very own Italian Maria. This was yet another sign that I was meant to be the Tony who a beautiful Maria fell in love with. The plot of the musical also reminded me of my unrequited love for Sinead from the Lower Falls at Butlin's in Mosney because Tony and Maria were from two divided tribes too. In fact *West Side Story* seemed to be based on my life, although there was no evidence of an Ormo Mini Shop in the script for the musical.

Everything was falling into place perfectly until an unexpected problem developed – my voice kept on getting lower and lower. For years I had wanted puberty to get a move on, but now that I needed to be a tenor to play the part of Tony I desired a temporary postponement. I could manage all the notes with P.J. Proby at first, but as the weeks went by the high notes became more and more of a strain. I was a good singer and I could reach a lot of high notes but I was no Bee Gee. When Garvin Wilson, Ian

Forrester, Thomas O'Hara and I arrived at the audition room I was crestfallen when, instead of being asked to perform my well-rehearsed rendition of 'Maria', Miss Baron asked us all to sing a C scale. I did my very best but I realised that I was struggling with one or two of the higher notes. I was seething that Miss Baron gave me no opportunity to show that I could project the emotions of a Roger Moore while singing with the voice of a P.J. Proby. The other auditionees struggled too because Ian was even more of a bass than me, Thomas was still a soprano and Garvin was ginger. Once the auditions were over all we could do was wait. The cast would not be announced until the New Year. It was as if Tom Baker with the big long scarf had decided to give up his sonic screwdriver and they were about to cast a new *Doctor Who*. For the whole of the Christmas holidays I dreamed of being the star of *West Side Story* – but in the meantime there was a talent contest and the heart of a certain girl to win.

In anticipation of the charity talent contest I asked my parents for early delivery of my Christmas present. This year I had requested a real electric guitar like on *Top of the Pops*. I had been going to guitar lessons round the corner with Mr Rowing for years now and I felt it was about time I graduated from my wee Spanish acoustic guitar with the crack up the middle of the wood to a proper grown up rock instrument like Paul McCartney. However I knew electric guitars were very expensive, even over sixty weeks from the *Great Universal Club Book*, so I wasn't sure how my parents could ever afford to buy me one. But overhearing my parents whispering one night in the kitchen, I realised this dream might come true.

'Sure, he's an awful good wee lad with his homework and all.'

'Aye, but his head's in the clouds, Betty love.'

'Ach, Eric, sure he works hard on that oul' bread van, so he does.'

'Aye, for buttons!'

'Sure it's a wee interest for him. It'll keep him off the streets.'

'Well, there's gonna be no more overtime in the foundry after Christmas.'

I could tell by my father's tone of voice that he was relenting and once it was eventually revealed that I was getting an electric guitar for Christmas it didn't take much further persuasion to ensure the instrument would be in my possession a few days before the talent contest. Until then I would have to practise my chosen song on my Rolf Harris stylophone. Choosing the right song was always important in a talent competition. Both Lena Zavaroni and Bernie Flint had been brilliant at this on *Opportunity Knocks*, so I decided to involve a few trusted friends in the process of song selection. I lured Titch McCracken and Philip Ferris round to our house one Saturday afternoon with the promise of a box of out-of-date gravy rings. Philip was wearing full punk regalia but he was still in bad form because his father had dropped him from the Boys' Brigade football team for refusing to remove his safety pins during the match. Titch was in a very good mood because he was wearing a brand new pair of gutties, which he had shoplifted from the bargain bucket outside McMurray's in North Street while he had been waiting for a black taxi. Titch was good at choosing what was going to be a hit in the charts, while Philip brought serious musical credibility. Of course I had some ideas of my own as well. I considered whether the charity talent contest might be a good opportunity to share the gospel with the whole school and get even a small proportion of them saved. I could do a punk version of 'What a Friend We Have in Jesus' and subvert the art form for Jesus the same way Cliff Richard did with rock and roll. Larry Norman with the long hair from America sang 'Why Should the Devil Have All the Good Music' so I could sing 'Why Should Punk be all Spitting and Fighting?'

'Wise a bap, wee lad!' was Philip's response to these sacred suggestions.

'What about doin' a Blondie?' asked Titch, clearly too blinded by his lust for Debbie Harry to realise that I was not a female lead vocalist.

This fact also ruled out any Bee Gee song. The chosen number would have to be easy enough for me to both sing and play on the electric guitar at the same time and this certainly reduced the options. Both 'Bohemian Rhapsody' and 'Rat Trap' were beyond my emerging abilities. 'Stairway to Heaven' was also out of the question because – according to Titch's cousin from Ballymoney – if you played it backwards it contained hidden messages in praise of Satan. I couldn't manage to play 'Stairway to Heaven' forwards so there was no danger of any devil worship at the BRA talent contest this year. I knew I could attempt a decent rock version of 'Hang Down Your Head, Tom Dooley' and perhaps one or two Status Quo songs because this required knowledge of only three chords but I wanted to perform something more edgy and right up to date.

'What about "Anarkeee in the You Kay"?' suggested Philip predictably.

'Stop you talkin' like a clampet!' answered Titch.

A fight ensued in which Philip's safety-pin nose scab started to bleed all over Titch's brand new gutties. It seemed both were being punished for their sins and when I urged them to join me in the way of non-violence they told me to wise up. Once they had inflicted sufficient damage on one another they calmed down and a more sensible conversation began.

'What about the Undertones, cause they're the only ones that sing in our accent?' suggested Philip.

'But they are a band and it's only me in the contest,' I explained.

'I know!' said Titch. 'What about "Jilted John"?'

This was a funny punk song about Jilted John who is going out with a girl called Julie who chucks him to go out with a love rival called Gordon.

'That's not serious punk. That's takin' the ballicks out of anarkeee!' shouted Philip, getting angry again.

Philip was starting to sound very political, although not at all like the Alliance Party.

'But it's funny, Philip. It's good craic, so it is. Are punks not allowed to laugh?' I said.

'Sell-outs!' said Philip with a sneer and a spit, and he walked out.

'He's had a face on him like a Lurgan spade ever since he went punk,' commented Titch.

'Well, I don't care what he says,' I announced, 'I'm goin' to do "Jilted John" at the talent contest.'

'But can you play it?' asked Titch.

'Wee buns!' I replied, with pretend confidence.

That night I recorded 'Jilted John' off Radio Luxembourg and for the next few weeks I practised it every day. Even though the song had not been written for the Rolf Harris stylophone I managed to grasp the tune and learn the lyrics and I practised singing in an English accent. Philip should have been proud of me! When my electric guitar finally arrived from the *Club Book* it was just a matter of restringing it upside down to make it a left-handed guitar and then transposing my performance to the new instrument. Next I had to practise standing up and playing at the same time, which wasn't as easy as yer man with the curly hair in Queen made it look on *Top of the Pops*. By the time the day of the talent contest arrived I was certain my recital of 'Jilted John' was very good. I performed the song to my whole family in a final dress rehearsal. I dressed up for the occasion in my oldest jeans, my plastic leather jacket and an old T-shirt with a rip covered in safety pins generously donated from the huge sewing kit inside Auntie Mabel's pouffe. With granny visiting, my family formed a very imposing judging panel. I forgot some of the lyrics in the dress rehearsal performance but I covered it up with a few 'na na nas', which was completely acceptable in the punk genre, and no one seemed to notice.

'Ach God love him. That was lovely, son!' said my mother.

'Aye, dead on!' was my father's muted critique, before returning to his home-made brewery kit in the garage.

'Class!' exclaimed my wee brother, clapping his hands excitedly.

Granny was uncharacteristically quiet for a moment. Her mouth was hanging open and as she hadn't put her teeth in that day she looked particularly shocked.

'For the love and honour of pig's gravy!' said Big Isobel. 'What in the name of blazes was that? I thought you were goin' to do one of your wee good livin' songs like that lovely wee Cliff Richards fella!'

'Loada shite!' said my big brother.

I accepted that the controversial nature of the punk movement would inevitably provoke a mixed response and so I proceeded to school for the charity talent contest undeterred. Daddy lent me the amplifier and speakers from the Westy Disco and Mammy gave me a lift to my first punk gig in the Ford Escort respray. In spite of her artistic reservations Granny gave me 50p for the charity to help the wee orphans.

The atmosphere was electric in the assembly hall that night. It may have been dark and windy outside and there may have been shooting in the distance but inside the hall it was like the night of the Oscars in America when rich film stars got prizes for good acting. My mother regularly showed her appreciation of my own acting talents because every time I was feeling too sick to go to school on the day of a maths test she told me I could win an Oscar. In the midst of the feverish last-minute preparations backstage it became clear that I had limited competition. Garvin Wilson was going to do some Irish dancing in a kilt like a girl. This was challenging too many gender and cultural norms to achieve mass popularity. I was sure his wee jig would earn him some laughs but not many decibels on the clapometer.

'Are you nervous about your performance?' I asked Garvin.

Before Garvin could respond, Frankie Jones laughed the filthiest of laughs.

Four of the spottiest school choir boys were going to be a barbershop quartet and sing about the Swanee River in straw hats and waistcoats. None of these boys had ever been anywhere near the barber shop I went to in Castle Street. Admittedly their harmonies sounded perfect during their backstage rehearsals but I doubted if the school would clap much for these four guys because they were swots who won prizes for Additional Maths. Meanwhile the girls gymnastic club was going to do a dance in leotards with ribbons to the music of 'Seasons in the Sun'. I realised that the leotards would attract a certain amount of appreciation because Frankie Jones was already backstage promising every dancer his full support and I knew for certain that my big brother would give the gymnastic girls the biggest clap. The only other competitors of note were a tiny Form 1 girl who did a squeaky Frank Spencer impersonation, a cross-eyed Form 2 boy who did a brilliant 'walk the dog' with his yo-yo and a Form 3 magician who knew which card you'd picked and made his balls disappear under three beakers from the dinner hall. I was going to be the most contemporary contestant by far. When the running order was revealed I discovered I was to be the final contestant. Of course, this could work in my favour if the other acts were wick but it gave me too much time to get nervous. I sat in the wings, peeking out through the blue velvet curtains to assess the level of applause for every act. Garvin's performance was by all accounts flawless but sadly misunderstood and the Form 1 impersonator forgot her lines and ran off the stage crying for her mammy. The barbershop quartet was perfect but nobody cheered and the magician lost all credibility when a jack of diamonds fell out of the sleeve of his blazer. The yo-yo boy was truly talented but had too few tricks to entertain an audience of two hundred teenagers for more than one minute. Only the gymnastics club appeared to receive anything close to a tumultuous reception in spite of the fact that two of the less experienced gymnasts got their ribbons badly entwined.

Finally it was my turn. I checked that my strings were in tune and that my flies were done and I walked on to the stage. I could feel my heart thumping as much with excitement as with fear. The first person I recognised in the sea of faces before me was Judy Carlton herself. She was sitting in the front row between Joanne Gault and Thomas O'Hara. I noticed with great delight that this trio applauded me as soon as I walked on to the stage. It was only when I heard the word 'gippo!' being cast in my direction that I noticed Timothy Longsley was also sitting in the front row.

I've been going out with a girl,
her name is Julie ...

I glanced towards Judy, hoping she would notice the uncanny similarity of her name with the object of my punk rock affections. She was smiling and clapping along to the drumbeat on the cassette tape I was singing and playing over. This boosted my confidence and I attempted to pogo and sing and play my electric guitar all at the same time with no mistakes whatsoever in the whole of the first verse. However my enthusiasm got the better of me in the second verse and I dropped my plectrum. Quickly bending down to pick up the plectrum I knocked the amp plug out of the guitar and for a few moments I became acoustic. Although I recovered remarkably quickly, this had been just the sort of mistake Timothy Longsley had been hoping for and he began to boo. All his rugger mates joined in because they copied everything Timothy did without question. I was ragin'! It was all unfolding right in front of me. Judy and Joanne and Thomas were still cheering while only a few seats away Timothy and assorted rugby-playing Klingons were booing. I had just reached the verse of 'Jilted John' where the lyrics about his love rival went 'But I know he's a moron, Gordon is a moron!' I sang the official lyrics one time, but the second time my emotions took over and I sang;

'Timothy's a moron!'

'Timothy's a moron!'

I lost track of the song and stared down at a shocked looking Timothy Longsley in the front row while repeating;

'Timothy's a moron!'

'Timothy's a moron!'

At first the audience loved this improvisation and cheered while Timothy and the Klingons stood up and booed even louder. But I could not stop repeating the lyric.

When I eventually ended my hate-filled mantra I noticed that it had gone very quiet in the assembly hall. The cheering and applause had ceased and everyone, including Judy, was looking straight at me with a puzzled and slightly concerned look on their faces. Thomas had hit a reddener and had put his head in his hands. Suddenly Timothy leapt up on the stage and jumped on top of me. Several Klingons followed and soon four rugger boys were beating me up on stage in front of the whole school. The audience began cheering again. They completely misunderstood. They thought this was all part of a punk performance and they joined in the applause with gladness. The teachers also assumed this was a pre-planned performance and did not intervene. I clung on to my precious new guitar to ensure that it would sustain no damage and I managed to knee one of the Klingons in the goolies, but it was a losing battle. At last several sixth formers emerged from backstage to remove my attackers and this act got even more applause because everyone thought it was all supposed to be a part of my wonderful representation of the culture of violence associated with a punk rock concert. The only teenage pacifist in West Belfast was providing the whole school with an orgy of violence.

By the time the attack was over and the bullies were being scolded backstage by the other performers I had a bloody nose and a split lip, but I was determined to finish the last few lines of 'Jilted John'. I couldn't look in Judy's direction because I was so ashamed. I collected myself and restored my dignity and sang the last words of the song, which now took on a tragic new poignancy.

Yeah yeah, it's not fair,
I'm so upset, I'm so upset, yeah yeah,
I ought to smash his face in.
Yeah, but he's bigger than me.

I departed the stage to thunderous applause.

'Feel wick, wee lad,' I thought.

Thomas ran up to congratulate me but I wasn't hanging around.

Within seconds I was locked in the teachers' toilet behind the stage mopping up tears and blood. I missed the announcement of the winning act but I knew it wasn't me when I heard the distant sound of Frankie Jones crying 'Go on ya girls youse!', followed by a refrain of 'Seasons in the Sun'. It wasn't fair! As I sat in the toilet gathering myself, I imagined what would happen if I left an anonymous note with Big Duff's bread delivery saying that Timothy Longsley was a secret IRA spy in the BRA rugby team. Not a single 'Thou Shalt Not' in the whole Bible could keep me from hating Timothy. But before I could develop the murder plot any further there was a quiet knock on the toilet door.

'Go away!' I shouted.

'It's me, Tony,' said a kindly female voice.

'Who's me?' I answered roughly.

'It's Joanne,' she said.

'What?' I asked.

'We saw that, Tony!'

'Saw what, wee girl?'

'We know that wasn't acting!' said Joanne.

'Aye, but he'll get away with it, won't he?' I replied.

'Don't worry about him, Tony. Sure you're gonna be Mr BRA, aren't you? You were picked.'

'S'ppose,' I said.

Joanne was correct. Out of the three entries I had won Mr

BRA. The other two boys who entered the beauty contest were Second Formers with buck teeth.

'Judy Carlton says you're the nicest boy in the school anyway.'

'Wha...?'

I stepped back in surprise, knocking over the teachers' toilet brush and a pile of Izal medicated toilet rolls. Perhaps my ill-fated punk performance had been worth it after all. Was it really possible that a girl like Judy would prefer a boy like me to a rugger playing hero like Timothy Longsley? I was shocked, so I was.

17

MR BRA

I jumped out of the Ormo Mini Shop with all the purposefulness of the Bionic Man jumping off a skyscraper to catch an evil Russian spy with a moustache and a nuclear bomb in his briefcase. This was the Saturday of the Belfast schools' charity fair and the final of Mr Belfast Grammar School. It was vital that Mr BRA arrive in good time to ensure the maximum number of votes. I admit I rushed my bread delivery duties that morning. I even avoided the usual conversation about the weather with Miss Adams.

'Gives rain, young man,' she said politely.

'Aye! See ya!' I replied hurriedly.

I even cut short my weekly visit with Naomi, even though she was very excitedly pointing to her recent birthday present of a *Grease* cassette. I left her house after only three rewinds of 'Sandy'. When Leslie began to tell me all the latest news about the security situation and Mrs Piper still having a fancy man from a gospel hall up the Newtownards Road and her good livin' and all, I resisted the temptation to ask any supplementary questions for fear of lengthening my working hours unnecessarily. I came across the McLarnon twins from my Sunday School class in the estate that morning. At first I was delighted to see them playing on the green in front of Big Duff's community centre singing 'Give Me Oil in My Lamp', a gospel song I had taught them in Sunday School. It was only as I drew closer that I noticed they had adapted the lyrics:

Give me oil in my lamp, keep me burning,
Give me oil in my lamp I pray.
Give me bullets in my gun and I'll shoot them every one
Because they're members of the I-R-A.

I had neither the time nor the energy to begin to challenge this blasphemy, today of all days, and I began to wonder if I was the least successful Sunday School teacher ever to have attempted to teach their charges to love their enemies. I knew that Jesus had said 'Suffer the little children to come unto me' but it seemed that the little children in my Sunday School class just wanted to make me suffer! As I departed the scene I felt a tap on my shoulder. It was Billy Cooper's granny with the curlers.

'A pan, a plain, two soda and two pataita.'

When I arrived back into our house my whole family was gathered around the television with a great sense of excitement. My father had just bought Pong for the Westy Disco and everyone was having a go. Pong was tennis on your TV. I watched in amazement as my big and wee brothers applied their customary ball skills to move a wee line up and down the sides of the TV screen. They were using buttons on a computer thingy my father had plugged into the back of the TV. Daddy looked awestruck at this advanced technology in our living room. He even stopped smoking for a few minutes to have a go, stubbing out his Hamlet cigar in the new tortoiseshell ashtray my wee brother had given him. (My wee brother had dug up the remains of Steve Austin from the pet cemetery under the holly tree at the bottom of the back garden on Father's Day, which was a ghoulish but practical use of my dearly departed pet.) This new technology was mind-boggling. If your wee line hit the ball it flew across the screen like in tennis and you won points like Bjorn Borg at Wimbledon. It looked like real tennis but when my big brother eventually let me have a go I found it far too fast. I preferred to play Space Invaders in the amusement arcade in Newcastle on the Sunday School excursion. Space Invaders was very fast and complicated too but it required no sporting ability and was a useful preparation for any possible alien invasion. It was good to see my family so happy while playing games on this modern marvel in our living room. Mammy even had a few gos and she laughed when Daddy said that Virginia Wade had nothing to worry about.

Ever since the shooting next door she didn't laugh as much and I kept overhearing Auntie Emma asking her about her nerves and 'the change'. Daddy had started to give off more and more about no more overtime at the foundry because the big bosses were as thick as champ, and about no hope for peace in Northern Ireland because the politicians were a shower of useless bigots. He began to bring home cans of Carlsberg Special from the Wine Lodge more often and when he drank too many cans he started to slabber. One night my mother got so angry with my father that she threw a carton of cottage cheese at him. It missed his head and plastered the living room wall behind him. Fortunately the texture of cottage cheese was the same as the woodchip wallpaper so nobody noticed. Henceforth every time my mother got cross we joked that she was going to splatter us with cottage cheese. I was glad to see my parents laughing today at 'Pong'. I wanted my family to live happily ever after like everyone in *The Waltons*, well except Grandpa Walton, but he was old. Amid all the excitement of playing tennis on TV I almost forgot about my imminent attempt to become the heartthrob of Belfast grammar schools. When I reminded my father that he had promised to give me a lift into town he sighed at the thought of a son of his participating in a beauty competition. But spurred on by the excitement of a future of TV and computers he quickly ferried me to Inst in the Ford Escort respray.

The schools' charity fair was held in the assembly hall of Inst, which was a school near the City Hall just for boys who passed the eleven-plus and played rugby. Inst was in a beautiful old Georgian building with a front lawn. It wasn't as old as BRA but it looked more refined than our rugged granite building. The schools' charity fair was held in Inst every year because it was in the city centre near the ABC cinema and all the best shops like the Athletic Stores. The school was just outside the city centre security cordon so you didn't have to queue up for ages to get frisked or have your bag searched to get into the fair. When I arrived at the hall, it was already full of nice families with clean prams going round the stalls buying home-made jam and caramel squares to help the babies in Africa. Most of the customers were pronouncing all their 'ings' as they haggled over the price of an old plate or a crocheted tea cosy. The Mr and Miss Belfast Schools' stalls were at the very front of the hall beside the tombola and I noticed that there was already a small crowd gathering. The rules of this annual beauty competition were very simple. The photograph of each finalist was pinned to the wall, with a large red bucket underneath. The public was invited to vote for their favourite by throwing coins into the respective bucket and the contestant who raised the most money for the African babies was deemed the winner. Of course most people just voted for their own school. It reminded me of politics in Northern Ireland. You just voted for your own side no matter what. Naturally, there was much more interest in the Miss Belfast Schools than the boys' competition because the three finalists were lovely, so they were. However it was hard to choose between the girls because all three were blonde and had their hair done like Purdey in *The New Avengers*. Miss BRA, Miss Methody and Miss Victoria College all stood beside their buckets smiling coyly and occasionally casting a glance of hatred towards their rivals. Their mothers stood beside them proudly, discreetly topping up their daughters' buckets from their purses. However, Mr Methody and Mr Inst were nowhere to be seen. This confirmed they had been given the same advice that my big brother had given me in relation to the competition: 'Don't let anyone see you there or they'll think you're a big Beirut!'

I was far too embarrassed to stand beside my bucket and request money for my good looks. Quite apart from not wanting to be a fruit I was not prepared to prostitute myself in such an undignified manner, even if it was to help the African babies. I was relieved to discover that Mr Inst and Mr Methody obviously shared my embarrassment. At least we were competing on an equally anonymous basis. As I approached the Mr Belfast Schools' stall stealthily, I saw that Joanne Gault was already standing beside my photograph loyally encouraging people to vote for me, although I think she was probably more interested in feeding the wee orphans than helping me. But when I looked at my photograph I was shocked at the specimen on display! This was the first time I had seen my picture since it had been taken by one of the skinny boys with glasses in the BRA photography club. It was horrible! In the photograph I had a very large head like when I looked in the funny mirrors at Barry's Amusements in Bangor. Had something gone seriously wrong in the dark room of the BRA photography club or was I really this ugly? The image made me think of the new movie coming soon about a person with a deformed head they called *The Elephant Man*. My main preoccupation before the photo was taken was my skin, so I had covered up the blemishes with my mother's talcum powder, but I had not even considered the possibility that I had a misshapen head. Who in their right mind would donate money for this monster? I thanked my lucky stars that my big brother had refused to attend the charity fair as I was certain that if he saw this picture he would start to call me *The Elephant Man* and I would be completely scundered. When I looked more closely at the competition I was even more depressed. Both Mr Methody and Mr Inst had blond hair and blue eyes and normal heads. Mr Methody looked like Blue out of *The High Chaparral* and all the girls loved him. Mr Inst looked so like Luke Skywalker from *Star Wars* that I almost wanted to vote for him myself. I could soon see that more coins were being dropped into their buckets than mine, in spite of Joanne Gault's valiant efforts.

'But he's gonna be lovely when he grows up a bit,' she pleaded with one potential voter who could not be dissuaded from donating 10p to Luke Skywalker.

Just as I was just about to slip out quietly, I felt a tap on my shoulder.

'What happened to your head Mr BRA?' asked Titch McCracken.

Even though he didn't go to my school or any grammar school or any school at all very much, Titch had come to support me. He stood out in the Inst assembly hall because he was the only person wearing a UVF badge in the lapel of his faux leather jacket from John Frazer's. He was accompanied by Heather Mateer, who had long since abandoned any school, and she was on fighting form.

'Are them wee lads in the photie club takin' the piss out of you, wee lad?' she enquired sympathetically.

Before I could even attempt to mount a defence of my deformities I noticed Titch approaching Mr Methody's bucket and placing his hand inside. I was about to challenge this apparent disloyalty when he immediately moved the same hand over my bucket and I heard a clatter of coins. He repeated the offence several times and no one seemed to notice. With each act of theft he lifted a larger handful of coins from my rivals' buckets and deposited them in mine. I never thought the day would come when I would appreciate Titch's exceptional talent for shoplifting and I was unsure whether or not to to take him to task about this flagrant theft. Finally I made a moral choice and spoke directly to Titch: 'Do it again, will ye?'

These were desperate times and so I permitted myself to become the chief beneficiary of Titch's predilection for theft. I satisfied myself with the justification that all the money was going to help the orphans in Africa no matter whose bucket it was in. Eventually Titch had to cease operations when Heather noticed that Miss Methody's mammy was starting to look at him very suspiciously over the rim of her swanky tortoiseshell glasses – good timing as who should swagger up to us but Timothy Longsley. He was here with his mother who was talking animatedly about antiques in her fur coat at the crockery stall.

'How's your split lip, Jilted Gippo?' he asked, with enough smarm to make me want to boke.

Before I could think up a suitably clever put-down in response my Westy Disco friends intervened.

'What's your problem, wee lad?' asked Heather.

This was going to be interesting. Heather versus Timothy was like Muhammad Ali versus Joe Frazier.

'Aye. Who you lookin' at?' asked Titch.

'Well, I can't quite tell what it is, but it's rather small and scruffy and it's certainly looking back,' smarmed Timothy.

'Here, wee lad,' intervened Heather, 'why don't you go and take a long walk off a short pier?'

'Oh, the Shankill millie can speak,' replied Timothy inadvisably, 'but I bet she can't read!'

Oh, I was never more delighted by any words that Timothy had ever spoken because I knew the likely consequences.

Heather pushed Titch out of the way and administered a powerful kick to the region of Timothy's jimmy joe.

'Awww!' moaned Timothy, falling to his knees and clutching his groin.

Personally I was fully satisfied by this level of retribution but it was not enough for Heather. She grabbed Miss Victoria College's bucket and swung it dangerously at Timothy's head. Now I was getting worried. As a pacifist I was happy enough to see Timothy humiliated but I didn't really want Heather to kill him. Poor Timmy ducked but the contents of the bucket spilled out noisily all over the floor of the Inst assembly hall, coins bouncing and rolling in every direction and suddenly everyone in the whole hall was looking straight at us. Titch ran for it, lifting a handful of sweets from the tuck shop on the way out. I later learned that he broke a tooth on one of the Highland Toffee bars he had swiped, which I suppose was a just punishment under the circumstances. Within seconds several members of the Inst Glorious First XV rugby team were carrying Heather Mateer from the building.

'Millie!' shouted Timothy after her, through real tears.

Yes, Timothy Longsley was now lying on the floor of the Inst assembly hall, holding his groin and crying tears of pain and humiliation in front of two hundred people from every good grammar school in Belfast. It was perfect! I owed Heather Mateer a pastie supper. Meanwhile Miss Victoria College's mother was running around the room fussily retrieving every coin that had been cast for her daughter.

'I hope this will be taken into account!' she kept saying, But the more she went on like this, the more I could tell she was losing the sympathy vote for her now distraught daughter.

'You have ruined my special day. You silly little boy!' cried Miss Victoria College into Timothy's reddened face.

She was crying so hard her snatters were running.

'I'm beautiful!' she roared.

This day had not turned out as expected. The beauty competitions were hurriedly completed to avoid any further incident. The Miss Belfast Schools' competition was judged a draw in case of legal action when it emerged that Miss Victoria College's uncle was a lawyer. As for me, Mr BRA came third behind Blue Boy and Luke Skywalker. This was typical because I never seemed to win anything. My disappointment was assuaged only by the vision of Timothy Longsley being decked by a girl in public.

As I left the Schools' Charity Fair that Saturday afternoon I wondered if I would ever win anything in my life. I wanted to win first prize in something, like Mairead Corrigan and Betty Williams did for peace. I dreamed of being a winner like those boys from Argentina in the World Cup. It wasn't fair! Why did people in this city always look down on you just because of where you came from? I was always too poor or too snobby or too Protestant or too good livin'! What was so wrong with being a wee good livin' Protestant pacifist breadboy from up the Shankill? When I went on like this at home my father told me not to have such a chip on my shoulder. But I didn't care. If I wanted to feel sorry for myself then I would. Maybe I should do what our headmaster always suggested and plan to leave Northern Ireland. Maybe I should just leave this place for good and go and live in Sweden, like ABBA, where they accepted everybody in fur coats in the snow. But just as I was leaving the ornate front gates of Inst with my head held low, Joanne Gault caught up with me.

'Cheer up, Tony!' she said, with a gentle pat on my shoulder. 'Sure, Judy Carlton was here and she put a 50p piece in your bucket instead of having five gos on the lucky dip – you missed it with the fight and all.'

I slowly lifted my head and smiled. I had never been more flattered in my life, so I hadn't.

18

HAPPY DAYS

I was worried, so I was. On my weekly bread round I sometimes forgot the odd Veda loaf as I dreamt I was Han Solo driving the *Millennium Falcon* past millions of stars. On dark mornings in snowstorms I pretended the incoming snowflakes were stars I was passing at warp speed. Occasionally I omitted a wheaten loaf as I imagined playing my electric guitar on *Top of the Pops* with The Undertones without dropping my plectrum. But on this frosty January morning I was more distracted by my worries than my dreams. I noticed this was happening more and more often. If this was a part of being all grown then I didn't like it. As I paced the streets of the Upper Shankill on Saturday mornings my mind used to be filled with movies and music and outer space and Olivia Newton-John. But now I had so much to worry about.

'He's an awful worrier, this wee lad of ours,' I overheard my mother say to my Auntie Doris one day over a cup of tea and a plate of Gypsy Creams.

I had money worries. What if Leslie gets a new wee lad from the Boys' Brigade Bible class to work for him for cheaper and I have no money to save up for ABBA's *Greatest Hits Volume 2* cassette? What if I fail all my GCEs and get chucked out of BRA and end up signing on the dole in Snugville Street forever? What if my father loses his job at the foundry and we end up dead poor and having to sell the Ford Escort respray?

I also had health worries. What if these bloody spots never go away, no matter how much Clearasil, Denim and toothpaste I put on them? What if my childhood heart murmur comes back and I have a cardiac arrest and die before I get even one chance to have a go at sex?

I worried about the health of my loved ones too. What if chain smoking Hamlet cigars gives my father cancer? What if granny's constant assertion that she is already in her coffin, only without the lid nailed on, finally comes true?

Then I had my worries about The Situation. What if they had got the wrong house and shot dead my father instead of Mr Oliver? What if my mother is walking past a car at the Co-op with her shopping when a bomb goes off? What if the provos make Protestant breadboys legitimate targets?

Of course I wasn't the only member of my family with worries. My father was always fretting about the foundry making him redundant and my mother was vexed about my granda and granny (who gave her a lot to worry about) and my father and her three sons and everyone. No wonder her nerves were bad!

My brothers didn't appear to worry quite as much as me. My big brother was doing dead hard A levels to go to Queen's University so, in theory, he had a lot more to worry about than me. He was going to become the first person in my whole family ever to go to university, which I thought was plenty to worry about. But he seemed more concerned about Manchester United's performance in the FA Cup final. My wee brother appeared to be too young for worries. The eleven-plus was a few years away and so all he had to be anxious about for now was the slow puncture in his space hopper and the possibility of being so busy flying down the hill on his bike with no hands that he missed *Chorlton and the Wheelies* on UTV.

However, on this particular Saturday morning I had one more immediate worry. This afternoon was finally the day of the announcement of the cast for Belfast Royal Academy's production of *West Side Story*. This could be the day when my acting talents were finally recognised. I was certain that Roger Moore once had a day like this. As a result of this all-consuming concern I delivered the bread absentmindedly that morning. Due to my wandering thoughts Mrs Piper had to run after the van demanding her frosted cream fingers and at first we couldn't even hear her calls over the sound of our 'diddledee dings'. Miss Adams had to remind me curtly that her sweet tooth was reserved for refined German biscuits and not vulgar Paris buns. I also forgot Naomi's can of Coke but this did not prevent the two of us from enjoying a duet over the final part of 'Summer Nights' when Travolta goes all Bee Gee. I was discovering so many competing priorities in my head that it occurred to me for the first time that I might not even want to be a breadboy forever. I completed my chores and bade farewell to Leslie, thanking him sincerely for the bonus of a box of shattered meringue nests. As I ran into the house I briefly noticed that Mr Oliver's rooster was now just an overgrown hedge. I rushed my father's Ulster fry to spend extra time in the bathroom preparing for the part of Tony in *West Side Story*. I splashed Denim on my spotty chin, noting with delight that some of my darkened facial hair was at last beginning to stiffen. A first shave had to be only weeks away – please! Then I applied the final remnants of Dad's ancient jar of Brylcreem to give my hair a hint of The Fonz as I felt this was appropriate for the male lead in a musical set in America in the fifties. My big brother had beaten me to a request for a lift in the car as he was playing in some big rugby match at Roughfort, so I took a black taxi down the Shankill and then caught a bus at the City Hall to get me up to school.

When I arrived in the BRA assembly hall, the scene of my recent 'Jilted John' decking, the other potential stars had already congregated, eagerly waiting to hear the exact nature of their stage musical debut. I sat down beside Thomas O'Hara and Ian Forrester and just behind Garvin Wilson, who was sitting beside Joanne Gault and Judy Carlton, as if he had a chance. Miss Baron was standing up on the stage with a clipboard in her hand containing the vital information. The dramatic tension reminded me of when the winners of the Oscars were announced, except Miss Baron was wearing a tweed maxi skirt rather than a sequinned evening gown. Everyone was chatting nervously and was slightly short of breath due to the excitement of the moment. I looked around to survey the competition and had a final surge of confidence. Thomas was too small, Ian couldn't sing and Garvin was ginger. The part of Tony was almost within my grasp. Miss Baron would say my name and everyone would congratulate me and laugh about me getting the part of the character with my own name and then it would all be about the rehearsals and learning lines and trying to reach the high notes at the end of 'Tonight, Tonight'. Suddenly the assembly hall became quiet. I had not experienced such a sudden hush in this room since the few seconds before inappropriate laughter broke out when Mr Jackson appeared to fart while saying 'Amen' at the end of the school prayer on Remembrance Day.

'The part of Maria goes to ...' teased Miss Baron, as Thomas attempted a drum roll on the back of Garvin's chair, '... Kimberly Stewart.'

Kimberly leapt from her seat with glee as a ripple of shock passed among the assembled girls. Several of the other school choir sopranos congratulated her with unusual fixed smiles on their faces that didn't quite match the look in their eyes. Kimberly could sing and act and I always noticed how attractive she looked when she took off her glasses for PE, but this choice was clearly a surprise to some of the sopranos who had not considered the possibility of a bespectacled leading lady. The kerfuffle ceased as Miss Baron moved on to my role.

'And the part of Tony goes to ...'

I could feel my heart beating fast, but time seemed to slow down, like when the Doctor got stuck in a time anomaly in the TARDIS.

'And the part of Tony goes to ... Garvin Wilson.'

Silence.

Cheers. Applause.

Garvin looked very surprised but eventually he stood up and took a genuinely humble bow, holding his glasses in place as he bent. I had frozen on the spot. Miss Baron had given the part of Tony to a ginger boy with glasses who wasn't even called Tony!

'I didn't get it because of where I come from,' I whispered to Thomas, bitterly. 'Yer man lives in a big house up the Cavehill Road, so he does.'

Overhearing this comment, Joanne Gault turned around.

'Don't be an inverted snob now, Tony,' she said.

I wasn't quite sure what an inverted snob was but Joanne was usually right so I hit a reddener, folded my arms and shut up. The problem was I liked Garvin Wilson so I couldn't really blame him, so I felt cross with Miss Baron instead. How could this woman be so blind to my talents? And speaking of blindness, how will Tony and Maria be able to sing 'There's a Place For Us' convincingly to one another if Kimberly and Garvin attempt to perform without their glasses and can't even see each other?

Before I could think of any further reasons for this great travesty of dramatic casting Miss Baron continued, 'And the part of Riff, the leader of the Jets, goes to … Tony Macaulay.'

Cheers. Applause.

I was shocked. It was not the romantic lead but it was not an old man either. Thomas patted me on the back enthusiastically and Garvin turned around and shook my hand so sincerely I couldn't hate him. From the corner of my eye I noticed Judy applauding gracefully. Ian seemed less impressed at the prospect of either Garvin or me as members of gangs of street fighters.

'They fight with flick knives, not friggin' handbags!' he said.

I quickly scanned the script to assess the size of my part. I was delighted to discover that Riff was very cool like The Fonz in *Happy Days* and was the lead singer in two of the songs in the musical. This was not a complete disaster. It seemed that I would be Han Solo to Garvin Wilson's Luke Skywalker. Perhaps the fact that Riff was a darker character than Tony, the romantic lead, was a sign that Miss Baron had finally recognised the hidden depths I could bring to the stage. Maybe this was recognition that I too could portray complex characters with a talent equal to that of Roger Moore. This scenario was not what I had been dreaming of but it was better than nothing. As the announcements continued Thomas and Joanne did not get speaking parts but they seemed happy enough. Ian got the part of the leader of the Sharks and took great pleasure in pointing out that he would be stabbing me to death at the end of act one in every performance.

As a curtain call to the drama of the afternoon, Miss Baron did a great act herself with a pep talk pretending that every person was 'equally important in this production', even the ones with no lines.

'Aye, right! Dead on!' I thought.

But then something truly unbelievable happened. Just as I was leaving the assembly hall, Joanne Gault stopped me at the door, offered me an Opal Fruit and whispered, 'Judy says you'll be brilliant as the leader of the Jets, so you will.'

I was more than flattered. The fact that Judy regarded me as brilliant in any way was a revelation. I was only just coming to terms with this news when Joanne continued with further sweet words.

'Judy says if you asked her to see you, she wouldn't say no, so she wouldn't.'

Silence.

I dropped my script. This was by far the biggest shock of the day! This was the biggest surprise of the year! In an instant the BRA assembly hall was transformed from a dull and formal space for grammar school education in Belfast into the cool and colourful schoolyard in *Grease*. I was John Travolta and one of Olivia Newton-John's girlfriends had just approached me with a message from Sandy to say 'You're the One that I Want'!

For a few seconds I lost confidence.

'Are you spoofin', wee girl?' I asked Joanne sincerely.

'Wise up, wee lad,' she replied. 'Sure she's always liked you, even when you're actin' the eejit.'

'But sure I don't play rugby and I'm from up the Shankill,' I protested.

'Sure her granda's from up there. Judy thinks you're lovely in your bomber jacket and all.'

The beauty of these words captivated me but I was unsure as to my next move. I noticed that Judy and several other girls were waiting behind at the back of the assembly hall, looking in our direction, whispering and giggling.

'Well. How do I ask her out?' I asked Joanne.

'I'll ask her for you,' she replied.

'Will ya?'

'Yes, Tony. I know the answer anyway!'

'Okay. Will you ask her to see me?'

Joanne did not hang around to reply. She conveyed the

requested to Judy faster than a Jedi Knight drawing his lightsaber. Within seconds she was back beside me, while a blushing Judy looked on.

'She says "Yes".'

I couldn't believe it!

I had got myself a real, live girlfriend. Not a millie or a boot but the loveliest girl in the whole school. This was better than Debbie Harry on my bedroom wall and all those ladies in the lingerie section of the *Great Universal Club Book*. My dream had come true! Judy Carlton had consented to be my own personal Wonder Woman!

'Well, are you not goin' to talk to her?' asked Joanne, gently pushing me in Judy's direction.

As I approached Judy the other giggling girls cleared from around her. As I walked between them I felt like Charlton Heston in the Bible striding to victory and parting the Red Sea.

What should I say?

What should be my first words to my new girl?

Should I just thank her for giving me a go?

Should I promise to reward her with gifts of bread and pastry from the Ormo Mini Shop?

Should I offer to take her to the Skandia Restaurant behind the City Hall for a chicken Maryland and a strawberry pavlova?

As I arrived in Judy's warm presence I took a deep breath, inhaled her lovely Charlie perfume and then the words just came to me. 'D'ya wanna come with me to the Westy Disco the night?'

Judy did not speak. She simply took me by the hand, smiled and nodded. We walked together out of the school grounds, holding hands for the very first time. I was so taken by the warmth and softness of her hand I almost tripped over the British soldier crouching at the school gate, taking aim at something. Behind us I could hear Joanne and the girls giggling and Thomas O'Hara and Garvin Wilson joining in a chorus of.

'Tony loves Judy, Tony loves Judy.'

The day was made perfect when the school minibus arrived back from rugger practice. As all the hateful forwards and hookers disembarked I could see the look of shocked admiration on my big brother's face when he noticed his wee brother hand in hand with Judy Carlton. He turned around to Timothy Longsley, who was behind him on the bus, pointed at me and, laughing, he shouted: 'Ha, ha! Look at that, Longsley, ya snobby sickener! She'd rather have a big fruit than you!'

The wholeheartedness of my big brother's loyalty only added to my elation.

An unforgettable Westy Disco was to complete this special day. Judy and I wore matching ocean blue Peter Storm anoraks and she held me close under her transparent Snoopy umbrella as we queued outside in the rain. I could hear ABBA singing 'Chiquitita' on the loudspeakers inside. Irene Maxwell, as an expert on all matters of art and culture, explained to the whole queue that 'Chiquitita' was Spanish for 'wee crater'. Irene looked Judy up and down dismissively and passed over her when she was sharing her Spangles with the rest of queue. I did not react to this snub as I understood how heartbreaking it must be for Irene not being in Judy's shoes. When we finally reached the front door of the Nissen hut, Uncle Henry smiled and warmly waved us through without asking either of us to blow into the breathalyser. This just proved that I was good livin' and Judy was no millie. He asked Titch McCracken to breathe into the breathalyser twice. When the red light came on Titch argued successfully that this was because the doctor had put him on a prescription of strong cough medicine – the wee chancer!

When we got inside the Nissen hut the Westy Disco was heaving with hundreds of teenagers as usual. This was the perfect venue to show off my lovely new girlfriend. Auntie Emma shook Judy's hand and said she was a lovely wee girl, so she was. Titch asked me sensitively if Judy was a good kisser. Philip Ferris pretended he wasn't interested in her but I noticed his eyes kept returning to Judy's breast magnets. My mother bought Judy a Ripple bar from the tuck shop and my father played a request for 'Heart of Glass' by Blondie, 'Just for young lovers – Tony and Judy'. Heather Mateer gave Judy a warm welcome by taking her to the girls' toilets for chewing gum and a chat. I hoped the girls' bogs weren't as smelly as the boys' bogs in case it put Judy off ever coming back.

The music was brilliant that night. After Blondie my DJ da put on the Boomtown Rats and then Meatloaf, who was a big fat fella my big brother liked who sang about bats and hell. Next my father introduced a brand new disco single by a black lady from America called Gloria Gaynor.

'You'll like this!' hissed my big brother on hearing the 'gay' syllable of Gloria's surname. This was in spite of the fact that I was actually sitting beside him with my new girlfriend trying to work out the best time to ask my father to stick on 'Hopelessly

Devoted to You' so I could have a first slow dance and hopefully get a decent snog with Judy. As the disco song began, suddenly Irene Maxwell appeared from the girls' toilets wearing a pair of roller skates.

'First I was afraid I was petrified …' began Gloria.

I was quite petrified myself at the sight of Irene.

'Roller discos are the next big thing!' she announced to the crowds of genuinely impressed teenagers, 'It says so in *Jackie*!'

Irene did her very best to dance on roller skates to 'I Will Survive' but she lost her balance when her half-filled sequinned boob tube began to slip and she tried to fix herself. Poor Irene ended up veering off course and crashing into Heather Mateer who was in the far corner of the Nissen hut snogging a flute player in blue flares from the Ballysillan Road. However Irene did survive and dragged Heather with her on to the dance floor. Eventually all of us (apart from a disgusted looking Philip Ferris, of course) were up on the sticky chewing gum surface of the Westy Disco dance floor, bopping. My wee brother even joined in and I knew right away he wanted a go on Irene's roller skates. Irene started to dance very close to Titch and I could tell she had decided to seduce him in her boob tube now that I was unavailable. I was more concerned that Titch was wearing so many paramilitary badges. I hoped he wasn't going to get involved or he would end up in prison or dead.

'I will survive,' sang Gloria.

Sammy Reeves joined us in his off-white Travolta suit and did the *Saturday Night Fever* pointy dance even though he had another black eye.

'As long as I know how to love I know I'll stay alive …'

Judy did not let go of my hand the whole time even though it was a fast dance.

'I've got all my life to live, I've got all my love to give …'

I looked around me at all my friends and family. My father stood proudly at the turntables with the satisfied smile he wore when he realised he had discovered the latest dance-floor filler. My mother was peeking in from the tuck shop enjoying the happiness her husband had produced by the push of a button. Auntie Emma joined in the dance with my wee brother and Uncle Henry chatted at the door with Leslie who had called in to update him about the latest security situation. Even from a distance I could lip read Leslie saying, 'C'mere til a tell ye!'

We all sang along with the chorus.

I will survive,
As long as I know how to love
I know I'll stay alive.

I wanted all of us to survive. I didn't want anyone to join the paramilitaries or start drinking too much or get cancer. I didn't want anyone to have bad nerves or get shot in the chest at their front door or get blown to pieces at the shops. I wanted us all to stay alive forever. I didn't know if I could to stay in Belfast much longer. I couldn't decide if I should stay or if I should go. I loved my city but I hated this war. I wanted to survive. The song seemed to say what all of us were feeling on a cold wet Saturday night in Belfast in 1979. It was wonderful end to an unforgettable happy day.

So what record did my father put on next to add to this feeling of hope and elation? 'Hit Me With Your Rhythm Stick' by Ian Dury and the Blockheads.

We all sat down, except for my big brother, and Philip Ferris joined him on the dance floor for a particularly masculine pogo as Ian Dury sang 'Hit me, hit me, hit me!' Eventually, after some encouragement from Heather Mateer, my father changed the atmosphere completely and he faded in the familiar introduction to 'How Deep Is Your Love?'

'D'ya wanna dance, Judy?' I asked my girl.

Judy smiled and nodded and so began our first slow dance. I decided not to rush into an immediate snog attempt to show Judy how much I respected her. I just held her close and we danced cheek to cheek as the Bee Gees sang:

Cause we're living in a world of fools,
Breaking us down
When they all should let us be …

I wanted Judy to be my girl forever. As we danced as one across the sticky chewing gum on the floor I was happier than I had ever been. I did not know what lay ahead. I could not predict the future or travel through time and space in a blue police telephone box that was bigger on the inside than on the outside. I had no idea what would happen after my days as a breadboy in the last Ormo Mini Shop in the whole wide world. I didn't even know whether bread would be replaced with wee vitamin pills by the year 2000. But on this happy day I was certain of one thing. I would survive, so I would.

ACKNOWLEDGEMENTS

I would like to thank the many individuals, festivals, voluntary organisations, schools, libraries and bookshops who have given me so much support since the publication of *Paperboy*.

I want to acknowledge my literary agents, Paul and Susan Feldstein, for their excellent advice and constant encouragement.

I would like to thank Helen Wright and the team at Blackstaff Press for their commitment, hard work and warm support in publishing *Breadboy*.

ALSO BY TONY MACAULAY

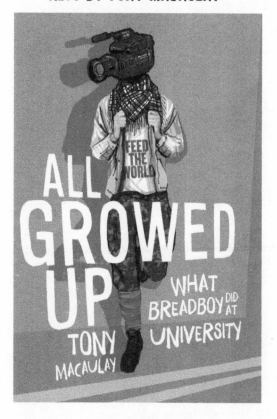

eBook
EPUB ISBN 978-0-85640-694-2
KINDLE ISBN 978-0-85640-706-2

Paperback
ISBN 978-0-85640-934-9

www.blackstaffpress.com

Follow Tony on Twitter @tonymacaulay